Jurisdiction and Admissibility in Investment Arbitration

International Investment Law and Arbitration

Volumes published in this Brill Research Perspectives title are listed at *brill.com/rpia*

Jurisdiction and Admissibility in Investment Arbitration

The Practice and the Theory

By

Filippo Fontanelli

BRILL

LEIDEN | BOSTON

This paperback book edition is simultaneously published as issue 1.3-4 (2017) of *International Investment Law and Arbitration*, DOI 10.1163/24055778-12340003.

Library of Congress Control Number: 2018932430

Typeface for the Latin, Greek, and Cyrillic scripts: "Brill". See and download: brill.com/brill-typeface.

ISBN 978-90-04-36648-0 (paperback)
ISBN 978-90-04-36649-7 (e-book)

Published by Koninklijke Brill NV, Leiden, The Netherlands.
Koninklijke Brill NV incorporates the imprints Brill, Brill Hes & De Graaf, Brill Nijhoff, Brill Rodopi, Brill Sense and Hotei Publishing.

This book is printed on acid-free paper and produced in a sustainable manner.

Contents

Jurisdiction and Admissibility in Investment Arbitration: The Practice and the Theory

Filippo Fontanelli
Senior Lecturer in International Economic Law, University of Edinburgh
filippo.fontanelli@ed.ac.uk

Abstract

This is the first half of a two-part essay on jurisdiction and admissibility in investment arbitration. It focuses on the arbitration practice, whilst the second part sets these concepts in the wider framework of public international law litigation. This essay maps the objections to the tribunal's jurisdiction (by *ratio: materiae, temporis, loci* and *personae*) and the claim's admissibility. It offers some preliminary conclusions: in certain areas there still is no consensus; tribunals are inclined to characterise objections as jurisdictional, and rarely resort to admissibility; findings of inadmissibility draw a judgment on the claimant or the claim's propriety (whilst jurisdictional decisions typically eschew value-judgment); tribunals failed to distinguish jurisdiction from admissibility. These findings are further explored, within a wider theoretical context, in the second part of the essay.

Keywords

admissibility – jurisdiction – investment arbitration – competence – *ratione materiae* – *ratione personae* – *ratione temporis* – *ratione loci*

* Senior Lecturer in International Economic Law, University of Edinburgh, filippo.fontanelli@ed.ac.uk.

 | DOI 10.1163/9789004366497_002

• • •

> … the Idols of the Market Place are the most troublesome of all—idols which have crept into the understanding through the alliances of words and names. For men believe that their reason governs words …[1]

> Expressions which bear multiple meanings often find themselves employed with promiscuous disregard to context and function.[2]

∵

Introduction

The practice of international investment tribunals with respect to the legal categories of admissibility and jurisdiction is irreversibly confused. These concepts being ultimately blurry, the words that are supposed to denote them are ambivalent. Yet, words and legal categories influence each other; the unclear application of the law is often the inevitable outcome of a tradition of terminological opacity.[3] This two-part essay sets out to chart the practice, expose and explain this confusion, and to propose a solution to it.

To appreciate the current state of uncertainty a simple instance is sufficient. In the dispute *Kılıç v. Turkmenistan*, the tribunal considered that the investor's failure to attempt local litigation for at least one year determined a lack of jurisdiction under the applicable bilateral investment treaty (BIT).[4] The investor sought annulment of the award, challenging—among other things—the tribunal's finding on the lack of jurisdiction. According to the investor, the failure

1 Francis Bacon, *Novum Organum*, Liber I, Aphorism LIX: '*At idola fori omnium molestissima sunt; quae ex foedere verborum et nominum se insinuarunt in intellectum. Credunt enim homines, rationem suam verbis imperare.*'

2 William W Park, 'The Arbitrator's Jurisdiction to Determine Jurisdiction' (2009) 1 Transnational Dispute Management 1.

3 Francis Bacon, above (n 1), describes the detrimental effect of the misalignment between the words and the reality they mean to represent, referring to the fallacies deriving from the use of the 'idols of the market' (*idola fori*). In particular, reliance on suboptimal language might grow into a habit and hamper the achievement of the truth.

4 *Kılıç İnşaat İthalat İhracat Sanayi ve Ticaret Anonim Şirketi v. Turkmenistan*, ICSID Case No. ARB/10/1, Award of 2 July 2013, para. 6.3.5.

to comply with the local litigation requirement could, at the most, cause the inadmissibility of the claim.[5]

The *ad hoc* committee looked into the tribunal's reasoning and the dissenting opinion of one member thereof. It took note of their respective strengths and the possible objections to each. Eventually, it threw up its figurative hands. The categories of jurisdiction and admissibility are so porous that it would be a stretch to consider either solution as mistaken. The tribunal simply noted that,

> [f]aced with the same question, other tribunals have decided differently on questions of jurisdiction and admissibility; it is not for the committee to favor one or the other of these positions.[6]

The state of the art, in treaty-based investment arbitration, is such that too often a determination on jurisdiction or admissibility is simply non-falsifiable. To the extent that these categories belong to a wider procedural tradition of general principles of procedure, an analysis of the practice outside investment arbitration can be helpful. This study seeks to inscribe the practice in investment litigation within the wider framework of public international law, accounting for the scientific fragility of both.

The essay is divided into two parts, each of which can be read on its own. **Part A** maps the practice of investment arbitration. It serves as up-to-date handbook, is primarily descriptive and informative, and could benefit practitioners and scholars of the discipline. It provides a gallery of selected jurisdictional issues and questions of admissibility, with which tribunals engage. Where necessary, a critique of the prevailing practice is provided, or a remark signalling the difficulty to identify a coherent case law. The purpose of **Part B** is to frame this practice in a wider theoretical context and to delve on the harder cases. It starts by examining the concepts of jurisdiction and admissibility in public international law. The goal is to reconnect the practice of investment arbitration to its normative background and to highlight the difficulties that emerge across the two disciplines. In the second half of Part B, a number of critical questions that have arisen in the practice are discussed, which share a critical aspect: in these cases, the conceptual confusion between jurisdiction and admissibility comes with a practical price.

Part A and Part B complement each other. Part A analyses a representative portion of the practice; it addresses several current or controversial issues

---

5 Which, in the investor's view, could have led to a suspension of the arbitration, rather than its dismissal.

6 *Kılıç İnşaat İthalat İhracat Sanayi ve Ticaret Anonim Şirketi v. Turkmenistan*, ICSID Case No. ARB/10/1, Decision on Annulment of 15 July 2015, para. 166.

and—in general—informs the reader of how jurisdiction and admissibility questions are handled in investment arbitration. The reader will gain insight more through example and inference than through principled reasoning. Part B, conversely, attempts to investigate the principles, and invites readers to interpret the practice with a certain degree of scepticism. This section illustrates the advantages and drawbacks of proceeding deductively, trying to assess whether the confusion in the practice is the result of unprincipled notions inherited from public international law or, instead, of a tinkering practice that overlooks taxonomies. In the final part of Part B, practice and theory are precipitated together: the 'hard' cases arise in the practice but reveal the flaws in the theory.

PART A The Practice: Jurisdiction and Admissibility in Investment Law Arbitration

Investment arbitration lies at the intersection between public international law adjudication and international commercial arbitration.[7] The hybrid nature has implications on its procedure and influences in particular the jurisdictional powers of investment tribunals, as well as the regime of admissibility of investment claims.[8] General principles of public international law regarding jurisdiction and admissibility can be useful tools for specific tribunals,[9] when their

7 Or, better, it consists of a '*combination of international commercial arbitration procedure and the substantive obligations arising under public international law*,' see Ian Laird and Rebecca Askew, 'Finality Versus Consistency: Does Investor-State Arbitration Need an Appellate System' (2005) 7 Journal of Appellate Practice and Process 285, 285. For a break-down of the laws applicable to the various elements of investment (treaty) arbitration, see For a fuller study, see Veijo Heiskanen, 'Forbidding Dépeçage: Law Governing Investment Treaty Arbitration' (2008) 32 Suffolk Transnational Law Review 367, 375, where the following categorisation is made: '*one must distinguish between:* (*a*) *the law governing the arbitration agreement;* (*b*) *the law governing the arbitral proceedings;* (*c*) *the law governing the arbitral tribunal;* (*d*) *the law governing the merits of the claim, or the subject matter of the dispute; and* (*e*) *the law governing the recognition, enforcement and execution of the award*.'

8 See, more extensively, Jan Paulsson, 'Jurisdiction and Admissibility' in Gerald Aksen et al. (eds), *Global Reflections on International Law, Commerce and Dispute Resolution: Liber Amicorum in Honour of Robert Briner* (International Chamber of Commerce 2005) 601.

9 The comprehensive analysis of these principles in public international law is addressed in Part B. For an instance, consider how the tribunal in *Pan American Energy LLC and BP Argentina Exploration Company v. The Argentine Republic*, ICSID Case No. ARB/03/13, Decision on Preliminary Objections of 27 July 2006, para. 169, rejected the possibility to hear '*hypothetical claims*,' echoing the practice of the International Court of Justice.

constituent instruments and the documents codifying State consent require interpretation in specific cases.[10] Whereas consent is the bedrock of jurisdiction, there is no space for presumptive interpretation of the relevant instruments against jurisdiction (*in dubio mitius*)[11] or in its favour.[12] Jurisdictional clauses in treaties must be interpreted, like all treaty norms, in accordance with the general rules of treaty interpretation.[13]

An element that complicates the analysis of consent in this field is the relevance of the investor's consent,[14] which is necessary to complement the home State's consent with respect to the specific jurisdiction of the tribunal over a

10 Robert Kolb, 'General Principles of Procedural Law' in Andreas Zimmermann et al. (eds), *The Statute of the International Court of Justice* (OUP 212) 871.

11 See *Abaclat and Others (Case formerly known as Giovanna Beccara and Others) v. Argentine Republic*, ICSID Case No. ARB/07/5, Decision on Jurisdiction and Admissibility of 4 August 2011, Dissenting Opinion of Abi Saab, para. 16: '*The requirement to ascertain the existence and scope of consent, while strict and exacting in international law, does not mean the restrictive interpretation of the jurisdictional title (the old theory of interpretation in favour of sovereignty, as far as the State party is concerned)*'.

12 *Amco Indonesia Corporation and others v. Republic of Indonesia*, ICSID Case No. ARB/81/1, Decision on Jurisdiction of 25 September 1983, 1 ICSID Reports 389 (1993), 394; *Government of the Province of East Kalimantan v. PT Kaltim Prima Coal and others*, ICSID Case No. ARB/07/3, Award on Jurisdiction of 28 December 2009, para. 171. See also *Fireman's Fund Insurance Company v. The United Mexican States*, ICSID Case No. ARB(AF)/02/1, Decision on the Preliminary Question of 17 July 2003, para. 64: '*The Tribunal does not believe that under contemporary international law a foreign investor is entitled to the benefit of the doubt with respect to the existence and scope of an arbitration agreement.*' This dictum is cited approvingly in *National Gas S.A.E. v. Arab Republic of Egypt*, ICSID Case No. ARB/11/7, Award of 3 April 2014, para. 117. See also *Eureko BV v Republic of Poland*, Ad Hoc Arbitration, Partial Award of 19 August 2005, para. 248 (the conclusion of thousands of BITs made the *in dubio mitius* principle obsolete).

13 *Mondev International Ltd. v. United States of America*, ICSID Case No. ARB(AF)/99/2, Award of 11 October 2002, para. 43; *Churchill Mining PLC and Planet Mining Pty Ltd v. Republic of Indonesia*, ICSID Case No. ARB/12/14 and 12/40, Decision on Jurisdiction of 24 February 2014, para. 151.

14 The relevance of the investor's consent is minimised in this study. Because investor-State arbitration is largely a one-way process, and the request of arbitration is normally considered to qualify as consent, the focus on the analysis is rather on the existence and limits of State's consent. See *Teinver S.A., Transportes de Cercanías S.A. and Autobuses Urbanos del Sur S.A. v. Argentine Republic*, ICSID Case No. ARB/09/1, Decision on Jurisdiction of 21 December 2012, para. 176. In a highly unusual case, the basis for jurisdiction being a contract and not a BIT, the host State launched a claim against the foreign investors. See *Government of the Province of East Kalimantan* above (n 12) para. 173–174.

dispute.[15] The existence and validity of the claimant's consent can be a matter of contention, especially in the case of mass claims.[16] Interestingly, the validity of claimant's consent is one of the few aspects in which general principles of law drawn from domestic systems bear directly on the tribunals' duty to determine their jurisdiction. The *Abaclat* tribunal held that, in the absence of any specific provision in the applicable BIT and the ICSID Convention, it was appropriate to review the validity of the claimant's consent on the basis of the general principles of contract law (*'requiring that any consent be genuine and intended, i.e., free from coercion, fraud and/or from any essential mistake'*).[17]

Most often, jurisdictional inquiries focus on the consent of the State. As a tribunal put it,

> ... it is of the utmost importance not to forget that no participant in the international community, be it a State, an international organisation or a physical or a legal person, has an inherent right of access to a jurisdictional recourse. For such right to come into existence, specific consent has to be given. As far as investment arbitration is concerned, such consent can be given in a contract, a domestic law or an international bilateral or multilateral treaty. In all these different hypotheses, the State can shape its consent as it sees fit by providing the conditions under which it is given—in other words, the conditions subject to which an "offer to arbitrate" is made to the foreign investors....
>
> An arbitral tribunal—just as the ICJ or any other international court—does not have a general jurisdiction; it only has a "*compétence d'attribution*," which has to respect the limits provided for by the States.[18]

---

15 In the ICSID field, consent must therefore exist with respect to the ICSID Convention, the relevant BIT (by way of ratification) and the parties' agreement to arbitrate the specific dispute. Abi Saab describes it as '*triple-layered consent*', above (n 11) para. 15.

16 *Abaclat* above (n 11) para. 428 ff. The issue of mass-claims in investment arbitration is specifically addressed in Part B.

17 Ibid., para. 436.

18 *ST-AD GmbH v. Republic of Bulgaria*, UNCITRAL, PCA Case No. 2011-06, Award on Jurisdiction of 18 July 2013, para. 337 and 362. For a comparable statement, consider *Menzies Middle East and Africa S.A. and Aviation Handling Services International Ltd. v. Republic of Senegal*, ICSID Case No. ARB/15/21, Award of 5 August 2016, para. 130: '*selon le droit international en général, et selon l'arbitrage d'investissement en particulier, un Etat souverain ne peut pas être assujetti à une juridiction internationale sans son consentement clairement exprimé et non-équivoque. Cette exigence découle du respect de la souveraineté des Etats et du principe qu'en matière de droit international, le consentement des Etats à l'arbitrage est l'exception et non pas la règle.*'

Tribunals must be satisfied that the State has expressed unequivocal consent to submit a dispute to arbitration.[19] In *Churchill v. Venezuela*, for instance, it was determined that the words '*shall consent*' in the applicable BIT indicated a precise obligation (as opposed to hortatory language) on the part of the State to agree to investor's request to arbitrate a dispute, after a painstaking perusal of the negotiating history.[20]

Investment arbitration proceedings often consist of two stages. In the first, the host State, more often than not, challenges the jurisdiction of the tribunal in a bid to halt the proceedings before they reach the merits.[21] Even when the proceedings are not subject to bifurcation, potential procedural objections are discussed preliminarily, because if any of them succeeds there is no need to discuss the merits.[22] In ICSID and UNCITRAL proceedings, jurisdictional objections cannot be raised after the counter-memorial or statement of defense.[23]

This essay offers a selective but illustrative overview of the practice of investment arbitration relating to the State's objection to the tribunal's jurisdiction (1) and the claim's admissibility (2). The overview cannot possibly be exhaustive and seeks simply to provide a roadmap of issues that are either controversial or recurrent, or both. Whereas other examples might be added to the list, the present section is designed to lay the foundation for the following Part B, which explores the doctrinal difficulty to draw a line between the two legal notions of jurisdiction and admissibility, and the attending complications. The lack of balance between the instances regarding competence and those on

---

19 In the case of State consent contained in a domestic law, the expression of consent by the investor might be inferred from the investor's reliance on the set of guarantees created by such statute, see *ABCI Investments N.V. v. Republic of Tunisia*, ICSID Case No. ARB/04/12, Decision on Jurisdiction of 18 February 2011, para. 119.

20 *Churchill* above (n 13) para. 181–230, resorting to the supplementary means of interpretation under Article 32 VCLT.

21 Ole K Fauchald, 'The Legal Reasoning of ICSID Tribunals-An Empirical Analysis' (2008) 19(2) European Journal of International Law 301, 304.

22 With the obvious exceptions of the *objections préliminaires du fond*. For a case where bifurcation was not granted but the award upheld some preliminary objections, see *Ampal-American Israel Corporation and others v. Arab Republic of Egypt*, ICSID Case No. ARB/12/11, Award of 1 February 2016. The tribunal acted under Article 41(2) of the ICSID Arbitration Rules and issued an award on jurisdiction only, mostly in order to defuse possible conflicts with the outcome of parallel arbitrations pending.

23 ICSID Convention, Article 41(1), UNCITRAL Rules, Article 21(3); Revised UNCITRAL Rules, Article 23(2). On this, see Judith Levine, 'Navigating the parallel universe of investor–State arbitrations under the UNCITRAL Rules' in Chester Brown and Kate Miles, *Evolution in Investment Treaty Law and Arbitration* (CUP 2011) 369, 395.

admissibility is not surprising: tribunals rarely address admissibility on its own right and often prefer not to draw a distinction at all.[24]

1 *Permutations of Jurisdictional Issues*

In the present essay, the notions of foundational and specific jurisdiction are employed. The former refers to the statutory competence of the body, the second on the body's power to decide a certain claim.[25] Both flow from the consent to arbitration granted by the host State, normally through a standing offer in an investment treaty. Therefore, to determine their scope the starting point is the arbitration clause of the applicable investment instrument (which could also be a domestic statute or a contract with the State or a State entity).

A long excerpt from the *Malicorp v. Egypt* decision illustrates with precision the task of an investment tribunal facing a set of objections to its jurisdiction. The attending review (carried out under the *Kompetenz-Kompetenz* principle) takes the shape of a checklist of legal and factual determinations.

> [Together, the compromissory clause of the applicable BIT and Article 25 ICSID] make the jurisdiction of an arbitral tribunal subject to a certain number of conditions, most of which ... are not in dispute in the present case:
>
> a) *The consent of the other Contracting State.* The respondent State must have consented in writing to submit the dispute to the Centre. By the first sentence of Article 8 of the Agreement, Egypt expressly and validly gave its consent to be subject to such an arbitration proceeding.
> b) *The consent of the investor.* The investor intending to take the action must also have consented in writing. Malicorp gave its consent, at the latest, by instituting this proceeding.
> c) *The nationality of the investor.* The investor must be a "national of the other Contracting State." Malicorp is a company incorporated "under the law in force in [a] part of the United Kingdom" ... and therefore a company of the other Contracting Party.
> d) *A legal dispute.* The dispute must be one that is legal and not political or other. This point is not in issue.

---

24 The doctrinal reasons of such blur and the implications are fully explored in Part B of this essay.

25 The distinction, which is discussed in-depth in Part B, is borrowed from Yuval Shany's work *Questions of Jurisdiction and Admissibility before International Courts* (CUP 2015).

> e) *Relating to an investment.* This point is not discussed by the Parties as such, but only from the standpoint of its relationship to the requirements of good faith....
>
> e) [sic] *In the territory of the other Contracting State.* The investment alleged to have been made by the party bringing the action must have been made in the territory of the other Contracting State. This is the case here with respect to the 28 investments Malicorp claims to have made, since they were intended for the construction and operation of the Ras Sudr Airport in Egypt.
>
> f) [sic] *An alleged violation of the Treaty.* The party bringing the action must allege that it was the victim of a violation of the underlying Treaty. In the present case, Malicorp alleges that Egypt breached the obligations prescribed in Articles 2 ("Promotion and protection of investments") and 5 ("Expropriation") of the Agreement ..., an allegation that cannot at this stage be rejected out of hand ...[26]

With the exception of requirements *ratione temporis*, the checklist touches upon the main tenets of the tribunal's jurisdiction. The full discussion of the jurisdictional dimensions (or *rationes*) of investment arbitration is beyond the scope of this study, but it is well researched already.[27] A discussion of selected problems will suffice here, for the purposes delineated above. This essay does not examine preliminary issues regarding consent, such as the possibility that State's consent to arbitration is not valid or effective (for instance because it is contained in a treaty that is terminated,[28] or in an invalid contract[29]), the allegation that the arbitration instrument does not contain a self-sufficient expression of consent,[30] or the '*unanswerable*' claims that an additional

26 *Malicorp Limited v. The Arab Republic of Egypt*, ICSID Case No. ARB/08/18, Award of 7 February 2011, para. 102. For a similar checklist based on the jurisdictional *rationes*, provided by the claimant, see *Copper Mesa Mining Corporation v. Republic of Ecuador*, PCA No. 2012-2, Award of 15 March 2016, para. 5.6.

27 See Michael Waibel, 'Investment Arbitration: Jurisdiction and Admissibility' in August Reinisch et al. (eds), *Handbook on International Investment Law* (Hart 2015) 212.

28 This is a habitual argument made with respect to intra-EU BITs, which respondents characterise as automatically terminated upon the entry into force of the Lisbon Treaty. See, for instance, *Jan Oostergetel and Theodora Laurentius v. The Slovak Republic*, UNCITRAL Decision on Jurisdiction of 30 April 2010, para. 65–68.

29 See for instance *World Duty Free Company v Republic of Kenya*, ICSID Case No. ARB/00/7, Award of 4 October 2006 (the contract under which the claimant brought the claim was obtained by bribery and was therefore held invalid).

30 See for instance *Millicom International Operations B.V. and Sentel GSM SA v. The Republic of Senegal*, ICSID Case No. ARB/08/20, Decision on Jurisdiction of 16 July 2010 (the host

expression of consent by a person with full powers must complement the arbitration clause in the BIT, or that the offer to arbitrate is invalid when it is incompatible with domestic law.[31]

1 Foundational and Specific Jurisdiction

The extract from *Malicorp* also shows the importance of the ICSID Convention in establishing the foundational jurisdiction of a tribunal in ICSID-based arbitration. The precise limits of its specific jurisdiction are normally determined by the rules of the applicable investment treaty. The *Alemanni* tribunal used a similar taxonomy while setting out to assess the preliminary objections. The language used by the tribunal hinted at a correspondence between *foundational jurisdiction* and competence, on one hand, and *specific jurisdiction* and jurisdiction, on the other:

> [there are] two types of limiting factor that go to determine whether a particular case may properly be heard by a tribunal established under the ICSID system, *the first being the overall scope of ICSID arbitration, and the second being the factors germane to the seizing of a specific tribunal to hear a specific dispute*. The first refers, that is to say, to Article 25 of the Washington Convention, as the foundation text, which like Article 41 is also phrased in terms of the "competence of the Centre" ('compétence' and 'jurisdicción' in French and Spanish, respectively); the second, by contrast, bears primarily on factors such as the consent of the parties, the nature of the particular dispute and the like, which would normally be thought of, in common parlance in English, as the elements necessary to ground the 'jurisdiction' of the tribunal.[32]

State claimed that the arbitral provision in the concession was hortatory, and required an additional expression of consent. The tribunal held that, on the basis of its language, the provision in the concession constituted a sufficient expression of consent). Likewise, see *Churchill* above (n 13), in particular para. 208 ff.

31 *Bureau Veritas, Inspection, Valuation, Assessment and Control, BIVAC B.V. v. The Republic of Paraguay*, ICSID Case No. ARB/07/9, Decision on the Objections to Jurisdiction of 29 May 2009, para. 65 ff.

32 *Giovanni Alemanni and Others v. The Argentine Republic*, ICSID Case No. ARB/07/8, Decision on Jurisdiction and Admissibility of 17 November 2014, para. 259 (emphasis added). The terminological distinction is not very convincing, given that both Article 41 and Rule 41 ICSID, instead, refer to the '*jurisdiction of the Centre*' and the '*competence of the tribunal*'.

With respect to *ad hoc* arbitration, foundational and specific jurisdictions flow from the same instrument and the same expression of consent instead. Whereas consent is normally provided *ex ante* by the host State, the framing of the case—crucial to circumscribe the tribunal's powers *in casu*—is left to the characterisation made by the claimant in the act of seisin of the tribunal and by the respondent's reaction thereto.[33]

It is clear that the practice of permanent courts, chief among them the ICJ, cannot easily apply as such to the jurisdiction of tribunals.[34] Investment tribunals' determinations are subject to review, and their competence is formulated *ad hoc*, for the resolution of a specific dispute. In the case of arbitration *ad hoc*, the foundational jurisdiction overlaps with the specific one (the tribunal does not exist outside the scenario of the specific dispute). It is moreover debatable whether *forum prorogatum* can operate in arbitration proceedings.[35] Not even an explicit consent of the parties can confer onto a tribunal competence that exceeds its statutory (foundational) jurisdiction.[36]

The Interplay between ICSID and the Instrument of Specific Jurisdiction

When the claim is brought under the aegis of the International Centre for the Settlement of Investment Dispute (ICSID), the foundational jurisdiction of the tribunal is *additionally* governed by the ICSID Convention, in particular by

33 See Juan Pablo Hugues Arthur, 'The legal value of prior steps to arbitration in international law of foreign investment: Two (different?) approaches, one outcome' (2015) 15 Anuario Mexicano de Derecho Internacional 449.

34 The parallel between investment tribunals and other international courts and tribunals is developed in Part B.

35 Chittharanjan F Amerasinghe, in his *International Arbitral Jurisdiction* (Brill 2011) 73, claims that it cannot.

36 *United States of America v. the Federal Republic of Germany* (Arbitral Tribunal for the Agreement on German External Debts) (16 May 1980) 59 ILR 495 (Young Loan Arbitration), 524. See also *Ambiente Ufficio S.p.A. and others v. Argentine Republic*, ICSID Case No. ARB/08/9 (formerly *Giordano Alpi and others v. Argentine Republic*), Dissenting Opinion of Santiago Torres Bernárdez of 2 May 2013, para. 349: '*... as a general proposition the "undertaking to arbitrate" in international law must be embodied in a written instrument excluding thereby the possibility of invoking forum prorogatum as a basis of jurisdiction in international arbitration.*' See also *Klöckner Industrie-Anlagen GmbH and others v. United Republic of Cameroon and Société Camerounaise des Engrais*, ICSID Case No. ARB/81/2, Award of 21 October 1983, 4 (the subject-matter of the dispute may be extended '*at any time, even in written submissions to the Tribunal ("forum prorogatum")*').

Articles 25 to 27 thereof.[37] In the case of ICSID, the 'double-keyhole' approach applies, in matters of competence and jurisdiction: the tribunal's powers is delimited by the applicable arbitration clause and the ICSID Convention,[38] much like the ICJ can hear a claim only if the parties' consent is recorded both in their membership in the Statute (foundational jurisdiction) and through a specific instrument relating to the dispute, normally a treaty or a declaration under the optional clause of Article 36 of the ICJ Statute.[39]

This double-keyhole approach has caused controversy over the treaty parties' ability to derogate from, and exceed, the outer jurisdictional boundaries[40] set in the ICSID Convention.[41] The *TSA v. Argentina* tribunal took a firm view on the matter, in a passage that seemed to rely precisely on the difference between foundational jurisdiction (of the ICSID Centre) and specific jurisdiction (subject to the parties' agreement):

37 It appears that the same double key-hole analysis applies to cases brought before ICSID's Additional Facilities, by virtue of Rule 4(2) of the Additional Facility, which refers to Article 25 of the ICSID Convention. See *MNSS B.V. and Recupero Credito Acciaio N.V. v. Montenegro*, ICSID Case No. ARB(AF)/12/8, Award of 4 May 2016, para. 186.

38 See for instance *Salini Costruttori s.p.a. and Italstrade s.p.a. v. Kingdom of Morocco*, ICSID Case No. ARB/00/4, Decision on Jurisdiction of 23 July 2001, para. 44; *Consortium RFCC v. Royaume du Maroc*, ICSID Case No. ARB/00/6, Decision on Jurisdiction of 16 July 2001, para. 51. See how this notion is phrased in the *SGS Société Générale de Surveillance SA v. Republic of the Philippines*, ICSID Case No ARB/02/6, Decision on Jurisdiction, 29 January 2004, para. 154: '*The jurisdiction of the Tribunal is determined by the combination of the BIT and the ICSID Convention*'; see also *Bayindir Insaat Turizm Ticaret Ve Sanayi A.S. v. Islamic Republic of Pakistan*, ICSID Case No. ARB/03/29, Decision on Jurisdiction of 14 November 2005, para. 122. It is sometimes suggested that, in the field of ICSID, the distinction between competence (of the tribunal) and jurisdiction (of the Centre) might be accurate, at least conceptually, see Veijo Heiskanen, '*Ménage à trois?* Jurisdiction, Admissibility and Competence in Investment Treaty Arbitration' (2014) 29 ICSID Review 231.

39 The combination of general jurisdiction (defined by the Convention) and specific competence (defined by a specific instrument) is acknowledged in Hanno Wehland, 'Jurisdiction and Admissibility in Proceedings under the ICSID Convention and the ICSID Additional Facility Rules' in Crina Baltag (ed), *ICSID Convention after 50 Years: Unsettled Issues* (Kluwer 2016) 230.

40 The expression '*outer limits*' is used in Aron Broches, Academy of International Law, Recueil des cours, vol. 136 [1973 II].

41 Judith Levine, 'Navigating the parallel universe of investor–State arbitrations under the UNCITRAL Rules' in Brown and Miles above (n 23) 369, 396 ff.

> Article 25 of the ICSID Convention defines the ambit of ICSID's jurisdiction. In other words, it defines the extent, hence also the objective limits, of this jurisdiction (including the jurisdiction of tribunals established therein) which cannot be extended or derogated from even by agreement of the Parties.[42]

This approach requires assessing the alignment between the Convention's and the investment treaty's jurisdictional dimensions. States could not, even if they wanted to, expand the foundational jurisdiction of the Centre through an *inter partes* agreement. Conversely, it is possible for the parties to restrict their consent to arbitration, excluding certain categories of disputes.[43] In principle, therefore, the foundational and specific requirements for jurisdiction apply cumulatively.[44] Some difficulties have occurred in the practice regarding the possible misalignment of the requirements in the ICSID Convention and the applicable investment treaty.

One such issue concerned the definition of 'investment' under the Convention (as opposed, and in addition to, the definition in the applicable treaty), and the rise and ruin of the arbitrator-made requirement that

---

42 *TSA Spectrum de Argentina SA v. Argentina Republic*, ICSID Case No. ARB/ 05/5, Award of 19 December 2008, para. 134. Similar statements can be found in *Joy Mining Machinery Limited v. Arab Republic of Egypt*, ICSID Case No. ARB/03/11, Award on Jurisdiction of 6 August 2004, para. 50; *Malaysian Historical Salvors, SDN, BHD v. The Government of Malaysia*, ICSID Case No. ARB/05/10, Award on Jurisdiction of 17 May 2007, para. 55.

43 See in particular Article 25(4) and Article 26 ICSID. As correctly pointed out in Shany above (n 25) 65, these allowed limitations can be construed, alternatively, as arrangements relating to the specific jurisdiction of the tribunal or variable limits to the foundational jurisdictional of the Centre. See also Robert N Hornick, 'The Mihaly Arbitration Pre-Investment Expenditure as a Basis for ICSID Jurisdiction' (2003) 20(2) Journal of International Arbitration 189, 194–195. A case that appears to allow the enlargement of the ICSID jurisdiction agreed *inter se* is *Autopista Concesionada de Venezuela, C.A. v. Bolivarian Republic of Venezuela*, ICSID Case No. ARB/00/5, Decision on Jurisdiction of 27 September 2001. In this case the State and the investor had agreed in a contract to consider the investor foreign by virtue of foreign shareholding (as opposed to foreign control, as required by Article 25(2)(b) ICSID). The tribunal accepted this characterisation (para. 119) but also made sure that the outcome would not be unreasonable (para. 122).

44 *Patrick Mitchell v. Democratic Republic of Congo*, ICSID Case No. ARB/99/7, Decision on the Application for Annulment of the Award of November 1, 2006, para. 31: '*the parties to an agreement and the States which conclude an investment treaty cannot open the jurisdiction of the Centre to any operation they might arbitrarily qualify as an investment. It is thus repeated that, before ICSID arbitral tribunals, the Washington Convention has supremacy over an agreement between the parties or a BIT.*'

investments contribute to the economic development of the host-state to fall under the Convention.[45] Currently, tribunals generally downplay this criterion.[46] More generally, the *Salini* tribunal's attempt to unpack the meaning of 'investment' under the Convention, which had met with some approval initially, has more recently been considered as an undue usurpation of the parties' right to shape the meaning of 'investment' through consent. A tribunal went as far as discarding the *Salini* criteria and holding that, given the silence of the Convention on what an investment is, only the definitions in the treaty are relevant.[47]

Another example of the interface between the Convention's and a treaty's jurisdictional *rationes* concerns the nationality requirement. On the one hand, Article 25(2)(b) ICSID requires the foreign nationality of the legal persons seeking to bring an investment claim to the Centre. This legal requirement points to the general principle of nationality by incorporation that prevails in

---

45 This criterion, listed by the *Salini* tribunal (*Salini v. Morocco* above (n 38) para. 37–40, but consider also the discussion in *Fedax N.V. v. The Republic of Venezuela*, ICSID Case No. ARB/96/3, Decision of the Tribunal on Objections to Jurisdiction of 11 July 1997, para. 43) was subsequently declassified as a descriptive but inessential feature of investments. See in particular *Malaysian Historical Salvors, SDN, BHD v. Malaysia* (ICSID Case No. ARB/05/10, Decision on the Application for Annulment of 16 April 2009). One member of the Ad Hoc Committee disagreed on this point and posited the necessity of the contribution requirement; see *Malaysian Historical Salvors, SDN, BHD v. Malaysia* (ICSID Case No. ARB/05/10, Dissenting Opinion of Judge Mohamed Shahabuddeen of 19 February 2009). See also *Mr. Saba Fakes v. Republic of Turkey*, ICSID Case No. ARB/07/20, Award of 14 July 2010, para. 111.

46 See the recent example in *İçkale İnşaat Limited Şirketi v. Turkmenistan*, ICSID Case No. ARB/10/24, Award of 8 March 2016, para. 295–296. See also *Consortium Groupement LESI-Dipenta v. People's Democratic Republic of Algeria*, ICSID Case No. ARB/03/8, Award of 10 January 2005, para. 13(iv); *Victor Pey Casado and President Allende Foundation v. Republic of Chile*, ICSID Case No. ARB/98/2, Award of 8 May 2008, para. 232; *Société Civile Immobilière de Gaëta v. Republic of Guinea*, ICSID Case No. ARB/12/36, Award of 21 December 2015, para. 207.

47 *Mr. Hassan Awdi, Enterprise Business Consultants, Inc. and Alfa El Corporation v. Romania*, ICSID Case No. ARB/10/13, Award of 2 March 2015, para. 199: '*Thus, the definition of "investment" in a treaty will determine its content in an exclusive way, with no room for additions or subtractions.*' The debate regarding the parties' autonomy to define investments in the ICSID framework is illustrated in *Ceskoslovenska Obchodni Banka, A.S. v. The Slovak Republic*, ICSID Case No. ARB/97/4, Decision of the Tribunal on Objections to Jurisdictions of 24 May 1999, para. 66–68. Conversely, a non-ICSID tribunal referred to the *Salini* criteria (minus the one about the contribution to the local economy one) to construe the term '*investment*' in the Energy Charter Treaty, see *Isolux Netherlands, BV v. Kingdom of Spain*, SCC Case V2013/153, Award of 17 July 2016, para. 686.

customary international law, but also allows States to agree to different nationality criteria, including effective seat, control, place of central management or registered office.[48]

On the other hand, under art 25(2)(b) of the ICSID Convention, States can agree to extend exceptionally the BIT's protection to investments with the nationality of the host State, which are controlled by nationals of the home State. The clause in the Convention setting an '*objective Convention limit*,'[49] the tribunal is allowed and required to pierce the veil of formal nationality, to ascertain the material control of the company.[50] If necessary, the tribunal is entitled to pierce the veil several times, i.e. '*up to the source of real control*'.[51] Even if the parties, in the BIT, have agreed to a more formalistic requirement, making the treaty applicable also to companies controlled only formally by foreign nationals, the threshold for jurisdiction in the Convention prevails.[52]

2 Ratione Materiae

Besides the constraints of the ICSID Convention (if applicable), consent *ratione materiae* in investment treaties is regulated directly by the arbitration clauses and indirectly by the clauses that set the conditions for the application of the treaty (e.g., the clauses with the definitions, the denial of benefits clauses,

48 For evidence of such flexibility, see *Orascom TMT Investments S.à r.l. v. People's Democratic Republic of Algeria*, ICSID Case No. ARB/12/35, Final Award of 31 May 2017, para. 266; *KT Asia Investment Group B.V. v. Republic of Kazakhstan*, ICSID Case No. ARB/09/8, Award of 17 October 2013, para. 113; *Mobil Corporation, Venezuela Holdings, B.V., Mobil Cerro negro Holding, Ltd., Mobil Venezolana de Petróleos Holdings, Inc., Mobil Cerro Negro, Ltd., and Mobil Venezolana de Petróleos, Inc. v. Bolivarian Republic of Venezuela*, ICSID Case No. ARB/07/27, Decision on Jurisdiction of 10 June 2010, para. 156; *The Rompetrol Group N.V. v. Romania*, ICSID Case No. ARB/06/3, Decision on the Respondent's Preliminary Objections on Jurisdiction and Admissibility of 18 April 2008, para. 113; *Soabi v. Republic of Senegal*, ICSID Case No. ARB/82/1, Decision on Objections to Jurisdiction of 19 July 1984, para. 29.

49 *Vacuum Salt Products Ltd. v. Republic of Ghana*, ICSID Case No. ARB/92/1, Award of 16 February 1994, para. 36. In this case, the clause granting the investor's right to resort to ICSID arbitration was contained in a lease agreement.

50 *TSA Spectrum* above (n 42) para. 147.

51 Ibid., para. 153.

52 This is the outcome of the *TSA Spectrum v. Argentina* arbitration, above (n 42). Under art 1(b)(iii) of the Dutch-Argentinean BIT the parties agreed to consider as investors of a Contracting Party all '*legal persons, wherever located, controlled, directly or indirectly, by nationals of that Contracting Party*.' The investor was formally owned by a Dutch company and considered this fact sufficient to obtain the protection of the BIT. However, since the Dutch company was held predominantly by an Argentinean national, the tribunal pierced the veil under Article 25(2)(b) of the ICSID Convention and declined jurisdiction.

the MFN and umbrella clauses). Investment treaties only extend protection to investments. Whereas sometimes treaties confer jurisdiction to international tribunals generically over all disputes in connection with an investment,[53] they more commonly limit the jurisdiction to disputes arising from the alleged breach of the treaty itself.[54] When the basis for jurisdiction is a contract, the terms of the arbitration clause and law chosen by the parties to govern the contract must be scrutinised to determine whether a claim based on customary international law is within the scope of the tribunal's jurisdiction (for instance, asserting a breach the minimum standard of protection, or seeking protection against unlawful or uncompensated expropriation).[55]

The scope *ratione materiae* of the tribunal's jurisdiction, of course, is also determined by the reach of the substantive obligations of the treaty. The following pages explore selected issues of jurisdiction *ratione materiae* that have arisen in the arbitration practice.

The Preliminary Oil Platforms *Test of Jurisdiction*

To establish its jurisdiction *ratione materiae*, the tribunal must be satisfied that the claim falls under the material normative scope of the applicable investment treaty. In other words, the tribunal must ascertain that a finding of breach against the respondent is at least legally possible.[56] This screening exercise aims to curb (a *species* of) patently hopeless claims' procession to the

53 Even when they concern general measures of public policy, such as taxes, which allegedly affect the investment in violation of the treaty, see *Spyridon Roussalis v. Romania*, ICSID Case No. ARB/06/1, Award of 7 December 2011, para. 490–493 (all matters, including breaches of domestic law or human rights violations, are within the jurisdiction of the tribunal, when they concern the investment). See ibid., para. 601, distinguishing from *Biloune v. Ghana Investments Centre*, Award of 27 October 1989 and 30 June 1990, XIX Yearbook Commercial Arbitration 11, 1994, para. 9 (in which the link with the investment was too remote to warrant the jurisdiction of the tribunal).

54 An overview of typical dispute settlement clauses in investment treaties is provided in August Reinisch, 'The Scope of Investor-State Dispute Settlement in International Investment Agreements' (2013) 21 Asia Pacific Law Review 3.

55 For instance, the tribunal decided in *Cambodia Power Company v. Kingdom of Cambodia*, ICSID Case No. ARB/09/18, Decision on Jurisdiction of 22 March 2011, para. 334–338 that the arbitration clause's language (covering '*any dispute ... in connection with this Agreement*') and the selection of English law entitled the claimant to bring claims based on customary international law.

56 The wording of Article 10.20(4) of the DR-CAFTA, which arguably codifies this procedural objection and assigns to it an inherently preliminary nature, are instructive, as they refer to an 'objection by the respondent that, as a matter of law, a claim submitted is not a claim for which an award in favor of the claimant may be made.'

merits, by preventing the possibility that the tribunal's jurisdiction *ratione materiae* is established automatically through the mere mentioning in the claim of a set of obligations on which the tribunal has jurisdiction. Given the preliminary nature of this endeavour, tribunals are called to carry out a *prima facie* analysis of the claim.[57] To do so, investment tribunals have borrowed from the ICJ the so-called *Oil Platforms* test, whereby they ascertain *prima facie* whether the alleged facts, if proven, are capable of constituting breaches of the applicable treaty.[58] If jurisdiction can be ruled out without looking at the evidence, the case can be dismissed. Conversely, if any determination need to be done that relies on controverted issues of facts, the jurisdiction *ratione materiae* of the tribunal is deemed established, and the analysis of the evidence will be performed at the stage of the merits.

The precise contours of the *prima facie* analysis are controversial. Inevitably, the non-prevailing party at this stage will argue that the determination was too superficial and that they *already* possess reliable evidence to rebut the outcome. Conversely, any look into such evidence will inevitably approximate a full analysis on the merits and engage the parties' equality of arms, legitimating each party's right to have contrary evidence considered. The task of tribunals is ultimately steeped in judicial discretion, but some principles are available. Whereas the tribunal will not consider the claimant's case at face value, it will ascertain whether it is '*decently arguable*'; whereas it will not look into the actual probability of success (which depends on the merits), it will verify that the case has '*a reasonable possibility as pleaded*'.[59] The *Cervin v. Costa*

57 In other jurisdictions, similar checks are ascribed to an admissibility analysis, see for instance Article 35(3)(a) of the European Court of Human Rights: '*The Court shall declare inadmissible any individual application submitted under Article 34 if it considers that: (a) the application is ... manifestly ill-founded*'. The reference to admissibility in these cases reflect the real nature of the test (which presupposes jurisdiction and effectively consists in an expedite analysis of the merits). The *Oil Platforms* case, instead, operates at an abstract level, as it expressly rules out the analysis of any controverted facts of the case.

58 See *Salini Costruttori S.p.A. and Italstrade S.p.A. v. The Hashemite Kingdom of Jordan*, ICSID Case No. ARB/02/13, Decision on Jurisdiction of 9 November 2004, para. 137 ff. The tribunal summarised the prevailing practice and concluded that the applicable test must take into account '*two opposing preoccupations: to ensure that courts and tribunals are not flooded with claims which have no chance of success and sometimes are even of an abusive nature; but to ensure equally that, in considering issues of jurisdiction, courts and tribunals do not go into the merits of cases without sufficient prior debate*' (para. 151).

59 *Chevron Corporation and Texaco Petroleum Corporation v. The Republic of Ecuador*, UNCITRAL, PCA Case No. 2009–23, Third Interim Award on Jurisdiction and Admissibility of 27 February 2012, part IV, para. 4.8. See also *Société Générale in Respect of DR Energy*

Rica tribunal issued further guidelines. A mere allegation that the respondent breached a treaty is insufficient: claimant must explain which facts would be attributable to the State and could establish a treaty breach.[60] The majority and a dissenting arbitrator differed on the degree of precision required in the allegation of facts at this stage.[61]

In TECO *v. Guatemala*, for instance, the tribunal in turn examined the prevailing interpretation of the minimum standard of protection in CAFTA,[62] which encompasses a duty of good faith, and noted that the investor's allegations against Guatemala pointed to a repudiation of the regulatory framework and bad faith behaviour.[63] Hence, the claim fell under the jurisdiction of the tribunal *ratione materiae*:

> There is in fact no doubt in the eyes of the Arbitral Tribunal that, if the Claimant proves that Guatemala acted arbitrarily and in complete and willful disregard of the applicable regulatory framework, or showed a complete lack of candor or good faith in the regulatory process, such behavior would constitute a breach of the minimum standard.[64]

Instead, the tribunal held in BIVAC *v. Paraguay* that the investor's claim of expropriation did not pass the *prima facie* test:[65] even if proved, the State's

---

Holdings Limited and Empresa Distribuidora de Electricidad del Este, S.A. v. The Dominican Republic, UNCITRAL, LCIA Case No. UN 7927, Award on Preliminary Objections to Jurisdiction of 19 September 2008, para. 61.

60 *Cervin Investissements S.A. and Rhone Investissements S.A. v. Republic of Costa Rica*, ICSID Case No. ARB/13/2, Decision on Jurisdiction of 15 December 2014, para. 322. See also *Telenor Mobile Communications A.S. v. The Republic of Hungary*, ICSID Case No. ARB/04/15, Award of 13 September 2006 para. 68; *Continental Casualty Company v. The Argentine Republic*, ICSID Case No. ARB/03/9, Decision on Jurisdiction of 22 February 2006, para. 61; *Saipem S.p.A. v. The People's Republic of Bangladesh*, ICSID Case No. ARB/05/07, Decision on Jurisdiction and Recommendation on Provisional Measures of 21 March 2007, para. 83; *Achmea B.V. v. The Slovak Republic, UNCITRAL, PCA Case No. 2013-12 (Number 2)*, Award on Jurisdiction and Admissibility of 20 May 2014, para. 217.

61 *Cervin* above (n 60) dissent of Ricardo Ramírez-Hernández, para. 3 ff (in particular para. 13, 21).

62 TECO *Guatemala Holdings,* LLC *v. Republic of Guatemala*, ICSID Case No. ARB/10/23, Award of 19 December 2013, para. 458.

63 Ibid., para. 460–461.

64 Ibid., 465. Other examples mentioned by the TECO tribunal are *Bayindir* above (n 38) para. 197; *Telefónica S.A. v. Argentine Republic*, ICSID Case No. ARB/03/20, Decision on Jurisdiction of 25 May 2006; *Impregilo S.p.A. v. Islamic Republic of Pakistan*, ICSID Case No. ARB/03/3, Decision on Jurisdiction of 22 April 2005.

65 *Bureau Veritas* above (n 31) para. 117.

alleged failure to honour a schedule of payments under a concession with the investor could not constitute expropriation under the BIT. Likewise, the majority of the *Cervin v. Costa Rica* tribunal rejected an FET/expropriation claim based on an alleged lack of clarity of the regulatory framework, because the reading of the regulation offered by the claimant was implausible. In any case, no breach of FET could derive from a supposed lack of clarity of the applicable regulations, '*in the absence of bad faith on the part of the regulator or of other special circumstances*.'[66] A claim of discriminatory treatment was similarly rejected *prima facie*.[67]

Ultimately, the *Oil Platforms* objection must succeed only in the rare occasion of implausible or frivolous claims, and the practice reflects such exceptional character.[68]

In the ICSID framework, Rule 41.5 affords the possibility to raise a preliminary objection against claims that are manifestly without legal merit, in separate incidental proceedings.[69] This possibility was introduced in 2006, and several recent treaties have included it since.[70] The objections are reviewed by the tribunals in an expedite fashion, and are therefore appropriate for consideration of *Oil Platforms* objections.[71] The appropriateness of Rule 41.5 proceedings for *Oil Platforms* objections can be demonstrated *a contrario*:[72] the tribunals often reject Rule 41.5 applications mentioning the need to resolve

66 *Cervin* above (n 60) para. 362. Arbitrator Ricardo Ramírez-Hernández dissented on this point.

67 Ibid., para. 379.

68 Ibid., see dissent, para. 57, noting that only 10% of the cases in which the *Oil Platforms* objection was raised led to a finding of lack of jurisdiction.

69 Under Rule 41(5), the respondent can raise an objection that the claim is 'manifestly without legal merit'. Such objections include, but are not limited to, a so-called *Oil Platform* objection (i.e., that the conduct described in the claim is unable to engage, even theoretically, the obligations invoked).

70 See for instance Article 10.20(4) of the DR-CAFTA; Article 8.32 of CETA; Article 9.23(4) of the TPP.

71 The proceedings can be used to raise other procedural objections too. In *Ansung Housing Company Limited v China*, ICSID Case No. ARB/14/25, Award of 9 March 2017 the respondent successfully raised an objection ratione temporis to the tribunal's jurisdiction; in *Rachel S. Grynberg, Stephen M. Grynberg, Miriam Z. Grynberg and RSM Production Company v. Grenada*, ICSID Case No. ARB/10/6, Award of 10 December 2010 the respondent succeeded in raising an objection based on abuse of process and *res judicata*; in *Global Trading Resource Corp. and Globex International, Inc. v. Ukraine*, ICSID Case No. ARB/09/11, Award of 1 December 2010, the tribunal found that the claimants had no investment.

72 As of date, no Rule 41(5) decision has rejected a claim for a manifest impossibility of the claim falling under the scope *ratione materiae* of the invoked instrument.

a legal issue through a complete survey of the evidence and the legal issues raised by the parties.[73] As explained above, this is precisely the kind of predicament that would certify the impossibility of upholding an *Oil Platforms* objection. An ICSID tribunal cared to comment on the potential interplay between Rule 41.5 objections and *Oil Platforms* challenges raised without recourse to the expedite proceedings. It remarked on the circumstances differentiating the two procedural scenarios,[74] but did not dismiss the practical possibility that they overlap in substance.[75] The point remains, at least, that raising a successful *Oil Platforms* objection after the corresponding objection has been rejected in Rule 41.5 proceedings is technically possible—the Rule 41.5 decision is no *res judicata* for any jurisdictional objection—but practically implausible.

Contractual Claims

In principle, investment treaty tribunals only have jurisdiction '*to hear and determine breach of treaty claims, not breach of contract claims.*'[76] Nevertheless,

---

73 For instance, see *Álvarez y Marín Corporación S.A. and others v. Republic of Panama*, ICSID Case No. ARB/15/14, Reasoning of the Decision on Respondent's Preliminary Objections pursuant to ICSID Arbitration Rule 41(5) of 4 April 2016, para. 96 (a dispute hinging on controverted facts cannot be resolved in expedite proceedings).

74 *Trans-Global Petroleum, Inc. v. Hashemite Kingdom of Jordan*, ICSID Case No. ARB/07/25, Decision on the Respondent's Objection Pursuant to Rule 41(5) of 12 May 2008, para. 103 (notes omitted): '*The Tribunal does not consider that the Respondent's submissions were materially advanced by the several ICSID decisions and awards applying Judge Higgins' dictum as to disputed facts in the ICJ's Oil Platforms case. These ICSID materials were directed at objections based on the tribunal's jurisdiction or competence under Article 41 of the ICSID Convention and Rule 41(1) of the ICSID Arbitration Rules—not Rule 41(5). Moreover, the procedure for such jurisdictional objections is also different from Rule 41(5): the timing of the respondent's jurisdictional objection can follow the claimant's first memorial, long after the request for arbitration and the first session; and the tribunal can postpone its decision or award by joining the objection to the merits of the dispute under Article 41(2) of the ICSID Convention and Article 41(4) of the ICSID Arbitration Rules.*'

75 For instance, the second Rule 41(5) objection raised by Panama in *Álvarez y Marín* above (n 73) is comparable to an *Oil Platforms* objection in substance (essentially, that the contested act could not produce legal effects, and was for this reason incapable of constituting a breach of the applicable treaty). Moreover, the reasons for rejecting this objection are redolent of the reasons commonly used to reject *Oil Platforms* challenges to the tribunal's jurisdiction (essentially, that the issue raised a '*complex issue [cuestión compleja]' that could not decided using the 'standard of burden of evidence applicable in this phase of proceedings [el nivel de alegación y prueba existente en la actualidad]*' (see para. 102).

76 *Tenaris S.A. and Talta—Trading e Marketing Sociedade Unipessoal Lda. v. Bolivarian Republic of Venezuela*, ICSID Case No. ARB/12/23, Award of 29 January 2016, para. 301.

it is common for the investor to impute to the host State a failure to perform a contractual commitment.[77] The relevant conduct, which might give rise to a contractual claim, could also underpin a treaty claim, without entailing a logical or legal contradiction.[78] For instance, the State's failure to comply with a concession contract could also entail a breach of the standard of fair and equitable treatment.[79] In other words, the same facts could be used to found multiple claims with different legal characterizations.[80] The prevailing view is that the two distinct aspects can coexist and that, therefore, there is no reason to reject a treaty claim only because it is based on State conduct which also amounts to a contractual breach,[81] or only because contract matters are relevant—as facts—to the outcome of the treaty claims.[82]

Respondents often attempt to characterise a claim as 'purely' contractual, as if the 'contractual purity' of the claim were a critical legal concept, preventing the possibility of framing the claim as treaty-based as well.[83] There are cases

---

See also AES *Corporation and Tau Power B.V. v. Republic of Kazakhstan*, ICSID Case No. ARB/10/16, Award of 1 November 2013, para. 192. Jurisdiction on contract claims might be warranted when the treaty contains an umbrella clause, or a widely-worded arbitration clause. These scenarios are discussed elsewhere in this essay.

77 Zachary Douglas, *The International Law of Investment Claims* (CUP 2009) para. 447.

78 *EDF International S.A., SAUR International S.A. and León Participaciones Argentinas S.A. v. Argentine Republic*, ICSID Case No. ARB/03/23, Award of 11 June 2012, para. 931: '*There is nothing mysterious about the fact that the same acts may constitute both a contractual breach and a violation of relevant treaty obligations*'.

79 For a recent example, see *MNSS v. Montenegro* above (n 37) para. 159: '*In determining claims for breach of the BIT, the Tribunal may examine as a question of fact whether the Privatization Agreement was breached, by way of background to a claim that does not have the nature of a contract or an umbrella clause claim. For example, the Tribunal is entitled to decide, as a question of fact, whether the Privatization Agreement was breached when deciding a claim for violation of the fair and equitable treatment standard in the BIT*.' See also AES above (n 76) para. 193.

80 On the analytical distinction between treaty and contract claims, with particular reference to the rules on attribution of State responsibility, see *Impregilo v. Islamic Republic of Pakistan* above (n 64) para. 262.

81 *Compañía de Aguas del Aconquija SA. and Vivendi Universal SA. v. Argentine Republic*, ICSID Case No. ARB/97/3, Decision on Annulment of 3 July 2002, para. 105; *Bayindir* above (n 38) para. 215; *Impregilo S.p.A. v. Islamic Republic of Pakistan* above (n 64) para. 219, 258.

82 *Bayindir* above (n 38) para. 235–236.

83 Among the many cases, see for instance *Ampal* above (n 22) para. 233: '*In view of the fact that the Gas Supply Dispute is purely contractual in nature, the Respondent submits that it thus falls outside the scope of the arbitration clauses in the Treaties*.'

which confirm this view in *dicta*,[84] but the attending principle, if any, is rarely applied in the practice. In fact, so long as a claim—which could be also contractual if framed differently—is plausibly based on the standards of protection of the treaty, it cannot be considered purely contractual, and the tribunal will normally retain jurisdiction on it. See the reasoning of the *Ampal v. Egypt* tribunal:

> the Tribunal accepts that, in order for it to find that there has been a breach of [the Treaty] standards in relation to the Gas Supply Dispute, it will need to determine as an incidental question whether the [concession contract] was validly terminated. However, this does not change the fact that the key issue under the Treaty in respect of a claim for unlawful expropriation or breach of the fair and equitable treatment is whether there has been a loss of property right constituted by the contract or whether legitimate expectations arose under the contract.[85]

This approach, however, complicates the coordination of parallel domestic and arbitration proceedings. Since there is no formal identity between the causes of action of each dispute, the principles of *lis pendens* or *forum non conveniens* cannot lead the tribunal to decline its jurisdiction when a contractual claim which revolves on the same factual circumstances has been brought to a national court,[86] or should be brought before

84 *Gustav F W Hamester GmbH & Co KG v. Republic of Ghana*, ICSID Case No. ARB/07/24, Award, 18 June 2010, para. 329; *Malicorp* above (n 26).

85 *Ampal* above (n 22) para. 255.

86 See Reinisch above (n 54) 16, referring to *CMS Gas Transmission Company v. Argentina*, ARB/01/8, Decision on Jurisdiction, 17 July 2003, para. 80 and other cases. When the triple identity test is used, even fork-in-the-road clauses are hardly effective. See for instance *Transglobal Green Energy, LLC and Transglobal Green Energy de Panama, S.A. v. The Republic of Panama*, ICSID Case No. ARB/13/28, Award of 2 June 2016, where the Respondent, at para. 88, complains that '*no tribunal that has applied the triple identity test has found the fork-in-the-road clause to have been triggered, thus depriving this clause of practical significance.*' A similar remark is made by the tribunal in *Chevron v. Ecuador* above (n 59) Part IV, para. 4.76. In this dispute, the fork in the road clause only applied to claims submitted by the claimant. The tribunal accordingly and did not decline jurisdiction on claims referring to situations on which national litigation had been launched by the responding State. An issue arose regarding the pleas in defense made by the investors in domestic proceedings, which could theoretically trigger the fork-in-the-road provision. The arbitration tribunal distinguished between autonomous claims (including counterclaims) and pleas in defense, holding that the latter fell outside the fork clause, see ibid., para. 4.82: '*The notion of 'submission' of a dispute connotes the making of a choice and a*

it.[87] For the same reason (a lack of identity between the causes of action of the domestic and the international claims), a fork-in-the-road provision will apply only rarely.[88] These clauses, which bar recourse to arbitration if the same claim has already been brought to domestic courts, only operate when the triple-identity test is satisfied,[89] unless the tribunal opts for a test based on the '*essential basis*' of the claim.[90] In *AES v. Kazakhstan*, the tribunal concluded that the claim before it differed from the one brought to domestic courts, under either test.[91] In *Hassan Awdi v. Romania* the tribunal stopped short of running the triple identity test. It noted that the claimant had indeed brought a claim before local courts, but the proceedings were discontinued before any hearings took place, for failure to pay court fees. As a result, there was no risk of parallel litigation, which fork-in-the-road clauses seek to prevent.[92]

When arbitration is launched in spite of an exclusive dispute settlement clause in the contract, the host State's attempt to label the claim as purely contractual seeks to achieve the result prefigured in a *dictum* of the *ad hoc* committee in *Vivendi*:

---

voluntary decision to refer the dispute to the court for resolution: as a matter of the plain and ordinary meaning of the term, it does not extend to the raising of a defence in response to another's claim submitted to that court'.

87 Commenting on the existence of an exclusive jurisdiction clause for contract claims, the tribunal in *Bayindir* above (n 38) reasoned (para. 150–151): '*it is undisputed that the 1997 Contract contains a dispute settlement clause providing for arbitration under the 1940 Arbitration Act of Pakistan.... As a matter of principle, this arbitration clause is irrelevant for the purpose of the jurisdiction of this Tribunal over the Treaty Claims*'. See also *Camuzzi International S.A. v. Argentine Republic*, ICSID Case No. ARB/03/2, Decision on Jurisdiction of 11 May 2005, para. 89.

88 See Christoph Schreuer, 'Consent to Arbitration', in Peter Muchlinski, Federico Ortino, and Christoph Schreuer (eds), *The Oxford Handbook of International Investment Law* (OUP 2012) 831, 848, and case-law referred to therein.

89 *Alex Genin, Eastern Credit Limited, Inc. and A.S. Baltoil v. The Republic of Estonia*, ICSID Case No. ARB/99/2, Award of 25 June 2001, para. 331.

90 In *Pantechniki S.A. Contractors & Engineers (Greece) v. The Republic of Albania*, ICSID Case No. ARB/07/21, Award of 30 July 2009, Paulsson (sole arbitrator) took issue with the formalistic requirements of the triple identity test and proposed a more substantive test, see para. 64: '*The Tribunal must determine whether the claim truly does have an autonomous existence outside the contract. Otherwise the Claimant must live with the consequences of having elected to take its grievances to the national courts.*' See also *Supervision y Control S.A. v. Republic of Costa Rica*, ICSID Case No. ARB/12/4, Final Award of 18 January 2017 para. 330.

91 *AES* above (n 76) para. 226–230.

92 *Hassan Awdi* above (n 47) para. 203–205.

> In a case where the essential basis of a claim brought before an international tribunal is a breach of contract, the tribunal will give effect to any valid choice of forum clause in the contract.[93]

Nonetheless, the lack of jurisdiction over contractual disputes cannot entail a lapse of competence over the potential treaty claims.[94] Even in a clear-cut case of exclusive jurisdiction of domestic courts, which was sanctioned by the investment contract and reinforced by an express safeguard in the applicable treaty,[95] the tribunal took pains to explain that the treaty-based jurisdiction of the tribunal was not affected, let alone excluded:

> … the Tribunal will note that the dispute settlement procedures provided for in the Contract could only cover claims based on breaches of the Contract. Those procedures cannot cover claims based on breaches of the BIT (including breaches of those provisions of the BIT guaranteeing fulfillment of contracts signed with foreign investors). Therefore Article 9(2) does not deprive the Tribunal of such jurisdiction, as it may have, to entertain treaty claims of this nature under other provisions of the BIT.[96]

The case *Getma v. Guinea* tested the limits of this approach.[97] The ICSID arbitration clause in the national investment law envisaged the possibility for the parties to agree on a different forum. The concession contract between the claimant and the host State, indeed, contained an exclusive commercial arbitration clause.[98] The tribunal considered this exclusive forum clause insufficient to undermine its competence *per se*: the arbitration clause in the concession contract covered only the claims arising from it, which could

93 *Vivendi I* annulment decision 2002 above (n 81) para. 98.

94 *Tenaris* above (n 76), para. 307, referring to the decision of the *Vivendi I* annulment committee, and to numerous arbitration awards. See also *Crystallex International Corporation v. Bolivarian Republic of Venezuela*, ICSID Case No. ARB(AF)/11/2, Award of 4 April 2016, para. 480.

95 See Article 9(2) of the Italy/Jordan BIT, which affords priority to the choice of forum in an investment contract, over the means of dispute settlement listed in the treaty itself.

96 *Salini v. Jordan* above (n 58) para. 96.

97 *Getma International and others v. Republic of Guinea*, ICSID Case No. ARB/11/29, Decision on Jurisdiction of 29 December 2012.

98 Which required the parties to submit any dispute arising from the concession to a tribunal established by the Cour Commune de Justice et d'Arbitrage, an arbitration institution based in Abidjan (Côte d'Ivoire).

not exhaust all the possible claims made under the investment statute.[99] Nonetheless, the concession contract governed expressly certain breaches of the contract that plainly entailed a breach also of the investment code which would be arbitrable before ICSID, such as an act of expropriation carried out through the unilateral termination of the concession. Therefore, the tribunal found that the clause '*contractualised*' certain treaty claims.[100] Accordingly, the tribunal lacked competence over the claims based on the State termination of the concession, even if it could otherwise qualify as expropriation and support an investment claim.[101] The ICSID tribunal's competence could be upheld residually on such act only insofar as the claimant could envisage, under the investment code, further consequences and damages arising from the termination other than those regulated in the concession, which included a cap on the recovery of damages.[102] The investor's attempt to seek before the ICSID tribunal damages arising from the unilateral termination of the contract, in excess of the contractual cap, did not succeed. In the tribunal's view, the claimants '*failed to explain why …, in spite of the clear agreement* [in the concession], *it would be sufficient to seise another tribunal and invoke the investment code to invalidate the contractual limitation on damages-interests*'.[103] In other words, the tribunal subscribed to the traditional view that exclusive forum provisions in the contract might in theory coexist with the jurisdiction of an investment tribunal; however, a purely contractual claim fell squarely within the competence of the selected forum. Since the contract expressly absorbed under its regulatory reach certain State acts, the tribunal found that these were removed

---

99 *Getma v. Guinea* above (n 97) para. 105: '*Or, les différends «découlant de la présente Convention» ne sont a priori pas nécessairement les mêmes que ceux «relatifs à l'application et l'interprétation du Code des investissements».*'

100 Ibid., para. 123: '*Dans la mesure où la résiliation est consécutive à un Acte de la Puissance Publique, l'article 32.5 «contractualise» les treaty claims qui, par voie de conséquence, doivent être soumis au Tribunal CCJA conformément à l'article 31 de la Convention.*' The reference to 'treaty' claims is perhaps inaccurate since the claim before the ICSID tribunal was based on an investment statute, not on a treaty.

101 *Getma International and others v. Republic of Guinea*, ICSID Case No. ARB/11/29, Award of 16 August 2016, para. 316.

102 *Getma v. Guinea* above (n 97) para. 125.

103 *Getma v. Guinea*, Award above (n 101) para. 332. My translation. The original text reads '[*l*]*es Demanderesses … n'ont pas expliqué … pourquoi, nonobstant l'accord clair, il suffirait de s'adresser à un autre tribunal et d'invoquer le Code des investissements pour que la limitation contractuelle des dommages-intérêts ne soit plus valable.*'

from its competence by the agreement of the parties,[104] unless the claimant could show that an investment claim would have entailed additional consequences and different remedies.

Ultimately, it is true that a treaty breach can result from a contractual breach, even if not necessarily all contractual breaches will result in a treaty breach.[105] The only defense available to the State, it follows, is not so much to prove that the claim is contractual (which is an irrelevant objection), but to prove that the claim has no connection with the treaty (which is an obvious objection).[106] Sometimes tribunals accept the treaty-nature of a claim only if the alleged conduct of the State goes '*beyond that which an ordinary contracting party could adopt*.'[107] In other words, the actions imputable to the State must transcend a case of mere non-performance that could be attributed to any contractual party, and must instead engage its sovereign authority or *puissance publique* (i.e., there must be a '*State interference with the operation of the contract involved*'[108]). This approach has gained traction and is now described as '*the main test ... to determine whether a contract claim has been disguised as a treaty claim*.'[109]

---

104 Ibid., para. 334: the jurisdiction of the tribunal '*concerne exclusivement les violations du Code des investissements à l'exception de celles qui ont été contractualisées*.'

105 *Consortium RFCC v. Royaume du Maroc*, ICSID Case No. ARB/00/6, Award of 22 December 2003, para. 48.

106 It might be helpful to distinguish between a breach of a contract binding the investor and the State, as opposed to the breach of a contract that the investor has with a State-controlled entity. The former breach could fall directly under the jurisdiction *ratione materiae* of the tribunal, when the relevant clause refers to '*all disputes ... relating to an investment*'. The latter kind, instead, is not covered as such by the offer to arbitrate, and a claim might be brought only if the breach also results in a treaty breach attributable to the State. See *Consortium RFCC v. Royaume du Maroc* above (n 38) para. 67–69.

107 *Salini v. Jordan* above (n 58), para. 155. See also *Impregilo v. Islamic Republic of Pakistan* above (n 64) para. 260; *Bureau Veritas* above (n 31) para. 125.

108 *Joy Mining v. Egypt* above (n 42) para. 72.

109 Stanimir A Alexandrov and James Mendenhall, 'Breach of Treaty Claims and Breach of Contract Claims: Simplification of International Jurisprudence' in Arthur W Rovine (ed), *Contemporary Issues in International Arbitration and Mediation: The Fordham Papers 2014* (Brill 2015) 24, 37. See also *Convial Callao S.A. y CCI—Compañía de concesiones de Infraestructura S.A. c. República del Perú*, ICSID Case No. ARB/10/2, Laudo Final of 21 May 2013, para. 501; *Kristian Almås and Geir Almås v. The Republic of Poland*, UNCITRAL, Award of 27 June 2016, para. 273–284 (the tribunal did not consider the contractual breach attributable to the State but noted that, even if it had been attributable, it would have constituted at most a contractual behaviour—even if allegedly wrongful—and could not entail in any event a treaty breach).

The only avenue available to States to found a jurisdictional objection on an exclusive jurisdiction clause in a contract might be to characterise it as a waiver, on the part of the investor, of the right to resort to arbitration.[110] This characterisation, however, should be assisted by unequivocal language:

> a waiver, if and when admissible at all, is never to be lightly admitted as it requires knowledge and intent of forgoing a right, a conduct rather unusual in economic transactions.[111]

Contracts with Non-State Organs and Umbrella Clauses

When a legal person other than the State is responsible for the contractual breach, it is necessary to consider some specific aspects. At the outset, it must be noted that a lack of privity (the State has no direct contractual dealings with the investor) is not necessarily a valid objection to jurisdiction over investment claims.[112] Before assessing whether there can be a breach of the treaty it is essential to ascertain the attribution of the alleged misconduct to the State, under the customary principles of State responsibility.[113] Unless the contractor is an organ of the State, it might be necessary to determine whether the contractual breach was committed *jure imperii*;[114] if so, the breach of contract could be attributed to the State and possibly engage its treaty obligations, since it was committed by an entity exercising governmental authority while '*acting in that capacity*'.[115] Matters of attribution, however, tend to be reviewed

---

110 See Alexandrov and Mendenhall above (n 109) 41–42.

111 *Crystallex* above (n 94) para. 481. See also *Aguas del Tunari, S.A. v. Republic of Bolivia*, ICSID Case No. ARB/02/3, Decision on Respondent's Objections to Jurisdiction of 21 October 2005, para. 119.

112 See *Yaung Chi Oo Trading Pte. Ltd. v. Government of the Union of Myanmar*, ASEAN Case No ARB/01/1, Award of 31 March 2003, para. 39: '*A dispute can arise directly from an investment whether or not the investment is made pursuant to a contract with the host State or one of its organs.*'

113 See in particular Articles 4, 5 and 8 of the ILC Articles on State Responsibility.

114 See *Sergei Paushok, CJSC Golden East Company and CJSC Vostokneftegaz Company v. The Government of Mongolia*, UNCITRAL, Award on Jurisdiction and Liability of 28 April 2011, para. 592: '*The Tribunal therefore has no hesitation in concluding that MongolBank acted de jure imperii, … Therefore, even if MongolBank were not to be considered an organ of the State but merely an entity exercising elements of governmental authority, Claimants would be entitled to pursue their claim against Respondent in connection with the actions mentioned above.*'

115 Article 5 of the ILC Articles. See, for instance, the award in *Vigotop Limited v. Hungary*, ICSID Case No. ARB/11/22, Award of 1 October 2014, para. 441.

at the stage of the merits and, therefore, exceed the present discussion on jurisdictional requirements.[116] It is just apposite to recall an obverse scenario: when the *investor*'s acts are attributable to the home State, for instance when a company discharges essentially governmental functions, the investor loses standing. Since the dispute is in fact an inter-state one, the claimant cannot be considered a national of the home State and access to investor-State litigation is, in principle, barred.[117] This principle can give way to the parties' agreement, when the applicable instrument recording the States' consent to arbitration expressly envisions the possibility of States or State entreprises acting as investors.[118]

Instead, if a State-owned company has a separate legal personality from the State and its acts are performed in a commercial capacity (*jure gestionis*), they are not attributable to the State.[119] A breach of a contract with a State company, therefore, will not *per se* engage the State's obligations under an investment treaty. Conversely, if it is possible to formulate a treaty-based claim against the State, an exclusive forum-selection clause in the contract with the State company will not bar the investor's resort to investment arbitration, since there is no identity between the parties to the two disputes at stake (the contract claim being directed at the State company, the treaty one at the State).[120]

116 It is common, however, for respondents to raise points of attribution in their preliminary objections, alleging a lack of passive standing (the State is not the rightful defendant in the case). For this reason, tribunals often enter, if only *prima facie* or *ex abundanti cautela*, into the analysis of attribution at the jurisdictional stage. See, for instance, *Helnan International Hotels A/S v. Arab Republic of Egypt*, ICSID Case No. ARB/05/19, Decision on Objection to Jurisdiction of 17 October 2006, para. 911 ff. See also *Tenaris* above (n 76) para. 303. In *Almås v. Poland* above (n 109), the tribunal expressly denied the jurisdictional nature of the objections on attribution, see para. 202.

117 *CSOB* above (n 47) para. 18–27. In that case, the tribunal recognised that the investor was controlled by the State and promoted the State policies, but carried out activities of essentially commercial character, and therefore qualified as investor.

118 Consider, for example, Article 1 of the US Model BIT of 2012, which expressly states that 'a Party or state enterprise thereof' enjoys protection when it makes an investment in the host State.

119 *Almås v. Poland* above (n 109) para. 253.

120 *Ulysseas, Inc. v. The Republic of Ecuador*, UNCITRAL, Interim Award of 28 September 2010, para. 154–156. See in particular para. 151: '*In order for the alleged contractual waiver by Claimant to be effective, the parties involved must be identical. The parties to the contracts which, according to Respondent, would have given effect to the waiver by Claimant of the BIT arbitration, i.e. the two Licence Contracts, should be Ulysseas, on one side, and the State of Ecuador, on the other.*'

Re-characterisation of a contractual claim into a treaty claim might not be necessary if the applicable BIT contains a so-called umbrella clause.[121] Under these provisions, all State commitments towards the investor[122] are safeguarded by a specific treaty obligation, hence expanding the BIT's material scope and, correspondingly, the jurisdiction *ratione materiae* of the tribunal seised. After the apparently incurable split between the *SGS v. Pakistan*[123] and *SGS v. Philippines*[124] tribunals, the subsequent awards could be grouped into two approaches, each tributary to the outcome and reasoning of either case. Some tribunals have espoused the reasoning of the former, i.e., that umbrella clauses do not automatically elevate contractual claims to the level of treaty claims and that other conditions must be met to bring a contractual claim to arbitration.[125] More often, tribunals have sided with the *SGS v. Philippines* case, mostly noting that additional conditions would render virtually superfluous the umbrella clause, the *effet utile* of which must lie precisely in its capacity to turn contractual claims into treaty claims.[126]

When the essential cause of action of a claim brought under an umbrella clause is a breach of a contract with the host State, any contractual forum-selection clause in favour of domestic courts, or any fork-in-the-road provisions in the treaty might apply. When a contract claim is 'treatified,'[127] indeed,

121 Whereas proper umbrella clauses normally require host States to '*observe*' or '*respect*' their undertakings vis-à-vis the investor, other clauses have a hortatory wording and do not empower investors to bring a contractual dispute to arbitration. See for instance Article 2(4) of the Italy/Jordan BIT, as discussed in *Salini v. Jordan* above (n 58).

122 Umbrella clauses cover specific undertakings relating to the investment, not general obligations found, for instance, in domestic law. See *CMS Gas Transmission Company v. The Republic of Argentina*, Decision of the ad hoc Committee on the Application for Annulment of the Argentine Republic of 25 September 2007, para. 95(a) and *WNC Factoring Limited v. The Czech Republic*, PCA Case No. 2014–34, Award of 22 February 2017, para. 345–347.

123 *SGS Société Générale de Surveillance SA v. Islamic Republic of Pakistan*, ICSID Case No ARB/01/13, Decision on Jurisdiction of 6 August 2003.

124 *SGS v. Philippines* above (n 38).

125 See, for instance, *El Paso Energy International Company v. Argentine Republic*, ICSID Case No ARB/03/15, Decision on Jurisdiction, 27 April 2006, para. 85. *Pan American* above (n 9) para. 113. *Salini v. Jordan* above (n 58).

126 *Noble Ventures, Inc v. Romania*, ICSID Case No ARB/O 1/11, Award of 12 October 2005, para. 53; *SGS Société Générale de Surveillance SA v. The Republic of Paraguay*, ICSID Case No ARB/07/29, Award of 12 February 2012, para. 91. *Contra*, see *Joy Mining* above (n 42) para. 81.

127 That is, presented as such (by virtue of an umbrella clause or a generic arbitration clause covering non-treaty disputes) rather than repackaged as a treaty claim.

there is triple identity (parties, object, cause of action) between the claim brought to arbitration and the claim that was brought or ought to be brought to local courts. In this respect, the umbrella clause cuts against the investor: the contractual obligations of the State are elevated together with the exclusive forum selection.[128] For this reason, investors are better advised, if they are able to formulate a treaty claim, to avoid invoking the umbrella clause altogether.[129]

If an umbrella clause is invoked, a problem arises when the underlying contract is not stipulated between the investor and the government of the host State. A lack of privity might occur when, for instance, the parties to the contract are the investor's domestic vehicle and/or a State-owned entity.[130] Tribunals tend to postulate the necessity of privity,[131] but the exact wording of the applicable umbrella clause (for instance, the use of '*investments*' instead of '*investors*') might be relevant and warrant its extension to contracts stipulated by entities connected to the investor:

> the protection of [the umbrella clause] goes beyond the simple direct contractual relationship between the investor and the host State, because such provision establishes that the State shall comply with the obligations undertaken '*… related to investments by investors of the other Contracting Party …*'. Such drafting is sufficiently broad to interpret that the obligations contracted by Costa Rica with Riteve, a company controlled by the Claimant and created exclusively to hold the rights of the

---

128 *Bureau Veritas* above (n 31) para. 148: '*the parties to a contract are not free to pick and choose those parts of the Contract that they may wish to incorporate into an "umbrella clause" provision such as Article 3(4) and to ignore others.*'

129 See, for instance, the claimant's emphatic refusal to rely on the umbrella clause in *Tulip Real Estate and Development Netherlands B.V. v. Republic of Turkey*, ICSID Case No. ARB/11/28, Award of 10 March 2014, para. 351–352.

130 The issue is discussed in Shotaro Hamamoto, 'Parties to the 'Obligations' in the Obligations Observance ('Umbrella') Clause' (2015) 30(2) ICSID Review-Foreign Investment Law Journal 449–464. For a case of a contract between a subsidiary of the investor and a State-owned company, see *Tenaris* above (n 76) para. 305.

131 *Duke Energy Electroquil Partners & Electroquil S.A. v. Republic of Ecuador*, ICSID Case No. ARB/04/19, Award of 18 August 2008, para. 323; *Burlington Resources Inc. v. Republic of Ecuador* (formerly *Burlington Resources Inc. and others v. Republic of Ecuador and Empresa Estatal Petróleos del Ecuador (PetroEcuador)*), ICSID Case No. ARB/08/5, Decision on Liability of 14 December 2012, para. 220; *WNC* above (n 122) para. 325: '*the dominant view is that in respect of contractual obligations, only parties entitled to enforce the obligation under the proper law of the contract may sue.*'

> Contract, are included under the scope of protection of the Treaty. As a result, the Tribunal has jurisdiction ratione materiae over the dispute.[132]

Conversely, the investor might want to enforce through the umbrella clause a contract stipulated by a State-owned entity that has a legal personality distinct from the host State. In *EDF v. Romania*, the tribunal observed that, in a similar scenario, the State has not entered into any obligation under the contract, hence the umbrella clause is inapplicable irrespective of whether the breach of the contract committed by the state-owned entity is attributable to the State.[133] In other words, attribution of responsibility is not the same as attribution of obligations: the former is only possible when the State is already bound by an existing obligation:

> Attribution does not change the extent and content of the obligations arising under the ASRO Contract and the SKY Contract, that remain contractual, nor does it make Romania party to such contracts.[134]

Lack of privity has not prevented some tribunals to entertain umbrella clause claims when the State-owned entity had entered into the contractual commitments on behalf of the State, i.e., to bind it directly.[135] In that scenario, it was possible to attribute the contractual arrangement to the State—as it were—and consider it bound by the deriving obligations. The attributability of the relevant conduct under the rules of State responsibility, in these scenarios, would effectively warrant the indication of the State as the correct defendant against an umbrella-clause claim.

Domestic Regulatory Disputes

Similarly to those hinging on the contractual/treaty divide, objections are sometimes made against domestic regulatory claims. Respondent States can argue that the claim revolves in fact around the application of domestic law

132 *Supervision v. Costa Rica*, supra (n 90), para. 287. Emphasis in the original. See also *AMTO v. Ukraine*, SCC No. 80/2005, Award of 26 March 2008, para. 110.

133 *EDF (Services) Limited v. Romania*, ICSID Case No. ARB/05/13, Award of 8 October 2009, para. 317–318.

134 Ibid., para. 319. Note that the tribunal had determined that there had been no breach of contract, therefore the claim under the umbrella clause would have failed even if privity had not been required.

135 *Noble Ventures* above (n 126) para. 85 (the State-owned entities did represent the State, in the framework of privatisation plans carried out with private investors); *Eureko* above (n 12) para. 248 ff.

and has therefore no international character. Tribunals normally make short shrift of similar objections: as long as there is a plausible treaty-based claim, the involvement of domestic law is not fatal to the jurisdiction *ratione materiae* of the tribunal.

This reasonable conclusion can be reached, *a contrario*, looking at the set of the applicable laws in treaty-based investment arbitration. If the necessity of determinations based on domestic law were sufficient to exclude treaty-based jurisdiction, the ICSID Convention (Article 42(1)) and several treaties would not explicitly include domestic law among the applicable sources.[136] Determinations based on domestic law (or other sources), which are necessary *en route* to the treaty-based review of State measures, are acceptable as a matter of applicable law (or incidental jurisdiction). Claims based, in part, on these determinations do not, as such, fall outside the tribunal's primary jurisdiction.[137] See the reasoning of the tribunal in *TECO v. Venezuela*:

> the Arbitral Tribunal's task is fundamentally to assess the legal relevance of the facts under customary international law [determining the minimum standard protected in the CAFTA]. As a consequence, although the decisions made by the Constitutional Court of Guatemala will have consequences on the findings that the Arbitral Tribunal will have to make under Guatemalan law, such circumstance cannot deprive the Arbitral Tribunal of its jurisdiction to decide the case under international law. In addition, as will be discussed further, the parties in the Guatemalan court proceedings were in any event different.[138]

Whereas the tribunal's primary jurisdiction only concerns the legality of the State's measure under international law, '*the facts in dispute*' include the content of domestic law as interpreted in domestic courts.[139] Obversely, when

136 *TECO* above (n 62) para. 469–470.

137 For instance, consider the case *Tidewater Inc., Tidewater Investment SRL, Tidewater Caribe, C.A., et al. v. The Bolivarian Republic of Venezuela*, ICSID Case No. ARB/10/5, Decision on Jurisdiction of 8 February 2013. The tribunal examined domestic law to determine whether a Venezuelan statute established the requisite consent under Article 25 ICSID (para. 106) and whether the dispute submitted to arbitration was merely the continuation of a previous dispute on matters of domestic law, which would have fallen outwith the application *ratione temporis* of the applicable treaty, because it had occurred before the claimant had acquired the Barbadian nationality which allowed the invocation of the Barbados—Venezuela BIT (para. 187).

138 *TECO* above (n 62) para. 475.

139 Ibid., para. 477.

the tribunal's jurisdiction goes beyond treaty claims (for instance, when an umbrella clause applies), claims based on domestic regulatory law might be entertained, subject to the applicable requirements.[140]

In the case *Iberdrola v. Guatemala*,[141] the host State's objection *ratione materiae* lamenting the purely internal nature of the dispute convinced the tribunal. Since the applicable BIT provided for international arbitration only over disputes '*arising ... over issues governed by* [the BIT itself]',[142] the tribunal interpreted accordingly the States' consent to arbitration and its own attending jurisdiction *ratione materiae*. The tribunal noted that '*issues governed by* [the BIT]'

> ... is not a broad formulation that includes any kind of dispute; it does not even refer to disputes arising out of or relating to an investment, **but only to disputes concerning matters covered by the Treaty.**[143]

The tribunal found that the investor's case, variously and erratically referring to the standards of the BIT, consisted mostly of a claim regarding Guatemala's mistaken interpretation of domestic law. It therefore dismissed the investor's attempt to '*label*'[144] the claim as a treaty-based one. Ultimately, the tribunal implemented the narrow reading of the arbitration clause and rejected the

140 In *Oxus v. Uzbekistan*, for instance, the claimant attempted to invoke the breach of certain municipal decrees, jointly with the umbrella clause, to establish the host State's responsibility under the BIT. The tribunal rejected the claim, holding that the umbrella clause entailed a privity requirement that the State obligations invoked be '*specifically entered into with Claimant*.' Accordingly, non-compliance with general regulations, or with obligations owed to the local vehicle of the foreign investors, could not establish a breach under the umbrella clause. See *Oxus Gold plc v. Republic of Uzbekistan, the State Committee of Uzbekistan for Geology & Mineral Resources, and Navoi Mining & Metallurgical Kombinat*, UNCITRAL, Award of 17 December 2015, para. 851.

141 *Iberdrola Energía S.A. v. Republic of Guatemala*, ICSID Case No. ARB/09/5, Award of 17 August 2012.

142 BIT Spain/Guatemala, Article 11(1). Our translation, the original reading: '*Toda controversia relativa a las inversiones que surja ... respecto a cuestiones reguladas por el presente Acuerdo*.'

143 *Iberdrola Energía S.A. v. Republic of Guatemala* above (n 141) para. 301. Courtesy translation, emphasis in the original. The original text reads: '*No se trata de una expresión amplia que comprenda cualquier tipo de controversias; ni siquiera se refiere a controversias derivadas de o relacionadas con una inversión,* ***sino solamente a controversias referentes a cuestiones reguladas por el Tratado***.'

144 Ibid., para. 349. In the Spanish original text: '*Más allá de* etiquetar *las actuaciones de la Demandada, la Demandante no presenta un razonamiento claro y concreto sobre cuáles*

claim on a *prima facie* review of competence (the *Oil Platforms* test). Even if Iberdrola's allegations would prove correct, they could not result in treaty breaches.[145] The finding of lack of jurisdiction was challenged in annulment, unsuccessfully.[146]

Narrow Arbitration Clauses and Carve-outs ratione materiae

Sometimes, jurisdictional clauses restrict the tribunal's competence. They can refer to a specific means of dispute settlement to the exclusion of others. If ICSID arbitration is excluded, for instance, the clause does not contain the State's consent to that specific arbitration method and, accordingly, an ICSID tribunal seised would not be competent. Conversely, resort to UNCITRAL arbitration might be precluded if the clause provides for the exclusive competence of ICSID tribunals or compulsory recourse to the ICSID Additional Facility.[147]

Arbitration clauses, moreover, can exclude certain subject matters[148] or narrow down the substantive jurisdiction of the tribunal to specific categories of cases,[149] such as the disputes relating to the amount of compensation for expropriation.[150] In the latter cases, the tribunal cannot entertain claims

---

son, a su juicio, los actos de imperio de la República de Guatemala que, en derecho internacional, podrían constituir violaciones del Tratado' (emphasis added).

145 Ibid., para. 357.

146 *Iberdrola Energía S.A. v. Republic of Guatemala*, ICSID Case No. ARB/09/5, Decision on Annulment of 13 January 2015.

147 This is the scenario discussed in *Nova Scotia Power Incorporated (Canada) v. República Bolivariana de Venezuela*, UNCITRAL, Decision on Jurisdiction of 22 April 2010, para. 137. The investor launched UNCITRAL arbitration even if the arbitration clause of the BIT made this means of dispute settlement available only if arbitration under ICSID (or its Additional Facility) was not available. Since the investor did not prove as much, the UNCITRAL tribunal declined jurisdiction.

148 Taxation being a common example, see for instance US/Latvia BIT, Article 10. In other (more recent) agreements, taxation measures are not just excluded from the arbitration clause, but also from the application of the treaty at large. See for instance the Canada/Serbia BIT, Article 14(1); Egypt/Mauritius BIT, Article 2(3)(a). See also the case *Vannessa Ventures Ltd. v. Bolivarian Republic of Venezuela*, ICSID Case No. ARB(AF)04/6, Decision on Jurisdiction of 22 August 2008, in which at stake was the exclusion from the arbitration clause of the Canada/Venezuela BIT of any decision, by the host States, not to permit the acquisition of an existing enterprise (see Annex to the BIT, Article II(3)(b)).

149 See August Reinisch, 'How Narrow Are Narrow Dispute Settlement Clauses in Investment Treaties?' (2011) 2 Journal of International Dispute Settlement 1–60.

150 Many BITs concluded by former centralised economy countries contain such clauses. Several cases have concerned the jurisdiction of tribunals entertaining claims based on Hungarian BITs, which have narrow arbitration clauses. See for instance *Emmis*

relating to other standards of protection (e.g., the FET), and it is doubtful whether it has jurisdiction to ascertain whether expropriation took place in the first place.

In the case *Sanum*[151] the tribunal concluded that determining the existence of expropriation (not just the *quantum* of compensation) fell within its jurisdiction, because the clause spoke of '*dispute*[s] involving'[152] the calculation of compensation for expropriation. The parties could have chosen a more restrictive language had they wanted the tribunal to only exercise jurisdictions only on disputes '*limited to*' the amount of damages.[153] Moreover, the BIT contained a fork-in-the-road provision barring access to arbitration for disputes on the *quantum* already submitted to domestic courts.[154] This, in the tribunal's view, was decisive in interpreting expansively the jurisdictional clause.[155] A restrictive construction of the arbitration clause would have produced the absurd effect of forcing the investor to first address the expropriation claim to domestic courts. The domestic courts, in turn, would have necessarily to look into the issue of compensation to determine the existence of expropriation and its legality. As a result, all matters of compensation having been presented to domestic courts by necessity, the arbitration clause would never allow re-submission to arbitration, not even of the compensation claim alone.[156] In other cases, in which the applicable BIT had no fork-in-the-road, the tribunal opted for the literal reading of the dispute settlement clause and declined to entertain questions regarding the existence of expropriation.[157]

International Holding, B.V., Emmis Radio Operating, B.V., MEM Magyar Electronic Media Kereskedelmi és Szolgáltató Kft. v. The Republic of Hungary, ICSID Case No. ARB/12/2, Decision on Respondent's Objection under ICSID Arbitration Rule 41(5) of 11 March 2013, para. 70: '*the plain text of the Treaties makes it manifest that, in the absence of other consent, the Non-Expropriation Claims fall outside the jurisdiction of this Tribunal.*'

151 *Sanum Investments Limited v. Lao People's Democratic Republic*, UNCITRAL, PCA Case No. 2013-13, jurisdictional award of 13 December 2013.

152 BIT between China and Lao, Article 8(3). Emphasis added.

153 *Sanum v. Laos* above (n 151) para. 329.

154 Article 8(3), second sentence.

155 *Sanum v. Laos* above (n 151) para. 340.

156 The same conclusion was reached in the case *Señor Tza Yap Shum v. The Republic of Peru*, ICSID Case No. ARB/07/6, Decision of Jurisdiction of 19 June 2009, para. 188.

157 See for instance *Vladimir and Moise Berschader v. The Russian Federation*, SCC Case No. 080/2004, Award of 21 April 2006, para. 153 and *Austrian Airlines AG v. The Slovak Republic*, UNCITRAL Final Award of 9 October 2009. In the case *ST-AD* above (n 18), the applicable rule allowed no margin for interpretation. Article 4(3) of the Germany/Bulgaria BIT reads, in the relevant part: '*the amount of the compensation shall ... be reviewed ... by*

In *Emmis v. Hungary*, the investor had framed the claim as one of expropriation, thus fitting within the narrow boundaries of the applicable arbitration clause. The claim was nevertheless rejected at the jurisdictional stage for a defect *ratione materiae*. The tribunal found that the investor could not prove to have a property right that was capable of being dispossessed. Whereas the investor's alleged rights might have been considered as investments protected by other clauses of the BIT, arbitration was possible only over expropriation claims. Accordingly, the tribunal had only competence *ratione materiae* over expropriable rights, of which the investor had none.[158]

Sometimes, specific subject-matters are carved out from the scope of application of the whole treaty, rather than the compromissory clause alone. Oftentimes, investment treaties do not cover taxation measures of the host State, curtailing the jurisdiction of tribunals accordingly. In *Ampal*, for instance, the tribunal upheld the limitation *ratione materiae* of Article XI of the US/Egypt BIT, noting however that the carve-out contained an exception for expropriatory measures.[159] The tribunal, therefore, retained jurisdiction on fiscal measure only insofar as deprivation of property might have occurred. Another issue concerning subject-matter carve-outs is whether domestic law categories are relevant to determine whether a claim is covered or not by the exception. In *Murphy v. Ecuador* (*UNCITRAL*),[160] the tribunal found that the domestic legal characterisation of a measure was not dispositive of the issue, but should be considered to interpret the treaty language.[161]

The Problem of MFN-based Jurisdiction

Through the most-favoured nation (MFN) clauses, the investor can demand to be granted the better standard of protection (i.e., the better 'treatment') that the host State grants to investors of third States. These clauses permit to 'import' the provisions of other BITs concluded by the host State into the

means of an international arbitral tribunal.' As the tribunal noted (para. 372), '*the BIT provide[d] a "narrow door" to enter the realm of international arbitration.*'

158 *Emmis International Holding, B.V., Emmis Radio Operating, B.V., MEM Magyar Electronic Media Kereskedelmi és Szolgáltató Kft. v. The Republic of Hungary*, ICSID Case No. ARB/12/2, Award of 16 April 2014, para. 255.

159 *Ampal* above (n 22) para. 266–267.

160 *Murphy Exploration & Production Company International v. Republic of Ecuador*, PCA Case No. 2012–16 (formerly AA 434), Partial Final Award of 6 May 2016.

161 Ibid., para. 161 and 185. See also *Burlington Resources Inc. v. Republic of Ecuador*, ICSID Case No. ARB/08/5 (formerly *Burlington Resources Inc. and others v. Republic of Ecuador and Empresa Estatal Petróleos del Ecuador (PetroEcuador)*), Decision on Jurisdiction of 2 June 2010, para. 159 ff.

applicable one.[162] The application of MFN clauses inevitably influences the jurisdiction *ratione materiae* of the tribunal.[163] Importing a better standard of protection might entail a better chance of success for the investor's claim on the merits (with wider obligations to observe, more State acts fall to be wrongful); sometimes, though, the use of an MFN clause can also result in an enlarged substantive scope of the BIT (when the State must observe additional obligations, more disputes fall to be covered by its jurisdictional clause).[164]

In *Société Générale v. the Dominican Republic*[165] the investor tried to secure the application of the wider definitions of investments contained in a comparator treaty. The tribunal did not allow this attempt, noting that the MFN applies to the treatment of investments, not to their definition.[166]

Often, MFN clauses are invoked to import advantageous procedural provisions from external treaties. The attempt is made, understandably, when the arbitration clause in the applicable treaty refers only to a specific category

162 Unless the parties agree, in the relevant text, that the provisions in a separate agreement shall not, *per se*, constitute treatment. See for instance Article 8.7.4 of CETA, which not only removes jurisdictional provisions from the scope of the MFN clauses, but clarifies that substantive provisions in other BITs, *per se*, do not constitute treatment.

163 See, below, how the MFN is sometimes used in relation to the jurisdiction *ratione temporis* of the tribunal.

164 See *RosInvestCo UK Ltd. v. The Russian Federation*, SCC Case No. V079/2005, award on jurisdiction of 1 October 2007, para. 131: '*indeed the application of the MFN clause ... widens the scope of [the arbitration clause] and thus is in conflict to its limitation, this is a normal result of the application of MFN clauses, the very character and intention of which is that protection not accepted in one treaty is widened by transferring the protection accorded in another treaty*'. *Nota bene*: if the arbitration clause refers to claims based on specific standards of the treaty other than the MFN, an MFN-based claim might fall outside the tribunal's jurisdiction. See *WNC* above (n 122) para. 353.

165 *Société Générale v. The Dominican Republic* above (n 59).

166 Ibid., para. 40–41. Other cases involving the invocation of an MFN clause to expand the applicable notions of investor or investments include *Yaung Chi Oo* above (n 112) para. 64; *HICEE B.V. v. The Slovak Republic*, UNCITRAL, PCA Case No. 2009-11, Partial Award of 23 May 2011, para. 149 ('[*the MFN clause*] *cannot legitimately be used to broaden the definition of the investors or the investments themselves*'); *Vannessa Ventures* above (n 148); *Rafat Ali Rizvi v Republic of Indonesia*, ICSID Case No. ARB/11/13, Award on Jurisdiction of 16 July 2013, para. 220 (the Tribunal took notice of the parties' agreement that the MFN cannot be used '*to alter the BIT's definition of "investment"*') and para. 225 (since the investment did not satisfy the admission requirements in the original BIT, there was no '*treatment*' thereunder to begin with, and the MFN clause could not apply); *MetalTech Ltd. v Republic of Uzbekistan*, ICSID Case No. ARB/10/3, Award of 4 October 2013, para. 145 ('*one must be* under *the treaty to claim* through *the treaty*') emphasis in the original.

of disputes (e.g., to disputes on the calculation of compensation for expropriation). The arbitration clause of an external treaty, covering all investment disputes without limitations, would serve the investor better. In *Sanum*, the tribunal rebuked the investor's attempt to use the MFN clause to bypass the narrow applicable arbitration clause and bring an expropriation claim. It refused to read into the MFN clause referring to '*protection*' an extensive dispute settlement provision, referring to the parties' assumed consent as the baseline:

> [hearing the MFN-claim] would result in a substantial re-write of the Treaty and an extension of the States Parties' consent to arbitration beyond what may be assumed to have been their intention, given the limited reach of the Treaty protection and dispute settlement clauses. Therefore, the Tribunal finds that it has no jurisdiction for claims submitted under [the MFN clause] of the Treaty.[167]

The *Rosinvestco* tribunal, instead, concluded differently, mainly based on the more comprehensive wording of the applicable MFN clause,[168] which also covered the investor's '*use*' and '*enjoyment*' of the investment.[169]

A more common occurrence is the investor's invocation of MFN to circumvent certain procedural duties that are not required in the external treaty.[170] MFN clauses have often been invoked to skip cooling-off periods and

167 *Sanum*, above (n 151). Note that, as clarified above, the tribunal had already found an alternative basis to entertain the expropriation claim under the arbitration clause of the China/Lao BIT, hence the rejection of the MFN-claim did not change the outcome of the jurisdictional decision. A similar rejection of the claimant's attempt to extend the arbitration clause occurred in the cases *Telenor* above (n 60) para. 81–82 and *Accession Mezzanine Capital L.P. and Danubius Kereskedöház Vagyonkezelö Zrt. v. Hungary*, ICSID Case No. ARB/12/3, Decision on Respondent's Objection under Arbitration Rule 41(5) of 16 January 2013, para. 74: '*In the instant case, the arbitrable scope of the basic treaty is expropriation, including fact and law questions related thereto. In that light, Claimants are entitled to rely on the MFN provisions of the BIT, but only insofar as such provisions relate to expropriation.*'

168 Art 3(2) of the UK-Russia BIT.

169 *RosInvestCo* above (n 164) para. 130.

170 The uncertainty in the case-law has served as fertile ground for scholarly commentaries. See Kaj Hober, 'MFN Clauses and Dispute Resolution in Investment Treaties: Have we reached the end of the road?' in Cristina Binder, Ursula Kriebaum, August Reinisch, Stephan Wittich (eds), *International Investment Law for the 21st Century* (OUP 2009) 31; Julie A Maupin, 'MFN-based Jurisdiction in Investor–State Arbitration: Is There Any Hope for a Consistent Approach?' (2011) 14(1) Journal of International Economic Law 157–190; Stephan W Schill, 'Allocating Adjudicatory Authority: Most-Favoured-Nation Clauses as

compulsory periods of domestic litigation. The arbitral practice in this respect is infamously ambivalent and has led States to expressly exclude this possibility in recent treaties and model BITs.[171] In *Maffezini v. Spain* the tribunal allowed the investor's use of the MFN to skip the 18-month cooling-off requirement in the Argentina/Spain BIT.[172] In *Salini v. Jordan*,[173] instead, the tribunal refused to apply the MFN of the Italy/Jordan BIT to extend the consent to arbitrate over contractual disputes (the Jordanian BITs with USA and UK contained wider litigation clauses[174]). The *Plama v. Bulgaria* tribunal similarly declined to accept MFN-based jurisdiction.[175] In that case, since the applicable BIT between Bulgaria and Cyprus only provided for arbitration regarding the amount of compensation, the claimant attempted to reach out for another Bulgarian BIT which contained a more comprehensive arbitration clause, and establish the tribunal jurisdiction on it.

The subsequent cases diverge in outcome, and the contradiction cannot be ascribed only to the textual differences between the treaties. Tribunals siding with the *Plama/Salini* approach[176] normally rely on the *ejusdem generis* principle, whereby the MFN can only operate with respect to clauses of the same

---

a Basis of Jurisdiction—A Reply to Zachary Douglas' (2011) 2(2) Journal of International Dispute Settlement 353–371.

171 For instance, see Article 9(3) of the TPP: 'For greater certainty, the treatment referred to [in the MFN clause] does not encompass international dispute resolution procedures or mechanisms, such as those included in Section B (Investor-State Dispute Settlement).' See also Article 8.7(4) of CETA.

172 *Emilio Agustín Maffezini v. The Kingdom of Spain*, ICSID Case No. ARB/97/7, Decision on Jurisdiction of 25 January 2000, para. 64.

173 *Salini v. Jordan* above (n 58).

174 For instance, Article IX(1) of the Jordan/US BIT reads, in the relevant part: '*an* investment dispute is a dispute … *arising out of or* relating *to an investment authorization,* an investment agreement *or an alleged breach of any right conferred, created or recognized by this Treaty with respect to a covered investment*' (emphasis added).

175 *Plama Consortium Limited v. Republic of Bulgaria*, ICSID Case No. ARB/03/24, Decision on Jurisdiction of 8 February 2005, para. 184.

176 *Berschader* above (n 157) (with a dissenting opinion on the point by Weiler); *Telenor* above (n 60); *Wintershall Aktiengesellschaft v. Argentine Republic*, ICSID Case No. ARB/04/14, Award of 8 December 2008; *Renta 4 S.V.S.A, Ahorro Corporación Emergentes F.I., Ahorro Corporación Eurofondo F.I., Rovime Inversiones SICAV S.A., Quasar de Valors SICAV S.A., Orgor de Valores SICAV S.A., GBI 9000 SICAV S.A. v. The Russian Federation*, SCC No. 24/2007, Award on Preliminary Objections of 20 March 2009 (with a separate opinion by Brower); *Tza Yap Shum* above (n 156); *Austrian Airlines* above (n 157) (with a dissenting opinion by Brower); *ICS Inspection and Control Services Limited (United Kingdom) v. The Republic of Argentina*, UNCITRAL, PCA Case No. 2010-9, Award on Jurisdiction of 10 February 2012;

kind[177] of those in the original BIT; since procedural rights are not 'treatment' (i.e., substantive treatment), MFN provisions cannot be used to enhance and expand them.[178] Another objection to the use of MFN to extend the jurisdiction of the tribunal is a logical one: if the claimant cannot show to enjoy protection under the original treaty, there cannot be any 'treatment,' less favourable or other, on which to plant the MFN clause to reach for a better treatment in a comparator treaty.[179] Finally, when the MFN refers to treatment '*in the territory*' of the host State, recourse to international arbitration appears ill-fitted to the text of the clause, since arbitration proceedings rarely if ever take place in the territory of the host State.[180]

The arbitral progeny of *Maffezini*, instead,[181] often notes that access to arbitration is one of the most important forms of protection of investors. As such, it falls under the notion of 'treatment' used in MFN clauses, and there is no analytically compelling value to the distinction between 'substantive' and 'procedural' provisions.[182] In truth, whereas the substantive/procedural divide is

---

Daimler v. Argentina, ICSID Case No. ARB/05/1, Award of 22 August 2012 (with a dissenting opinion by Brower).

177 For an overview of the principle, see Endre Ustor, 'International Law Commission: The Most-Favoured-Nation Clause' (1977) 11(5) Journal of World Trade 462; the International Law Commission is currently working on a report on MFN clauses, see Article 9(1) of the UN Draft Articles on the MFN Clause. See also *Yearbook of the International Law Commission*, 2015, vol. II. Unsurprisingly, as of 2015, one of the conclusions of the ILC was that '[t]*he central interpretative issue in respect of the MFN clauses relates to the scope of the clause and the application of the* ejusdem generis *principle*.'

178 See, for instance, *Telenor* above (n 60) para. 90 ff.

179 *ST-AD* above (n 18) para. 397–398: '*consent has to be exchanged first, under the conditions stated in the BIT, before the Tribunal can even discuss the scope of the MFN clause*.' In this case, the MFN clause was in contained in the same article providing for arbitration, weakening the *ejusdem generis* objection to its use.

180 *Berschader* above (n 157) 185; *ICS* above (n 176) para. 309.

181 *Camuzzi* above (n 87); *Suez, Sociedad General de Aguas de Barcelona S.A., and InterAguas Servicios Integrales del Agua S.A. v. The Argentine Republic*, ICSID Case No. ARB/03/17, Decision on Jurisdiction of 16 May 2006; *Telefónica* above (n 64); *National Grid plc v. The Argentine Republic*, UNCITRAL, Decision on Jurisdiction of 20 June 2006; *AWG Group v. The Argentine Republic*, UNCITRAL, Decision on Jurisdiction of 3 August 2006; *Hochtief AG v. Argentina*, ICSID Case no. ARB/07/31, Decision on Jurisdiction of 24 October 2011 (with a dissenting opinion on the point by Thomas); *Teinver* above (n 14) (with a dissenting opinion by Hossain).

182 Tomoko Ishikawa, 'Interpreting the Most-Favoured-nation Clause in Investment Treaty Arbitration: Interpretation as a Process of Creating an obligation?', in Charles J G Sampford, Spencer Zifcak, Derya Aydın Okur (eds), *Rethinking International Law and Justice* (Ashgate 2015) 127, 129. See *Werner Schneider, acting in his capacity as insolvency administrator of Walter Bau Ag (In Liquidation) v. The Kingdom of Thailand*, UNCITRAL

descriptively valid, it is not clear why it should self-evidently correspond to the outer limits of the MFN's reach. Nor is it clear why, as the *White Industrial v. India* tribunal seemingly conceded, the use of MFN clauses to import dispute settlement provision should '*have the effect of fundamentally subverting the carefully negotiated balance of the BIT in question*'[183] more than the importation of substantive standards of protection would. In both cases, ultimately, the host State would be bound by international obligations it did not bargain expressly for in the original treaty, but this is not inherently troublesome: the carefully negotiated balance of a treaty in fact incorporates, if an MFN clause is inserted, the parties' wish that their obligations evolve and expand.[184]

In the *EDF* case[185] a further permutation was attempted: the use of an MFN clause to import into the basic treaty an umbrella clause.[186] The tribunal upheld the investor's attempt; it recognised the divergence of opinions regarding the use of MFN to import dispute settlement clauses but ultimately noted that by permitting the importation of an umbrella clause the tribunal simply brought '*into consideration the clearly substantive provisions requiring respect for explicit host state undertakings such as concession agreements.*'[187] A similar attempt failed in *Paushok v. Mongolia*, because the MFN clause in the applicable BIT operated only with respect to the FET treatment; hence, it could

(formerly *Walter Bau AG (in liquidation) v. The Kingdom of Thailand*), Award of 1 July 2009, para. 9.71. See also the Separate Opinion of Charles N Brower to *Austrian Airlines* above (n 157), para. 4–5, on why the word 'treatment' cannot be held to implicitly exclude procedural benefits.

183 *White Industries Australia Limited v. The Republic of India*, UNCITRAL, Final Award of 30 November 2011, para. 11.2.1–3, referring to India's reliance on a passage of Campbell McLachlan, Laurence Shore and Matthew Weininger, *International Investment Arbitration* (OUP 2007) which had gained the endorsement of the Wintershall tribunal, see *Wintershall* above (n 176) para. 188–189.

184 The precise function of MFN clauses is to expand the obligations of the treaty parties. It allows each treaty party to benefit from the progresses in draftmanship and standard-setting that are necessary to align future treaties to the ever-evolving economic practice. See Georg Schwarzenberger, 'Most Favored-Nation Standard in British State Practice' (1945) 22 Brit. YB Int'l L. 96–121, 99–100: '*the use of the m.f.n. standard leads to the constant self-adaptation of such treaties and greatly contributes to the rationalization of international affairs.*'

185 *EDF* above (n 78).

186 On the issue, see the analysis in Tarcisio Gazzini and Attila Tanzi, 'Handle with care: Umbrella clauses and MFN treatment in investment arbitration' (2013) 14 Journal of World Investment and Trade 978–994.

187 *EDF* above (n 78) para. 931. The attempt was also granted in *Mr. Franck Charles Arif v. Republic of Moldova*, ICSID ARB/11/23, Award of 8 April 2013. The tribunal confirmed the substantive nature of the umbrella clauses in para. 395.

not be used to invoke '*completely new substantive rights, such as those granted under an umbrella clause*'.[188] In *Impregilo*, the tribunal noted that the investor was challenging the breach of contracts into which it had entered not with the host State, but with its instrumentalities. Therefore, the importation of an umbrella clause, even if accepted *arguendo*, would have not assisted its claim, for lack of privity.[189] In *Teinver v. Argentina*, the MFN clause covered '*all matters governed by [the original BIT]*' and, since the original treaty did not include an umbrella clause, the importation of one such clause from a third treaty was not warranted.[190] In other words, the language of the treaty codified an *ejusdem generis* requirement that left no space to interpretation. The Tribunal took pains to distinguish *MTD* and *Bayindir*, which apparently reached a different conclusion. In *MTD v. Chile*, the MFN clause was internal to the FET one, and the tribunal considered the imported treatment[191] to fall under the FET standard of protection.[192] In *Bayindir v. Pakistan*, the tribunal allowed the importing of an FET clause, even if there was none in the original treaty. However, the preamble of the original treaty referred to fair and equitable treatment, and the MFN clause was not expressly restricted to the matters covered by the treaty.[193] As a result, this line of awards is not at odds with the *ejusdem generis* principle. The claimant in *Teinver* succeeded, however, to import the full protection and security standard from a comparator treaty.[194]

At the moment, it is impossible to reconcile the different schools of thought through hair-splitting distinguishing or conceptual discrimination (for instance, arguing that an MFN can successfully circumvent pre-litigation requirements, but not create a competence that does not exist in the original treaty).[195] It is, perhaps, not a coincidence that treaty parties are increasingly resorting

188 *Paushok v. Mongolia* above (n 114) para. 570. See Articles 3(1) and 3(2) of the Russia/Mongolia BIT. A similar conclusion was reached in *WNC* above (n 122) para. 349, because the arbitration clause did not list the MFN clause among the clauses that might be invoked, hence ruling out altogether the possibility of MFN-based jurisdiction.

189 *Impregilo v. Islamic Republic of Pakistan* above (n 64) para. 223.

190 *Teinver S.A., Transportes de Cercanías S.A. and Autobuses Urbanos del Sur S.A. v. Argentine Republic*, ICSID Case No. ARB/09/1, Award of the Tribunal of 21 July 2017 para. 884.

191 Regarding the obligation to award permits to an approved investment.

192 *MTD Equity Sdn. Bhd. & MTD Chile SA v. Chile*, ICSID Case No. ARB/01/7, Award of 25 May 2004, para. 104.

193 *Bayindir* above (n 38) para. 155.

194 *Teinver* above (n 190) para. 896–897.

195 Schreuer 2012, above (n 88) 855.

to a more sophisticated language in MFN clauses, for the avoidance of doubts,[196] and that tribunals are increasingly reluctant to pronounce on the matter, using judicial economy to avoid it when possible[197] or questioning the possibility that a treaty investment clause, as such, constitutes treatment.[198] Occasionally, the tribunals can sidestep the controversy relying on the text of the applicable MFN, which expressly extends to the dispute settlement provisions of the original treaty. One such case is *Garanti Koza v. Turkmenistan*,[199] in which the tribunal—not without expressing some relief[200]—upheld the investor's attempt to accede ICSID arbitration, which was unavailable under the original BIT but was offered as an alternative in the comparator BIT.[201] This conclusion was reached based on the text of the applicable MFN clause, which confirmed '[*f*]*or the avoidance of doubt … that the treatment provided for in* [*the MFN clause*] *shall apply to the provisions of Articles 1 to 11 of* [*the BIT, Article 8 being the provision codifying the States' consent to arbitration*]'.[202] The same outcome was reached in *Venezuela US v. Venezuela*, where a similarly worded

196 Whereas the more common occurrence is the exclusion of dispute settlement provisions from the application of the MFN clause, sometimes drafters opt for the opposite clarification, i.e., they include expressly the consent to arbitration under the treatment covered by the MFN. See, for instance, Article 3(3) of the UK Model BIT 2008, available at http://investmentpolicyhub.unctad.org/Download/TreatyFile/2847, and the comment in Chester Brown and Audley Sheppard, 'United Kingdom' in Chester Brown (ed), *Commentaries on Selected Model Investment Treaties* (OUP 2013) 697, 728. See also CETA, 2016, Article 8.7.4.

197 In some recent cases, the tribunals held that pre-arbitration requirements were not compulsory, thus rendering the attempt at circumventing them through an MFN clause unnecessary. See *Alemanni* above (n 32) para. 317; *Muhammet Çap Sehil Inşaat Endustri Ve Ticaret Ltd. Sti. v. Turkmenistan*, ICSID Case No. ARB/12/6, Decision on Respondent's Jurisdiction under Article VII(2) of 13 February 2015, para. 282.

198 *İçkale* above (n 46) para. 332 (the tribunal observed that MFN-based treatment can only be invoked to remedy actual discrimination and not to import treaty provisions in the abstract, in light of the '*in similar situations*' language of the applicable MFN clause).

199 *Garanti Koza LLP v. Turkmenistan*, ICSID Case No. ARB/11/20, Decision on the Objection to Jurisdiction for Lack of Consent of 3 July 2013.

200 Ibid., para. 42: '*Fortunately, perhaps, the present case does not require this Tribunal to take a position on the policy issues implicated in deciding whether an MFN clause ought to be applied to the investor-state arbitration article of a BIT*.'

201 Ibid., para. 75–76. Boisson de Chazournes appended a dissenting opinion to the award, arguing that the investor's claim sought to bypass the requirement of consent (ibid., para. 78) but the tribunal found that consent to arbitration had been given, the MFN only operating to expand the choice of procedural venues available to the investor.

202 See Article 3(3) of the UK/Turkmenistan BIT.

MFN clause was found to grant access to UNCITRAL arbitration, unavailable in the original treaty but offered in the comparator BIT.[203]

The latter case highlights a bolder use of the MFN clause: whereas in *Garanti Koza v. Turkmenistan* access to ICSID arbitration was simply preferable for the investor than *ad hoc* arbitration, in *Venezuela US v. Venezuela* the MFN-based access to UNCITRAL arbitration was vital for the investor's claim, the original BIT offering no viable arbitration system. For this reason, the tribunal took pains to highlight that Venezuela had indeed '*given its consent*'[204] to arbitration in the original BIT, and the MFN only assisted the investor to bypass '*the conditions for resorting to arbitration*' therein,[205] which had become unfulfillable after Venezuela's withdrawal from ICISD. The dissenting arbitrator took issue with this decision, noting that the MFN had been used to import an arbitration offer into a treaty that had none (better: none available any longer).[206]

In *Menzies v. Senegal*, the investor made an extreme attempt to use an MFN clause in the absence of an applicable BIT. It invoked the MFN clause of the GATS agreement[207] to benefit from the arbitration clauses of BITs between the host State and third States. The tribunal found that the attempt to '*compose*' the State's consent by '*gluing together*' several instruments '[*wa*]*s a manifest example of a "consent" to arbitration that is equivocal and doubtful*.'[208] In any event, it noted that even if the MFN clause in the GATS could be construed to cover arbitration, it created an obligation to consent (which the State could chose to disregard), not a valid expression of consent (that the investor could accept).[209]

Some of the cases in which the MFN clauses are invoked to elude pre-arbitration procedural requirements raise critical issues for the present study. These are discussed in detail in the next Part.

---

203 *Venezuela US, S.R.L. (Barbados) v. Bolivarian Republic of Venezuela*, PCA Case No. 2013-34, Interim Award on Jurisdiction on the Respondent Objection to Jurisdiction *Ratione Voluntatis* of 26 July 2016.

204 Ibid., para. 109.

205 Ibid., para. 111.

206 Dissenting Opinion of Professor Marcelo G Kohen (on the Respondent's Objection to Jurisdiction *Ratione Voluntatis*), para. 5.

207 Stipulated in the framework of the World Trade Organisation. General Agreement on Trade in Services, Annex 1B of the WTO Agreement, 1869 UNTS 183; 33 ILM 1167 (1994), see Article II.

208 *Menzies* above (n 18) para. 135.

209 Ibid., para. 140.

Investments of Financial Nature

What counts as investment determines in practice the scope of the tribunal's jurisdiction. Hence, the instrument that records the parties' consent to arbitration (the investment treaty or the investment statute) is the starting point of any inquiry into whether the asset of the claimants qualify as protected investments.[210] The analysis usually involves understanding what 'investment' means in the applicable source, a task often facilitated by the inclusion of a clause providing a definition. When the claim is brought before the ICSID, the applicability of the Convention is a further condition for establishing the tribunal's jurisdiction. As a result, what 'investment' means in the Convention is also relevant, in addition.[211]

Respondent States might challenge the notion that intangible assets—like financial interests—are protected investments. Economic interests with no physical medium complicate the analysis *ratione loci* (there might be an investment, but is doubtful whether it is made in the relevant territory, see below) and are often challenged as investments *tout court*.

Already in 1997 did the *Fedax* tribunal find that promissory notes were investments.[212] It relied on the negotiating history of the ICSID Convention and the consensus regarding long term loan contracts with public authorities. Essentially, it discarded the idea that only direct investments were covered by the ICSID Convention and by open-ended BITs, confirmed that the requirement *ratione loci* can be satisfied also when the investment's economic contribution is not physically transferred into the territory of the host State,[213] and pointed out that transactions backed-up by the State's exercise of governmental powers cannot be considered ordinary commercial transactions.[214]

---

210 Such inquiry is moot, of course, when the arbitration clause is contained in an investment contract. In that case the parties have expressly confirmed their consent to make arbitration available to disputes relating to the underlying asset (the problem might remain to ensure the application of the ICSID Convention, when the claim is brought before the Centre).

211 See above, part 1.1 titled *The interplay between ICSID and the instrument of specific jurisdiction*.

212 *Fedax* above (n 43).

213 Ibid., see para. 41: '*The important question is whether the funds made available are utilized by the beneficiary of the credit, as in the case of the [host State], so as to finance its various governmental needs.*' Likewise, see *Gold Reserve Inc. v. Bolivarian Republic of Venezuela*, ICSID Case No. ARB(AF)/09/1, Award of 22 September 2014 para. 261: '*According to the ordinary meaning of the words, "making an investment in the territory of Venezuela" does not require that there must be a movement of capital or other values across Venezuelan borders.*'

214 Ibid., para. 42.

On several occasions, it has been disputed whether loans could qualify as investments.[215] In *Deutsche Bank v. Sri Lanka*,[216] at stake was whether an oil hedging agreement[217] was an investment. The tribunal rejected the host State's contention that '*claims to money*'—one of the investment's definitions in the treaty—needed to relate to a separate investment to obtain protection under the relevant BIT.[218] It then turned to the requirements *ratione materiae* inherent in Article 25 ICSID. The tribunal found that the hedging agreement was no ordinary commercial transaction,[219] given the lengthy negotiation which preceded it and the involvement of several high-rank State officials. Critically, the tribunal also rejected the argument that the hedging agreement was in fact a speculative transaction and, as a consequence, was null *ab initio*.[220] This conclusion was particularly delicate because an English court[221] and a commercial tribunal established at the London Court of International Arbitration[222] had reached opposite conclusions in similar disputes initiated by other banks against Sri Lankan entities. Other financial transactions which did not satisfy the minimum objective criteria of an investment (duration, financial contribution, risk) were not accepted by other arbitral tribunals, such as the temporary transfer of shares[223] or the purchase of fiscal credits.[224]

215 *CSOB* above (n 47) para. 77; *Alpha Projektholding GmbH v. Ukraine*, ICSID Case No. ARB/07/16, Award of 8 November 2010, para. 273.

216 *Deutsche Bank AG v. Democratic Socialist Republic of Sri Lanka*, ICSID Case No. ARB/09/2, Award of 31 October 2012.

217 Oil hedging agreements are derivative transactions, essentially oil future contracts. The Sri Lankan state oil corporation sought to offset the financial risk deriving from the expected increase of oil price and concluded the agreement with Deutsche Bank. The agreed strike price (the threshold used to determine which party should compensate the other for flotation in the price) was 112.5$ per barrel, at a time when the price on the market was comfortably higher (137$). In July 2008, however, oil price dropped by roughly 60%. Accordingly, the State company was bound contractually to make massive payments to the investor and tried to restructure the agreement—hence the dispute.

218 *Deutsche Bank v. Sri Lanka* above (n 216) para. 286.

219 Ibid., para. 310.

220 Since the State company that entered the agreement had no power to conclude speculative transactions, the distinction was critical for the validity of the investment under domestic law.

221 *Standard Chartered Bank v Ceylon Petroleum Corporation* [2011] EWHC 1785 (Comm) (11 July 2011).

222 *Citibank N.A. v. Ceylon Petroleum Corporation*, First Partial Award, LCIA ab# 81215, 31 July 2011.

223 *Saba Fakes* above (n 45) para. 140–148.

224 *Nations Energy Corporation, Electric Machinery Enterprises Inc., and Jamie Jurado v. The Republic of Panama*, ICSID Case No. ARB/06/19, Award of 24 November 2010, para. 430.

In the case of *Poštová Banka v. Greece*,[225] the tribunal held that sovereign bonds did not constitute protected investments under the applicable BIT. This conclusion was reached even though the Slovakia—Greece BIT defined investments as '*every kind of asset*',[226] and provided an illustrative list of '*particular*' though '*not exclusive*[ ]' examples which included '*loans*' and '*claims to money*.' The tribunal reasoned that the list had a narrowing function in spite of its open-endedness (otherwise it would have served no purpose).[227] Varying lists in different treaties might point to a different constellation of investments under each instrument. Whereas the *Fedax*, *Abaclat* and *Ambiente Ufficio* tribunals drew reassurance from the illustrative lists of the respective BITs (which pointed at public securities, listing '*obligations*' and '*public titles*'[228]), the Slovakia/Greece BIT only referred to loans of a commercial kind, and would not cover State bonds.[229] This conclusion is not very compelling: the *effet utile* of an illustrative list can very well be to avoid doubts rather than delimit the application *ratione materiae* of the treaty contrary to its express language (which embraces '*every kind of asset*').[230] Moreover, interpretation based on the comparison with treaties concluded by different parties is not sanctioned by the VCLT and appears to stretch the notion of context in an unwarranted way.[231]

The case *Alps Finance v. Slovakia* is even more interesting because it was resolved through UNCITRAL proceedings, hence without the necessity to impose the objective, inferred requirements of the ICSID Convention on the notion of investment. At stake was the possibility to qualify a contract of purchase

---

The claimant had indeed made an actual investment in a company, but the tribunal paused to consider whether the expropriated asset (the fiscal credits) could be regarded as an investment in its own right.

225 *Poštová Banka, a.s. and Istrokapital SE v. The Hellenic Republic*, ICSID Case No. ARB/13/8, Award of 9 April 2015.

226 Article 1(1).

227 *Poštová Banka* above (n 225) para. 288.

228 Ibid., para. 306–307.

229 Ibid., para. 303.

230 In *Hassan Awdi* above (n 47), para. 198–200, for instance, the tribunal took the view that since the US/Romania BIT covered '*every kind of investment*,' it was sufficient to find an economic contribution by the claimant to be satisfied as regards the investment requirement.

231 On this procedure, see Andrew D Mitchell and James Munro, 'Someone Else's Deal: Interpreting International Investment Agreements in the Light of Third-Party Agreements' (2017) 28(3) European Journal of International Law 669.

of receivables as investment under the loose terms of the applicable BIT.[232] Nevertheless, the tribunal adopted the now-familiar *Salini* criteria to conclude that the contract did not satisfy the minimum requirements that an investment should satisfy (duration, risk, contribution) and was better characterised as a one-off transaction.[233] The tribunal also observed that since ICSID arbitration was available under the BIT, the parties '*must have inevitably intended to refer to what constitutes "investment" under the ICSID Convention*'.[234] A similar approach permeated the reasoning of the *Nova Scotia v. Venezuela* (ICSID AF) tribunal.[235] Convinced that the definition of investments must hinge on some inherent meaning, irrespective of the BIT's open-endedness and the applicability (or not) of Article 25 ICSID, the tribunal noted:

> It cannot be the case that the scope of "investment" in a bilateral investment treaty changes depending on the arbitral forum. No matter what the forum, the ordinary meaning of investment in the relevant bilateral investment treaty derives from something more than a list of examples and calls for an examination of the inherent features of an investment.[236]

232 *Alps Finance and Trade AG v. The Slovak Republic*, UNCITRAL, Award of 5 March 2011. The BIT between Slovak Republic and Switzerland, referring to '*every kind of assets*' under Article 1(2).

233 Ibid., para. 241–245. See also *Malaysian Historical Salvors* above (n 42) para. 107–146. Likewise, see *Romak S.A. (Switzerland) v. The Republic of Uzbekistan*, PCA Case No. AA280 (UNCITRAL Rules), Award of 26 November 2009, para. 205: '*Contracting States can even go as far as stipulating that a "pure" one-off sales contract constitutes an investment, even if such a transaction would not normally be covered by the ordinary meaning of the term "investment." However, in such cases, the wording of the instrument in question must leave no room for doubt that the intention of the contracting States was to accord to the term "investment" an extraordinary and counterintuitive meaning.... the wording of the BIT does not permit the Arbitral Tribunal to infer such an intent in the present case.*' The presumption that sale contracts cannot qualify as investments is such that an ICSID tribunal dismissed through the expedite proceedings of Rule 41(5) a case in which the claimants claimed to hold investments in the form of sale and purchase contracts with the government of the host State. See *Global Trading* above (n 71).

234 *Alps Finance* above (n 232) para. 239.

235 *Nova Scotia Power Incorporated v. Bolivarian Republic of Venezuela*, ICSID Case No. ARB(AF)/11/1, Award of 30 April 2014.

236 Ibid., para. 80. See also the illuminating treatment of the subject by Paulsson in *Pantechniki* above (n 90) para. 32–49. However, the tribunal seemed to do precisely what it professed to avoid: determining the meaning of investment through an analysis of the procedural rules—rather than the intent of the parties. Its conclusion proceeds from the concern to make one notion of investment applicable to disputes governed by different procedural

In ultimate analysis, the essential elements of an investment (duration, risk and economic contribution) may now be inevitably considered by some to represent the non-negotiable minimum in investor-State arbitration.[237] Even when the objective standards inferred from the ICSID Convention do not apply, the definitions of the treaty may nonetheless imply certain *de facto* minimum requirements. Consider the reasoning of the tribunal in *Mytilineos*[238] with respect to certain contractual rights of the claimant. Since the applicable treaty covered '*every kind of asset*' including '*claims to money*,' the tribunal held that it was unnecessary to investigate the entrepreneurial risk shouldered by the claimants or its commitment of capital, or to make sure that the investment entailed something more than a sale of services.[239] The tribunal was content with noting that the language of the treaty (the only requirement which needed to be met, given the inapplicability of ICSID[240]) would include any economic activity. Nevertheless, it took pains to note, somewhat unnecessarily, that the claimant's contracts provided for the '*establishment of a long-term business relationship*' and entailed '*a significant contribution to* [the host State's] *development*,' that the claimant expected '*various returns and profits*' and that the engagement '*was substantial in monetary terms and also not without risks*'.[241]

3 Ratione Temporis

The time at which several relevant facts occur (e.g., the making of the investment, the entry into force or the termination of a treaty, the alleged breach, the acquisition of a different nationality, the arising of a dispute, the bringing of a claim, its registration) might therefore also affect the jurisdiction *ratione temporis* of the tribunal.[242] A few aspects of this proposition are discussed below.

---

rules. However, one could argue that the notion selected is, in fact, derived from the interpretation of the ICSID Convention.

237 See also *Orascom* above (n 48) para. 372, using the three elements as the minimum and sufficient test, and rejecting the suggestion that an indirect participation obtained through a corporate restructuring could not qualify as investment, for lack of a genuine investing mind-set (para. 376).

238 *Mytilineos Holdings SA v. The State Union of Serbia & Montenegro and Republic of Serbia*, UNCITRAL, Partial Award on Jurisdiction of 8 September 2006.

239 Ibid., para. 104–105.

240 Ibid., para. 118.

241 Ibid., para. 124.

242 For a full study of the topic, see Nick Gallus, *The Temporal Jurisdiction of Tribunals* (OUP 2017).

The Critical Dates

Treaty-based protection of investments starts with the entry into force of the applicable treaty,[243] unless otherwise specified.[244] As a result, the jurisdiction of a tribunal seised with a treaty claim will exist only with respect to violations and disputes arisen after that date,[245] sometimes subject to an explicit time bar for the submission of the claim after the claimant has constructive knowledge of the breach.[246] This is the conclusion dictated by the principle

243 *Société Générale v. The Dominican Republic* above (n 59) para. 80; *ST-AD* above (n 18) para. 300.

244 The obligation not to defeat the object and purpose of the treaty, codified in Article 18 of the Vienna Convention on the Law of Treaties 1969, cannot be construed to entail the retroactive application of the treaty's obligation since its signature, see *M.C.I. Power Group L.C. and New Turbine, Inc. v. Republic of Ecuador*, ICSID Case ARB/03/6, Award of 31 July 2007, para. 117. Specific treaties might contain express provisions requiring the provisional application before ratification, like the Energy Charter Treaty (see Article 45 and the award in *Hulley Enterprises Limited (Cyprus) v. The Russian Federation*, UNCITRAL, PCA Case No. AA 226, Interim Award on Jurisdiction and Admissibility of 30 November 2009, para. 394–395.

245 *Société Générale v. The Dominican Republic* above (n 59) para. 84.

246 For instance, Article 1116(2) NAFTA disallows investment claims made after three years from the date of the breach (or the date the investor knew or should have known about it). See *Apotex Inc. v. The Government of the United States of America*, UNCITRAL, Award on Jurisdiction and Admissibility of 14 June 2013, para. 314. Likewise, the investor's claim was rejected under ICSID Rule 41(5) in the case *Ansung* above (n 71), because the institution of ICSID proceedings occurred more than three years after the claimant first acquired knowledge of its loss (see Article 9(7) of the China-Korea BIT). A similar provision was included in Article XII of the Canada/Venezuela BIT, see *Rusoro Mining Ltd. v. Bolivarian Republic of Venezuela*, ICSID Case No. ARB(AF)/12/5, Award of 22 August 2016, para. 190 ff. The tribunal considered whether acts committed more than three years before the claim could be considered jointly with the acts occurring after. Because the two sets of measures were factually distinct, the tribunal accepted to consider the investor's claims separately, and bar the claims relating to the measures occurred before the cut-off date (para. 231). See also *William Ralph Clayton, William Richard Clayton, Douglas Clayton, Daniel Clayton and Bilcon of Delaware Inc. v. Government of Canada*, UNCITRAL, PCA Case No. 2009–04, Award on Jurisdiction and Liability of 17 March 2015, para. 266. There have not been cases in which a claim was considered time-barred in application of general considerations of procedural fairness, see *Wena Hotels LTD. v. Arab Republic of Egypt*, ICSID Case No. ARB/98/4, Award of 8 December 2000, para. 104–105; *Ioannis Kardassopoulos v. Republic of Georgia*, ICSID Case No. ARB/05/18, Award of 3 March 2010, para. 104–106, 261, 264–268. In fact, the available information regarding the cases *World Wide Minerals v. Kazakhstan* suggests that time bars do not operate implicitly over treaty claims (a Canadian investor seeking to obtain redress from Kazakhstan for acts occurred

of non-retroactivity of treaties.[247] Consider how the *Berkowitz v. Costa Rica* tribunal set out the critical dates, when called to determine two concurring jurisdictional objections *ratione temporis*, i.e., that a) the breach had occurred before the treaty's enter into force and b) that the claim was filed more than three years after the claimant knew or should have known about the breach:

> If the Claimants cannot establish, to an objective standard, that they first acquired knowledge of the breaches and losses that they allege in the period after 10 June 2010 [i.e., three years before the claim], they fall at the first hurdle. To surmount this obstacle, each claimant must show, in respect of each property claim, that they have a cause of action, a distinct and legally significant event that is capable of founding a claim in its own right, of which they first became aware in the period *after 10 June 2010*. If they can establish this, a further jurisdictional question arises, namely, whether, in the circumstances of each claim presented, that post-critical limitation date cause of action can be *sufficiently detached from acts or facts that pre-date the* CAFTA*'s entry into force on 1 January 2009* so as to be independently justiciable, even if *it may be appropriate still to have regard to pre-1 January 2009 conduct* and developments for purposes of determining whether there was a subsequent breach of a CAFTA obligation.[248]

In other words, the tribunal noted that for the tribunal to have jurisdiction the claimant must show two things. First, that a distinct breach breach occurred after the treaty's enter into force, which is sufficiently unrelated to prior events. Second, that knowledge of such breach occurred after the critical date of three years before the claim.[249]

---

in the late '90s first saw its claim thrown out due to a statutory time bar in the domestic investment law, then succeeded at the jurisdictional stage when it invoked a Russian BIT as jurisdictional basis *in lieu* of the domestic statute, see respectively *World Wide Minerals v. Republic of Kazakhstan*, UNCITRAL (Case 1), Award of 22 December 2010 and *World Wide Minerals v. Republic of Kazakhstan*, UNCITRAL (Case 2), Decision on Jurisdiction of 15 October 2015). See also CAFTA Article 10.18.1, as applied in *Aaron C. Berkowitz, Brett E. Berkowitz and Trevor B. Berkowitz* (formerly *Spence International Investments and others*) *v. Republic of Costa Rica*, ICSID Case No. UNCT/13/2, Interim Award of 25 October 2016, para.

247 *Lao Holdings NV. v. The Lao People's Democratic Republic*, ICSID Case No. ARB(AF)/12/6, Decision on Jurisdiction of 21 February 2014, para. 113–118.

248 *Berkowitz* above (n 246) para. 163, footnotes omitted, emphases added.

249 Given the heavily fact-specifity of the jurisdictional analysis, the tribunal expressly declared that its findings would have limited 'precedential' effects, see ibid., para. 166.

Normally there is no precise indication in the applicable treaties of the chronological interplay between the tenets of jurisdiction—nationality, investment, breach, dispute, filing of the claim—, other than the requirement that the protected nationality must exist at the time of the claim (or its registration with ICSID).[250] In a basic sense, which does not exhaust the facets of the analysis *ratione temporis*, the application of a treaty's obligation and the competence of the tribunal correspond. Normally, the starting element of the analysis is the time at which the obligations are allegedly breached by the State:

> Because the BIT is at the same time the instrument that creates the substantive obligation forming the basis of the claim before the Tribunal and the instrument that confers jurisdiction upon the Tribunal, a claimant bringing a claim based on a Treaty obligation must have owned or controlled the investment when that obligation was allegedly breached.[251]

The application of a treaty to investments made before its entry into force is a common occurrence,[252] but it does not imply any retroactive effect. Simply, it avoids arbitrary discriminations: after the treaty comes into force, it applies prospectively to all existing investments, whatever their date of establishment. This is, in essence, a specification of the application *ratione personae* of the treaty, not a limit to the competence *ratione temporis* of the tribunal. *Dicta* referring to the non-identity between application of a treaty *ratione temporis* and competence *ratione temporis* of a tribunal simply refer to this possibility: pre-BIT investments can be protected, but only with respect to post-BIT events.[253]

---

250 See Article 25(2)(a) and (b) ICSID; see for instance Article 8(3) of the France/Peru BIT, referring to the possibility of considering locally incorporated companies as nationals of the '*other State*' when they are controlled by the other State's national '*before the claim arises/is brought*.'

251 *Renée Rose Levy and Gremcitel S.A. v. Republic of Peru*, ICSID Case No. ARB/11/17, Award of 9 January 2015, para. 147.

252 See for instance Article II(2) of the Argentina/Spain BIT: 'This agreement shall apply also to capital investments made before its entry into force by investors of one Party in accordance with the laws of the other Party in the territory of the latter. However, this agreement shall not apply to disputes or claims originating before its entry into force.'

253 See, for instance, *Ping An Life Insurance Company, Limited and Ping An Insurance (Group) Company, Limited v. The Government of Belgium*, ICSID Case No. ARB/12/29, Award of 30 April 2015, para. 173.

Furthermore, State measures can only fall under a tribunal's jurisdiction after an investment of the right nationality has come into existence[254] and before its dissolution.[255] Before a treaty's entry into force, or without an investment of the right nationality, or when the investment was made before a cut-off date,[256] an investment-protection treaty cannot apply and, therefore, the host State has no obligation *vis-à-vis* the (non) investor.[257] Conversely, the State's consent to arbitration granted unilaterally might be revoked, but the revocation will only affect future investments, not existing ones.[258] In *Nordzucker v. Poland*, an issue arose regarding the jurisdiction of the tribunal *ratione temporis* over a FET claim. Whilst FET protection was available to the investor at the time of the alleged breaches, arbitration was not: the arbitration clause was reserved for claims about expropriation and transfers of money. The treaty was subsequently amended and its arbitration clause extended to all standards of treatment in the treaty,[259] whereupon the claimant brought an FET claim. The tribunal upheld its competence on the claim, and took the opportunity to specify the critical dates with respect to each genre of treaty provisions:

> For a provision creating a right/obligation to arbitrate, this is the bringing of the claim. For a provision creating a substantive obligation, this is the breach of such obligation. Each obligation, the substantive obligation, on the one hand, and the procedural obligation to submit to arbitration,

254 *Phoenix Action Ltd v. Czech Republic*, ICSID Case No. ARB/06/5, Award of 15 April 2009, para. 67: '*It does not need extended explanation to assert that the Tribunal has no jurisdiction ratione temporis to consider Phoenix's claims arising prior to December 26, 2002, the date of Phoenix's alleged investment, because the BIT did not become applicable to Phoenix for acts committed by the Czech Republic until Phoenix "invested" in the Czech Republic*'. See also *Gami Inv., Inc. v. The Government of the United Mexican States*, UNCITRAL-NAFTA, Final Award of 15 November 2004, para. 93. *Société Générale v. The Dominican Republic* above (n 59) para. 106: '*Thus, the investment could not be protected by this Treaty until both this Treaty entered into force and Claimant, as a French company, acquired the investment and it became a French investment*.' Likewise, see *Cervin* above (n 60) para. 278.

255 *Phoenix* above (n 254) 71.

256 For instance, the Russia/Mongolia BIT (entered into force in 2006) applies to investments made since 1949, see Article 9. The Italy/Pakistan BIT applies to investments made after 1954, see Article 1(1).

257 *Société Générale v. The Dominican Republic* above (n 59).

258 *AES* above (n 76) para. 223. Consent to arbitration was contained in a domestic statute. This approach is dubious as it does not require that the investor has already consented to arbitration, to keep the State's consent effective even after revocation.

259 Without any specification regarding the transitional regime applicable to previous breaches.

on the other hand, has to be assessed in relation to the respective date at which it took effect.[260]

A similar scenario, relating to two subsequent treaties, led to a different conclusion in the *ABCI v. Tunisia* case, since the latter treaty expressly provided that all disputes arisen before its entry into force would be governed by the previous treaty, including its less-favourable arbitration clause.[261]

A first order of issues concerns the distinction between the facts underlying the controversy, the legal dispute and the submission of a claim. The sequence that leads from a certain factual framework to the solidification of a legal controversy and, later, to the submission of a claim to arbitration '*has to be taken into account in establishing the critical date for determining when under the BIT a dispute qualifies as one covered by the consent necessary to establish ICSID's jurisdiction*'.[262] Normally, the tribunal has jurisdiction over disputes arisen or crystallised after the entry into force of the treaty, even if some of the underlying events predate it.[263] Whereas the existence of a legal dispute does not correspond to the presentation of a claim which can result from it, the difference between the two relevant times is not critical for the jurisdiction of the tribunal, which must cover both.[264] Obviously, a claim submitted before the entry into force of the treaty falls outside the tribunal's jurisdiction.[265]

The pivot of the analysis is the date of occurrence of the challenged State measures which underlie the dispute, but some *caveats* are in order. First, it is possible to envisage a treaty breach resulting from a series of acts and facts occurring over a long period of time, whose lawfulness under the treaty must be assessed as a whole. Second, it is possible to resort to the concept of continuing (or composite) breach—shifting the attention from the instantaneous wrongful act to its permanent effects.[266] Accordingly, it is possible to envisage

260 *Nordzucker v. Poland*, UNCITRAL, Partial Award on Jurisdiction of 10 December 2008, para. 107.

261 *ABCI* above (n 19) para. 163.

262 *Maffezini* above (n 172) para. 96.

263 Ibid., para. 97; *Levy v. Peru* above (n 251) para. 149: '*It is not uncommon that divergences or disagreements develop over a period of time before they finally "crystallize" in an actual measure affecting the investor's treaty rights.*'

264 *Sanum v. Laos* above (n 151) para. 84–86.

265 *Tradex Hellas S.A. v. Republic of Albania*, ICSID Case No. ARB/94/2, Decision on Jurisdiction of 24 December 1996, para. 47.

266 See Barton Legum et al, 'Ratione Temporis or Temporal Scope,' in Barton Legum (ed), *The Investment Treaty Arbitration Review* (Law Business Research 2016) 30 ff.

breaches that are somewhat connected to acts occurred before the entry into force of the treaty, but that either materialise or persist thereafter:

> ... there might be situations in which the continuing nature of the acts and events questioned could result in a breach as a result of acts commencing before the critical date but which only become legally characterized as a wrongful act in violation of an international obligation when such an obligation had come into existence after the effective date of the treaty.... If it is merely the continuing effects of a one-time individual act that as such has ceased to exist that is involved, then the non-retroactivity principle fully applies, but when both the existence of the wrongful act and its effects continue both before and after the critical date, then the non-retroactivity principle will not exclude the application of the obligations of the treaty to the acts and omissions that occur after its effective date.[267]

Conversely, when the first knowledge of a breach constitutes a critical date (for time-bars), the continuous nature of a breach is not relevant, and knowledge of the inception of the breach is the only relevant element.[268]

In ultimate analysis, the tribunal has jurisdiction over acts committed after the critical date (the latter between the entry into force of the treaty, the acquisition of protected nationality, the acquisition of the investment and the relevant cut-off date if there is a time bar),[269] and can award damages only regarding those.[270] The time at which the dispute arises, which normally follows such acts or omissions, might be additionally relevant. The timing of the

---

267 *Société Générale v. The Dominican Republic* above (n 59) para. 87–88, footnotes omitted. See also *Técnicas Medioambientales Tecmed, S.A. v. United Mexican States*, ICSID Case No. ARB (AF)/00/2, Award of 29 May 2003, p. 22; *Walter Bau v. Thailand*, UNCITRAL, Award of 1 July 2009, para. 9.84; *ABCI* above (n 19) para. 165, 178; *Paushok v. Mongolia* above (n 114) para. 491. Certain treaties expressly exclude their application to disputes or facts that predate their entry into force, even with respect to injurious effects that persist over time, see for instance Article 11(1) of the Spain-Colombia BIT.

268 *Berkowitz* above (n 246) para. 208: '*While it may be that a continuing course of conduct constitutes a continuing breach, ... such conduct cannot without more renew the limitation period as this would effectively denude the limitation clause of its essential purpose, namely, to draw a line under the prosecution of historic claims.*'

269 Ibid., para. 217: '*Pre-entry into force conduct cannot be relied upon ... to found liability in-and-of-itself in circumstances in which liability could not properly rest on the post-entry into force breach that has been alleged and on which the Tribunal's jurisdiction was founded.*'

270 Ibid., para. 212.

dispute matters when the instrument defining jurisdiction links to it another essential element, such as the requirement of protected nationality,[271] and when the tribunal's jurisdiction is premised expressly on the existence of a dispute—as in Article 25(1) ICSID.[272] Acts occurred before the critical date might be taken into account—in the absence of a specific expression to the contrary[273]—to colour the assessment of liability, especially in the case of continuing situations, or to calculate damages.[274] For instance, in *Berkowitz v. Costa Rica*, the tribunal declined jurisdiction over certain conduct—i.e. expropriation—that occurred before the treaty's entry into force and/or the critical time-bar, and on other acts that post-dated those critical dates but could not constitute an autonomous cause of action—i.e., the court decrees liquidating insufficient compensation in the wake of the expropriation.[275] Instead, it upheld jurisdiction over the FET claims relating to the unfair conduct of the domestic court proceedings regarding expropriation, which occurred after the critical dates and were sufficiently independent from the expropriation claim (i.e., they did not hinge on the necessary determination of liabilities for claims falling outside the tribunal's jurisdiction *ratione temporis*).[276]

---

271 See for instance Article 26(7) of the ECT.

272 *Duke Energy International Peru Investments No. 1 Ltd. v. Republic of Peru*, ICSID Case No. ARB/03/28, Decision on Jurisdiction of 1 February 2006, para. 148: '*What is decisive of the Tribunal's Jurisdiction ratione temporis is the point in time at which the instant legal dispute between the parties arose, not the point in time during which the factual matters on which the dispute is based took place.*' See also *ABCI* above (n 19) para. 168. Treaties often provide expressly that their application does not extend to disputes that have already arisen before their entry into force, but even in the absence of specific language this conclusion is warranted as a matter of interpretation, see *M.C.I. v. Republic of Ecuador* above (n 244) para. 61.

273 *Empresas Lucchetti, S.A. and Lucchetti Peru, S.A. v. Peru*, ICSID Case No. ARB/03/4, Decision on Annulment of 5 September 2007, para. 94–95. The Committee noted that it would take a special provision in the applicable treaty to remove from the jurisdiction of the tribunal disputes that, despite having arisen after the entry into force of the treaty, related to facts or situations occurred before.

274 *Berkowitz* above (n 246) para. 217–218. This interpretation cannot, for instance, extend the jurisdiction of the tribunal over disputes that have arisen before the entry into force of the BIT, just because they continue thereafter. See *M.C.I.* above (n 244) para. 61–67. Earlier events might be relevant to assess the breach, but '*it must still be possible to point to the conduct of the State after that* [*critical*] *date which is itself a breach*', see *Mondev* above (n 13) para. 70. See also, in the context of time bars, the clarification of the tribunal in *Rusoro* above (n 246) para. 233.

275 *Berkowitz* above (n 246) para. 280.

276 Ibid., para. 286.

In *ST-AD*, the claimant acquired the investment after the critical dates—all breaches had occurred already and the dispute had already crystallised. The claimant tried to recoup the tribunal's jurisdiction *ratione temporis* instituting before the domestic courts a claim identical to one that had been rejected six years earlier. The purpose of this choice was to obtain a State breach (in the form of a second adverse judicial decision) after the cut-off date for jurisdiction. The tribunal dismissed the claim:

> it is not acceptable for a claimant to artificially create a new act of the State allegedly interfering with its rights by simply "mirroring" events that occurred before it became a protected investor. For example, if a claimant, before coming under the protection of a given BIT, had asked for and been refused a license, it could not simply purport to create an event posterior to it becoming a protected investor by presenting the very same request for a license that would, no doubt, be similarly refused.[277]

The tribunal in *Paushok v. Mongolia* followed a similar approach, and cautioned against the expansion of jurisdiction over a dispute relating to pre-BIT actions, even when it arises after the treaty entered into force:

> … the Treaty should not be interpreted as granting it jurisdiction concerning disputes which arose after the entry into force but which are based on actions that have occurred before such entry into force, except for the particular situation of continuing or composite acts.[278]

Whether the dispute presented to the tribunal is in fact a re-hash or a continuation of a previously existing one can be hard to tell. Essentially, tribunals ascertain whether there is identity between the two: a treaty-based dispute is not the same as a domestic dispute, especially if the domestic judgment delivered in the latter is singled out as a specific treaty breach in the former[279]; a pre-BIT divergence (different views) is note the same as a post-BIT dispute (formalised attempt to resolve the difference) even if the latter develops from the former.[280]

277 *ST-AD* above (n 18) para. 332.

278 *Paushok* above (n 114) para. 467–468. See also *M.C.I.* above (n 244) para. 66.

279 *Jan de Nul N.V. and Dredging International N.V. v. Arab Republic of Egypt*, ICSID Case No. ARB/04/13, Decision on Jurisdiction of 16 June 2006, para. 117: '*the original dispute has (re) crystallized into a new dispute when the Ismaïlia Court rendered its decision.*'

280 *Helnan* above (n 116) para. 52.

The sequencing of the relevant elements of the dispute could determine the lapse of the tribunal's jurisdiction. For instance, if treaty-based protection expires after the breach but before the raising of the claim which signals the investor's consent to arbitration, the tribunal might lack jurisdiction because the investor might have lost the opportunity to accept the State's consent to arbitration when it was still available.[281] Likewise, when there are stricter requirement *ratione temporis* in the instrument of consent, the lapse of jurisdiction might occur as early as the rising of the dispute. For instance, the ECT contains the parties' consent to arbitration regarding claims brought by local companies controlled by foreign investors, and requires foreign control to exist '*before the dispute*'.[282] If foreign control existed at the time of the breach but is not maintained until the dispute arises, the claimant would be barred from bringing a claim.[283]

The non-retroactivity of arbitration clauses over existing disputes might cause issues when there are two successive treaties: the latter one cannot in principle be used to bring a pre-existing claim to arbitration. In *Jan de Nul v. Egypt*[284] the tribunal accepted jurisdiction because the dispute had crystallised after the entry into force of the latter BIT, but noted that some of the State measures challenged by the investor fell under the application of the substantive provisions of the former BIT. In *Walter Bau v. Thailand*,[285] instead, the tribunal concluded that the dispute had come into existence before the second BIT had come into force. The latter treaty afforded investor with the possibility to launch investor-State arbitration, which was unavailable under the former

281 *ABCI* above (n 19) para. 93: '*Il est bien établi que l'offre de consentement faite par l'Etat hôte, soit dans un TBI, soit dans sa législation nationale, doit être acceptée par l'investisseur tant que cette offre est en vigueur.*' See also *Southern Pacific Properties (Middle East) Limited v. Arab Republic of Egypt*, ICSID Case No. ARB/84/3, Decision on Jurisdiction of 27 November 1985, para. 66.

282 Article 26(7) ECT.

283 This scenario is at stake in the pending case *Eskosol S.p.A. in liquidazione v. Italian Republic*, ICSID Case No. ARB/15/50, since the claimant, which sought to use the exception under Article 25(2)(b) ICSID and Article 26(7) ECT on grounds of control by a Belgian investor, entered bankruptcy after the alleged breaches (but before it notified the State of the dispute), thus handing control of the company over to the Italian receiver. For a preliminary commentary, see Filippo Fontanelli, 'Foreign control and ICSID jurisdiction on Energy Charter Treaty Claims of Local Companies: The *Eskosol* Case,' in EJIL: Talk!, 12 June 2017.

284 *Jan de Nul N.V. and Dredging International N.V. v. Arab Republic of Egypt*, ICSID Case No. ARB/04/13.

285 *Werner Schneider* above (n 182) para. 9.67 ff.

one. The tribunal held that the arbitration clause in the latter treaty was a '*substantive provision*' which could not apply retroactively, and rejected the claim for lack of jurisdiction *ratione temporis*.[286]

In *Ping An v. Belgium*,[287] instead, the latter treaty expressly regulated the transition between two consecutive treaties. It provided that the new treaty would not apply to any dispute '*which was already under judicial or arbitral process before its entry into force*'.[288] There was no express provision, instead, regarding disputes that had arisen and had been notified under the previous treaty, but had not yet been brought to arbitration. The tribunal held that one such dispute could not be covered by the latter treaty. It found among other things that the much wider scope *ratione materiae* of the new arbitration clause (which was not limited to the amount of compensation for expropriation, like the old one) advised against approving its retroactive effect.[289]

A peculiar problem *ratione temporis* arose in the dispute *Venezuela US v. Venezuela*,[290] hinging on the Barbados/Venezuela BIT. The peculiarity of the case revolved around the atypical language of the arbitration clause, the denunciation of ICSID by the respondent,[291] and the bold attempt by the investor to use the MFN clause to circumvent jurisdictional problems. The bilateral treaty was signed after Venezuela had signed the ICSID Convention, but before it had ratified it. The parties therefore inserted a clause in the arbitration provision making ICSID Additional Facility arbitration available '[*a*]*s long as the Republic of Venezuela has not become a Contracting State of the Convention*'. If the Additional Facility proved unavailable for any reason, recourse could be had to UNCITRAL arbitration.[292] Venezuela reasoned that its consent to non-ICSID arbitration applied only to the period *prior to its accession* to ICSID; the investor argued instead that it could apply *also after Venezuela denounced*

---

286 Ibid., para. 9.71.

287 *Ping An* above (n 253).

288 Article 10(2) of the 2009 China/Belgium BIT. See, conversely, the arbitration provision in the Netherlands/Tunisia 1998 BIT, which expressly stated that even disputes merely *arisen* before its entry into force would be governed by the previous treaty. See *ABCI* above (n 19). A similar provision is contained in the Netherlands/Egypt BIT of 2002, Article 12.

289 Ibid., para. 230–231.

290 *Venezuela US, S.R.L. v. Venezuela* above (n 203).

291 Venezuela, a Contracting State of the ICSID Convention since June 1995, denounced the Convention in January 2012, hence exiting the multilateral instrument as of July 2012, in accordance with Article 71 thereof. After that date, ICSID arbitration has become unavailable even if a BIT concluded by Venezuela is still in force and provides for this avenue of arbitration.

292 Article 8(2) Barbados/Venezuela BIT.

the Convention, and launched UNCITRAL arbitration. The tribunal sided with Venezuela as regards the non-availability of UNCITRAL arbitration in the original BIT (which had lapsed as soon as Venezuela had joined ICSID). Nonetheless, it granted access to UNCITRAL arbitration under the MFN clause, which expressly applied to procedural rights.[293]

Acquisition of Nationality and Jurisdiction Ratione Temporis

Assuming for ease of argument that breach and dispute are contemporaneous and that in any case the dispute follows the breach,[294] the distinction between the emergence of dispute and the formal submission of a claim has often been relevant when the investor acquired the qualifying nationality shortly before launching proceedings, but after the dispute had already materialised. In certain cases, jurisdictional objections were raised when a change in nationality seemed aimed precisely at acquiring treaty protection with the view of bringing a dispute. The objections hinted at an abusive use of the jurisdictional requirements *ratione personae* (the investor was not a genuine national) and/or *temporis* (the investor's nationality was obtained too late).

Nationality planning is, *per se*, permissible (as discussed below in relation to personal jurisdiction). Sometimes, however, a precipitous attempt to acquire the qualifying nationality can fail. In *Banro v. DR Congo* the Canadian investment was transferred to a US subsidiary to launch ICSID arbitration (Canada is not party to ICSID). The tribunal found that the resulting investor was not a national of an ICSID member, and declined jurisdiction.[295] Given the chronological succession, the tribunal regarded the transfer an assignment of a (defective but already existing) claim, rather than an acceptable restructuring occurring before the dispute had arisen.[296] The tribunal in *Phoenix v.*

293 See above, in the section relating to MFN clauses and jurisdiction *ratione materiae*.

294 It is possible that the dispute precedes the breach. For instance, if the dispute arises when a State measure is announced, but long before it is actually adopted. The difference might be crucial: the tribunal might decline jurisdiction if the investor acquired the protected nationality after the dispute had emerged, even if the measures had not been adopted yet. See *Venezuela Holdings, B.V., et al. v. Venezuela* (case formerly known as *Mobil Corporation, Venezuela Holdings, B.V., Mobil Cerro Negro Holding, Ltd., Mobil Venezolana de Petróleos Holdings, Inc., Mobil Cerro Negro, Ltd., and Mobil Venezolana de Petróleos, Inc. v. Venezuela*), ICSID CASE NO. ARB/07/27, Award of 9 October 2014, para. 210.

295 *Banro American Resources, Inc. and Société Aurifère du Kivu et du Maniema S.A.R.L. v. Democratic Republic of the Congo*, ICSID Case No. ARB/98/7, Award of 1 September 2000.

296 A similar conclusion had been reached in *Mihaly International Corporation v. Sri Lanka*, ICSID Case No. ARB/00/2, Award of 15 March 2002, para. 24.

Czech Republic invoked precisely a defect of jurisdiction[297] when the investor acquired a treaty-protected nationality only after the dispute had fully materialised. Although framed as an analysis *ratione materiae* (hinging on whether there was a protected investment) the reasoning revolved critically on the timing of the claim.[298] In general, whereas prospective nationality planning is allowed, it is harder to '*create a remedy for existing grievances*'.[299] Speculating on a corporate transaction that turned out to be wholly fabricated, but that would have granted the investor the requisite nationality 12 days before the critical date of the State breach, the tribunal in *Cementownia v. Turkey* reasoned:

> Even if they did occur, the share transfers would not have been *bona fide* transactions, but rather attempts (in the face of government measures dating back some years about to culminate in the concessions' termination) to fabricate international jurisdiction where none should exist.[300]

In the case *Philip Morris v. Australia*,[301] the investor had restructured the company in Hong Kong to gain protection under the Hong Kong/Australia BIT. The restructuring entailed the acquisition of the qualifying nationality shortly before the challenged measures occurred (and the ensuing dispute arose with the host-State). Correctly, the tribunal referred to a strand of cases which distinguished between objections based on jurisdiction *ratione temporis* and abuse of rights. Namely,

> if a company changes its nationality in order to gain ICSID jurisdiction at a moment when things have started to deteriorate so that a dispute is highly probable, it can be considered an abuse of process, but for an objection based on *ratione temporis* to be upheld, the dispute has to have actually arisen before the critical date to conform to the general

297 Whereas the tribunal observed no flaw with the jurisdiction *ratione personae*, i.e., with the newly acquired nationality, see para. 65.

298 Ibid., para. 138.

299 Christoph Schreuer, 'Nationality of investors: legitimate restrictions vs. business interests' (2009) 24(2) ICSID review 521–527, 526.

300 *Cementownia "Nowa Huta" S.A. v. Republic of Turkey*, ICSID Case No. ARB(AF)/06/2, Award of 17 September 2009, para. 117.

301 *Philip Morris Asia Limited v. The Commonwealth of Australia*, UNCITRAL, PCA Case No. 2012–12, Award on Jurisdiction and Admissibility of 17 December 2015.

> principle of non-retroactivity in the interpretation and application of international treaties.[302]

The tribunal therefore concluded that the critical date for jurisdiction was that of the enactment of the challenged measures.[303] Even if obtained with abusive intent, the Hong Kong nationality was obtained in time for the tribunal to have jurisdiction, before the alleged treaty breach occurred. The tribunal turned therefore to matters of admissibility to analyse the investor's tactic as a possible abuse of rights (see below).[304]

In *García and García v. Venezuela*, the claimants did not have Spanish nationality at the time of making the investment, but they had acquired it when the breaches occurred and subsequently retained it, continuously, until the request for arbitration. The tribunal did not consider this to be a problem for its jurisdiction.[305]

MFN and Jurisdiction Ratione Temporis

An MFN might be invoked to found the jurisdiction on the clauses of another treaty, which might have entered into force at a later time. The issue was at stake in the *Maffezini* case (where certain jurisdictional hurdles in the Argentine-Spain BIT were overcome relying on the later Chile-Spain BIT). However, in that case, the tribunal found that both BITs had entered into force before '*the conflict of legal views and interests came to be clearly established*'.[306] There is no publicly known case in which the treaty made applicable through the MFN clause entered into force after the critical time of the dispute, giving

302 *Levy v. Peru* above (n 251) para. 182. See also *Pac Rim Cayman LLC v. Republic of El Salvador*, ICSID Case No. ARB/09/12, Decision on the Respondent's Jurisdictional Objections of 1 June 2012, para. 2.101, 2.107 and *Lao Holdings* above (n 247) para. 76.

303 *Philip Morris* above (n 301) para. 533.

304 Ibid., para. 535 ff.

305 *Serafín García Armas and Karina García Gruber v. The Bolivarian Republic of Venezuela*, UNCITRAL, Caso CPA No. 2013–3, Decision on Jurisdiction of 15 December 2014, para. 214–215. Subsequently, the Court of Appeal of Paris set aside the award, noting that, under the BIT, the requirement of foreign nationality of the investor was an essential element of the 'investment' at the time of 'investing'. Decision of the Paris Court of Appeal on the Set Aside Application of 25 April 2017, *Venezuela v. García Armas et García Gruber*, Reg. no. 15/01040, 8. The applicable BIT provision (Article 1(2)) reads: '*Por «inversiones» se designa todo tipo de activos, invertidos por inversores de una Parte Contratante en el territorio de la otra Parte Contratante*' ('investments' indicates all assets, invested by the investors of one Contracting Party in the territory of the other Contracting Party).

306 *Maffezini* above (n 172) para. 98.

rise to a hiatus *ratione temporis* with respect to the original treaty. In *ST-AD*, the investor tried to invoke pre-investment protection reaching back to the time of its preliminary contract of investment. The tribunal found that the investor failed to elaborate on this claim, noting that '*it ha[d] not presented any treaty entered into by [the host State] granting such rights*'.[307] This dictum appears to suggest that, through an MFN clause, it might be possible to achieve pre-investment protection, thus extending retroactively the jurisdiction *ratione temporis* of the tribunal. In *Tecmed*,[308] instead, the attempt was made to use the MFN clause to extend the tribunal's jurisdiction *ratione temporis* (the comparator treaty had—allegedly—retroactive effects). The tribunal noted that the attempt sought to extend the application of the treaty and jurisdiction of the tribunal, and rejected the MFN-based claim.[309] In *MCI v. Ecuador*,[310] the applicable BIT had entered into force in 1997, after the dispute had arisen. The investor attempted to use the MFN clause to import the treatment granted in the comparator BIT, which had entered into force in 1995. The attempt hinged on a creative reading of the imported provision (which obviously referred to the '*Contracting Parties*' of the comparator BIT, not to any contracting parties of any future treaty as the claimant suggested) and was disallowed.[311]

In *Ansung v. China*,[312] the investor sought to invoke an MFN clause to avoid the three-year time bar in the applicable BIT. The tribunal rejected the attempt, noting that the relevant MFN provision limited its operation '*to investment and business activities*,'[313] which the applicable BIT defined as including '*the expansion, operation, management, maintenance, use, enjoyment, and sale or other disposal of investments*'.[314] According to the tribunal, therefore, matters of access to arbitration lay outside the ambit of the MFN clause.[315]

307 *ST-AD* above (n 18) para. 313.

308 *Técnicas Medioambientales Tecmed* above (n 267).

309 Ibid., para. 55: '[*the Tribunal*] *deems that matters relating to the application over time of the Agreement, which involve more the time dimension of application of its substantive provisions rather than matters of procedure or jurisdiction, due to their significance and importance, go to the core of matters that must be deemed to be specifically negotiated by the Contracting Parties*.' See also *ABCI* above (n 19) para. 174.

310 *M.C.I.* above (n 244).

311 Ibid., para. 127–128.

312 *Ansung* above (n 71).

313 Article 3(3) of the China-Korea BIT.

314 Ibid., Article 3(1).

315 *Ansung* above (n 71) para. 141.

The Effects of Denunciation of the ICSID Convention

Article 71 ICSID allows contracting parties to withdraw from the Convention.[316] The denunciation takes effect six months after the State gives written notice to the World Bank. Article 72 ICSID protects investors from the effects of the State's unilateral action, providing that the denunciation shall not affect the State's obligations arising out of consent to the jurisdiction of Centre given before the denunciation. This undoubtedly means that investors who have already accepted the State's offer to arbitrate are unaffected by the denunciation (the 'offer-and-acceptance' approach). According to a wider construction, Article 72 ICSID applies also to the consent given unilaterally by the State, for instance in a BIT arbitration clause, hence even if the investor has not accepted it yet (the 'firm offer' approach).[317] Both readings would expose States to ICSID arbitration after their withdrawal from the Convention comes into effect. Following the 'firm offer' approach, the State would not be spared from its obligations under ICSID for as long as there are treaty arbitration clauses (or other instruments like contracts and laws) in force which provide for ICSID arbitration.[318] The crux of the interpretive issue is whether a unilateral standing offer is enough to entail the '*consent to the jurisdiction of the Centre given by [the State]*' (from which Article 72 ICSID derives post-denunciation obligations) or, instead, the combination of State's offer and investor's acceptance is necessary to create consent.[319]

---

316 For an overview of the withdrawal mechanism, see Christoph Schreuer, 'Denunciation of the ICSID Convention and Consent to Arbitration' in Michael Waibel et al. (eds), *The Backlash against Investment Arbitration: Perceptions and Reality* (OUP 2010) 353–368.

317 A vocal endorsement of this approach is Christer Söderlund, who attached a Separate Opinion dated 13 April 2017 to the *Blue Bank International & Trust (Barbados) Ltd. v. Bolivarian Republic of Venezuela*, ICSID Case No. ARB 12/20, Award of 26 April 2017, even if the question was not critical in that case. See in particular para. 39–45, explaining that mutual consent is perfected by the BIT provisions and would survive ICSID denunciation.

318 Given that many investment treaties have clauses that preserve their effects for many years after their termination, the scenario is very likely.

319 The hermeneutic controversy over Article 72 ICSID is explored in detail in Frederic G Sourgens and Michael D Nolan, 'The Interplay between State Consent to ICSID Arbitration and Denunciation of the ICSID Convention: The (Possible) Venezuela Case Study' (2007) Transnational Dispute Management. Schreuer above (n 316), opts for the 'offer plus acceptance' option, whereas Emmanuel Gaillard, 'The Denunciation of the ICSID Convention' (2007) New York Law Journal, 26 June 2007, 8, distinguish between firm unconditional offers to arbitrate (which entail consent) and optional offers (which do not). A more recent overview of the question is Frederic G Sourgens, 'Keep the Faith: Investment Protection Following the Denunciation of International Investment Agreements' (2012) 111 Santa Clara Journal of International Law 335.

After Venezuela's denunciation of the ICSID Convention, tribunals have had to determine their jurisdiction *ratione temporis*[320] over investment claims aimed at Venezuela under the surviving BITs, applying the rules in Articles 71 and 72 ICSID. In *Venoklim v. Venezuela*,[321] the investor filed an ICSID claim on 23 July 2012, almost six months after the respondent State's ICSID denunciation of 24 January 2012. The tribunal rejected Venezuela's attempt to evaluate the jurisdiction of the tribunal at the date of the notice of registration of the claim by the Secretariat, which occurred after the critical cut-off date.[322] The investor's right to launch ICSID proceedings was granted by Article 71 ICSID, since the claim was filed when Venezuela was still an ICSID member, if only for two days.[323] It is worth noting the tribunal's finding, made in passing, that under Article 72 ICSID the State's consent is simply the unilateral offer to arbitrate (resulting from the joint effects of the national investment law and the BIT with the Netherlands), rather than the consent resulting from the investor's acceptance of that offer.[324] The tribunal remarked that a State must comply with its offer to arbitrate, even during the six months that follow the

320 The issue could be characterised as well as an obstacle *ratione personae*. The respondent State might claim that the withdrawal from the Convention is an obstacle to the possibility to sue it in arbitration proceedings.

321 *Venoklim Holding B.V. v. Bolivarian Republic of Venezuela*, ICSID Case No. ARB/12/22, Award of 3 April 2015.

322 Ibid., para. 78–79. A similar scenario emerged in the *Blue Bank* case (above n 317, para. 107), in which the request for arbitration was made on 22 June 2012, before the critical date of 25 July 2012. However, because ICSID required additional clarification from the Claimant, the registration occurred only after it, on 7 August 2012. The tribunal found that consent had crystallised before the denunciation entered into effect, see para. 120.

323 At the time of writing, the award is being challenged in annulment proceedings.

324 It can be suggested that the tribunal in *Pan American Energy LLC v. Plurinational State of Bolivia* (ICSID Case No. ARB/10/8) might have reached the same conclusion, given that Bolivia's denunciation of ICSID came into effect in November 2009, and the claim was brought in April 2010. Whereas the details of the case are confidential, it is known that the tribunal issued a decision regarding the jurisdictional objections in November 2013 and the parties requested thereafter a suspension of proceedings, which led ultimately to a settlement. It could be inferred that the respondent's jurisdictional objections were rejected, and that the negotiation is evidence that the tribunal was ready to look into the merits. If so, it would mean that Article 72 ICSID was interpreted to refer to 'firm-offer' consent, allowing recourse to arbitration on the basis of the US/Bolivia BIT after the denunciation of ICSID came into effect. It cannot be known, however, whether the claimant had accepted the offer to arbitration before the critical date of November 2009, in a separate act different from the filing of the claim.

denunciation of ICSID.[325] This conclusion on Article 72 ICSID is plausible and lends credence to the 'firm-offer' school of thought, but it is unclear why the tribunal took pains to specify that the State's obligations flowing from its unilateral consent must be observed '*even during the six-month period*' after denunciation. This specification is at least irrelevant, at most misleading: the 'firm-offer' approach entails that the State's obligation extends *even after* the withdrawal and its six-month incubation period, surviving for as long as there is an offer to consent to ICSID arbitration (in the BIT, the national law, or any other pre-denunciation instrument).

In the *Rusoro* case, the request for arbitration was submitted a week before Venezuela's denunciation came into effect. Arbitration under the ICSID Additional Facility was still available.[326] Conversely, in *Nova Scotia v. Venezuela* the investor's attempt to launch UNCITRAL arbitration was rejected, precisely because recourse to the ICSID Additional Facility was still available.[327] Whereas the role of the Secretariat is considered as merely administrative at this stage, it is possible to envision circumstances in which a claim is made after the six-month period and the Secretariat refuses registration, implicitly endorsing the offer-and-acceptance approach. Conversely, the Secretariat might limit itself to register the case and leave the jurisdictional objection to the tribunal. In such latter scenario, the risk is that the Secretariat's conduct might be read as a preference for the firm offer approach.

4 Ratione Loci

Investments Made 'In the Territory'

Whereas it is not often at the centre of litigation, the restriction *ratione loci* of a treaty's application speaks to the essence of foreign investment protection:

> it is quite plain that NAFTA Chapter Eleven was not intended to provide substantive protections or rights of action to investors whose investments are wholly confined to their own national States, in circumstances

325 *Venoklim* above (n 321) para. 65–66: '*considera el Tribunal que el consentimiento al que se refiere el Artículo 72 es, en este caso, el del Estado en sí, es decir la simple oferta unilateral de arbitraje, y no el consentimiento del Estado perfeccionado con la aceptación del inversionista de dicha oferta al presentar su solicitud de arbitraje.... Una vez que un Estado ha hecho una oferta de arbitraje internacional válida, una de sus principales obligaciones es la de cumplir con la misma, inclusive durante el periodo de seis meses previsto por el Convenio CIADI para que la denuncia surta efectos.*'

326 *Rusoro* above (n 246) para. 269–273.

327 *Nova Scotia* above (n 147). The case has since been registered under the ICSID Additional Facility, see *Nova Scotia* above (n 235).

> where those investments may be affected by measures taken by another NAFTA State Party. The NAFTA should not be interpreted so as to bring about this unintended result.[328]

This territorial nexus[329] is often expressed in the applicable treaty, which covers investments made '*in the territory*' of the host State.[330] Even when the definition of investor does not expressly refer to the location of the investment (see for instance Article 1101(1)(a) NAFTA), foreign investors are protected by investment treaties only insofar as they have an investment in the host State.[331] The territorial link normally pertains to the investment rather than the investor. Therefore, in the absence of specific restrictions, that the investor has no substantial business in the host country is irrelevant: shareholding in an investment made there, even indirect, would be sufficient.[332]

---

328 *Bayview Irrigation District et al. v. United Mexican States*, ICSID Case No. ARB(AF)/05/1, Award of 19 July 2007, para. 103; see para. 104: '... *The economic dependence of an enterprise upon supplies of goods—in this case, water—from another State is not sufficient to make the dependent enterprise an 'investor' in that other State*'; *Grand River Enterprises Six Nations, Ltd., et al. v. United States of America*, UNCITRAL, Award of 12 January 2011, para. 87–89. See also Abi Saab's dissenting opinion above (n 11) para. 74: '*A territorial link or nexus is inherent in the concept of "investment" in article 25 of the ICSID Convention. The whole idea behind the Convention was to encourage the flow of private foreign investment to developing countries by offering an international guarantee in the form of an alternative neutral adjudication of disputes arising out of such investment in the territory of the host States, typically subject to its laws and courts.*'

329 On which, see diffusedly Christina Knahr, 'The Territorial Nexus between an Investment and the Host State', in Marc Bungenberg, Jörn Griebel et al. (eds), *International Investment Law: a Handbook* (Nomos/Hart Publishing/C.H. Beck 2015) 590.

330 See for instance Article 1 of the Canada/ Côte d'Ivoire BIT: '*"covered investment" means, with respect to a Party, an investment in its territory of an investor of the other Party* ...' (emphasis added). See also *Philippe Gruslin v. Malaysia*, ICSID Case No. ARB/99/3, Award of 27 November 2000, para. 13.11.

331 *The Canadian Cattlemen for Fair Trade v. United States of America*, UNCITRAL (formerly *Consolidated Canadian Claims v. United States of America*), Award of Jurisdiction of 28 January 2008, para. 169. The review of the territorial element does not depend on its inclusion in the treaty, see *Inmaris Perestroika Sailing Maritime Services GmbH and others v. Ukraine*, ICSID Case No. ARB/08/8, Decision on Jurisdiction of 8 March 2010, para. 113–121; *Philippe Gruslin v. Malaysia* above (n 330) para. 13.9–13.12 (the territoriality objection was ultimately not reviewed by the sole arbitrator).

332 *Flemingo DutyFree Shop Private Limited v the Republic of Poland*, UNCITRAL, Award of 12 August 2016, para. 342: '*It is also not an impediment for the Tribunal to exercise jurisdiction if Claimant, an Indian company, allegedly does not deploy commercial activities in India and is not involved in the Polish operations of the Flemingo Group.*'

Jurisdictional issues *ratione loci* tend to overlap with others *ratione materiae* (e.g., the existence of an investment) and *ratione personae* (e.g., the identification of the correct respondent, and of the claimant's nationality). The requirement that investments be made in the territory of the host State, indeed, excludes business operations that are entirely carried out abroad. In the case of trans-border operations, at issue might be the relevance of the elements that are located in the host State. Thus, the critical question might be framed interchangeably as one about the place of the alleged investment (there is an investment, but not in the host State), one about its substance (what is located in the host State is not an investment), or one about the identification of the host State (the investment is made in the territory of a State different from the putative respondent).

A pertinent case in point is the dispute *Apotex v. USA* (UNCITRAL).[333] The claimant (a Canadian pharmaceutical company) challenged the import alert issued by the US authorities, which prevented the company from shipping goods to the US for two years. The tribunal ultimately found that the part of the operations occurring in the US did not qualify as investment under NAFTA's Article 1139. In other words, what took place in the US was not an investment (but, at most, a trade operation, mostly consisting of importing and distributing goods from Canada); conversely, what was indeed an investment was not located in the US (i.e., the developing and production of pharmaceutical products).[334] The NAFTA tribunal in the *Grand Rivers v. US* case faced a similar set of circumstances. The claimants' main asset, a tobacco manufacturing plant, was located in the home State. Three of the four claimants' purported investment in the US allegedly consisted in an enterprise to distribute cigarettes, which operated in the '*undocumented manner customary among indigenous peoples*'.[335] The tribunal rejected this characterisation.[336]

The cognate issue of whether damages must arise in the host State to be recoverable (which presupposes the existence of a foreign investment[337] and of a breach) was considered briefly by the *SD Myers* NAFTA tribunal, which simply noted that '[*t*]*here is no provision that requires that all of the investor's losses must be sustained within the host state in order to be recoverable*'.[338]

333 *Apotex* UNCITRAL above (n 246).

334 Ibid., para. 176.

335 *Grand River* above (n 328) para. 91.

336 Ibid., para. 106.

337 On whether the claimants held an investment in Canada, see Partial Award of 13 November 2000, para. 231.

338 *S.D. Myers, Inc. v. Government of Canada*, UNCITRAL, Second Partial Award of 21 October 2002, para. 118.

Another controversial instance occurred in the *Abaclat* case (and in the germane disputes *Ambiente Ufficio* and *Giovanni Alemanni*). At stake was whether Argentinean sovereign bonds bought by Italian citizens were made in the territory of Argentina. In spite of Abi Saab's strenuous arguing to the opposite,[339] the majority sided with the claimants in light of the nature of the investments considered:

> With regard to an investment of a purely financial nature, the relevant criteria [to identify its location] cannot be the same as those applying to an investment consisting of business operations and/or involving manpower and property. With regard to investments of a purely financial nature, the relevant criteria should be where and/or for the benefit of whom the funds are ultimately used, and not the place where the funds were paid out or transferred.[340]

The '*benefit*' criterion, in the tribunal's account, is inherited from a line of cases.[341] Of particular relevance is the case *S.G.S. v. the Philippines*, where the tribunal held that the investment was made in the territory of the host State, even if it mainly consisted in the carrying out of pre-shipment inspections abroad. The inspections, critically, were instrumental to obtain a certificate which would ease importing operations into the country, issued by a liaison office based in the host State. Resultantly, '[*a*] *substantial and non-severable aspect of the overall service was provided in the Philippines*'.[342] It appears clearly that the *S.G.S. v. the Philippines* tribunal did not deal with purely financial investments; moreover, it rejected outright the relevance of benefit as a territorial nexus:

> investments made outside the territory of the Respondent State, however beneficial to it, would not be covered by the BIT.[343]

339 See Abi Saab's dissenting opinion above (n 11) para. 73 ff.

340 Para. 374. This approach was followed in the case *Deutsche Bank v. Sri Lanka* above (n 216) para. 288 ff. Abi Saab contested this interpretation and claimed that even if financial investment are covered by the BIT, they must be linked to the funding of '*specific economic projects, enterprises or activities which, had they been undertaken directly by these foreign financial investors, would have constituted foreign direct investment*' in the territory of the host State. See Abi Saab's dissenting opinion above (n 11) para. 98.

341 *Fedax* above (n 43) para. 41. See also *SGS v. Pakistan* above (n 123) para. 136–140, where emphasis was laid on the fact that the aim of SGS's activity was to raise the financial revenue of the State (para. 139); *SGS v. Philippines* above (n 38) para. 111.

342 *SGS v. Philippines* above (n 38) para. 102. See also *Bureau Veritas* above (n 31) para. 103–104.

343 Ibid., para. 99. This passage was highlighted in Abi Saab's dissenting opinion above (n 11) para. 100.

A more fitting analogue is the *Fedax v. Venezuela* case, described above, in which the tribunal considered the debt instruments issued by the host State to be investments; the territorial requirement was met because the investor's contribution was made available to the government of the host State.[344] The same approach was used by the *CSOB v. Slovak Republic*, with reference to a loan made by the investor to a State-owned company of the host State.[345] Likewise, in *Inmaris Perestroika v. Ukraine*,[346] the tribunal did not consider it necessary to investigate whether there is a direct transfer of funds into the host State, as long as '*the transaction accrues to the benefit of the State itself*.'[347]

Treaty Application over a Specific Territory

A different set of issues *ratione loci* can arise when the nexus between respondent's rights and obligations and the territory is contested. Contestation could derive from an episode of unlawful occupation, or when the application of a treaty depends on treaty succession. It could also arise in case of concurrent application of investment treaties stipulated by different host States with respect to the same territory. These problems could be repackaged as *ratione personae* impediments, as they call into question whether the State indicated as respondent is really bound by investment protection obligations for conduct occurred in a specific place.

After Russia's *de facto* annexation of Crimea in 2014, a number of Ukrainian investors brought claims against Russia relating to the acts of Russian authorities in Crimea.[348] These claims imply the applicability of the Ukraine—Russia BIT to the facts of the dispute, including their location.[349] Russia has not participated in these proceedings, but sent a letter to the PCA stating that the BIT

344 *Fedax* above (n 43) para. 41.

345 *CSOB* above (n 47) para. 78–91.

346 *Inmaris* above (n 331) para. 123.

347 Ibid., para. 124 (the investor renovated a boat and subsequently used it jointly with the host State government). Likewise, see *Gold Reserve* above (n 213) para. 262.

348 For a full list of these claims, and an overview, see Odysseas G Repousis, 'Why Russian investment treaties could apply to Crimea and what would this mean for the ongoing Russo-Ukrainian territorial conflict' (2016) 32(3) *Arbitration International* 459–481; Richard Happ, Sebastian Wuschka, 'Horror Vacui: Or Why Investment Treaties Should Apply to Illegally Annexed Territories' (2016) 33(3) *Journal of International Arbitration* 245–268.

349 Article 1(1) of the Russia-Ukraine BIT provides that 'investments' are those '*put ... on the territory of the other Contracting Party,' and Article 1(4) extends the notion of territory to each Contracting Party's territory,* EEZ *and continental shelf, 'as defined in conformity with international law.'*

cannot '*serve as a basis for composing an arbitral tribunal*' seised with such claims.[350] Russia's characterisation of the Crimea events (lawful annexation or accession) would warrant the application of Russia's investment obligations on that territory—by virtue of succession in Ukraine's obligations. However, the consensus is that Crimea was unlawfully occupied. As a result, and under the rules of nullity and non-recognition[351] reflected also in Article 53 VCLT and Article 41(2) of the ILC State Responsibility Articles,[352] the occupied territory must not be considered part of Russia. This conclusion might deal a fatal blow to the claims of the Ukrainian investors, insofar as their investments would be considered to be '*put*' in Ukraine and, accordingly, be divested of treaty protection.

It is known that at least in one case the Tribunal upheld jurisdiction.[353] This decision might have relied on one of these reasons (or a combination of them): the Tribunal did not examine the territorial objection, since neither party raised it; the tribunal considered that the duty of non-recognition cannot benefit the wrongdoer; and/or the Tribunal considered that Russia's *de facto* control over Crimea warranted the extra-territorial application of its obligations. The former circumstance should be ruled out: not only can Tribunals examine jurisdictional flaws *proprio motu*, they must do so (*ex officio*).[354] The second circumstance would engage the principle that Russia cannot benefit from its own wrongdoing, or a sort of estoppel: given Russian claims to sovereignty over Crimea's territory, a territorial objection would be precluded. Since no such objection was effectively raised, this argument is doubtful. The more pertinent question would be whether the Ukrainian investors could benefit from Russia's wrongdoing (i.e., deriving from it unanticipated treaty protection). The third circumstance would draw inspiration from the doctrine of extra-territorial application of human rights obligations, employed by human

350 Permanent Court of Arbitration, *Aeroport Belbek LLC and Mr. Igor Valerievich Kolomoisky v. Russian Federation*, Press Release of 6 January 2016, available at http://www.pcacases.com/web/sendAttach/1553.

351 UN General Assembly, Declaration on the Strengthening of International Security, UN Doc. Res 2734 (XXV) (16 Dec. 1970): '*no territorial acquisition resulting from the threat of use of force shall be recognized as legal.*'

352 Reading: '*No State shall recognize as lawful a situation created by a serious breach within the meaning of article 40, nor render aid or assistance in maintaining that situation.*'

353 *PJSC Ukrnafta v. The Russian Federation*, UNCITRAL, PCA Case No. 2015–34, Award on Jurisdiction of 4 July 2017, see PCA Press Release.

354 *Contra*, see Repousis above (n 348) 470: '*an investment tribunal would not have to determine whether it has jurisdiction over the dispute in hand, since the parties would not oppose the application of the Russia–Ukraine BIT to Crimea.*'

rights bodies[355] and endorsed by the ICJ.[356] According to this doctrine, a State exercising jurisdiction outside its territory is bound by the same human rights obligations it must uphold internally. The parallel is imperfect: this doctrine typically operates to rule out a lapse in human rights protection, hence it assumes that one State must necessarily be in charge. The territorial State being effectively ousted, the occupying one takes upon the responsibility, lest the individuals suddenly lose their rights. BIT-derived obligations, however, are not granted by State parties to '*everyone within their jurisdiction*,'[357] but only to qualified subjects: when the territorial requirement is a specific requirement of jurisdiction it cannot be replaced by *de facto* control. Moreover, there would be no issue of rights' discontinuation; in the cases against Russia, the Ukrainian investors did not hold treaty-derived rights beforehand, so there is no compelling reason of fairness to create them *ex novo* after the occupation. Reportedly, the tribunals have extended this doctrine to investment treaties, and supported its use noting that the word—'territory' in the treaties might also cover '*de facto*' territories.

An issue of State succession arose also in the *Sanum v. Laos* case.[358] The investor was an entity incorporated in the Macao Special Administrative Region, which sought to invoke the China–Laos BIT in the dispute. The Respondent, however, argued that investors from Macao do not fall under the territorial scope of the 1993 China–Laos BIT, because Macao is not part of China for the purposes of that treaty, as illustrated by its ability to conclude autonomous investment treaties.[359] The question hinged on the extension of the pre-existing China-Laos BIT to the territory of Macao,[360] which Portugal handed over to China in 1999, and on whether some circumstance would impede such

355 Human Rights Committee (1981) ICCPR Comm. No. 52/1979, para. 12.3, referring to Art. 2 of the UN Covenant on Civil and Political Rights; European Court of Human Rights, *Bankovic and Others v Belgium and 16 Other Contracting States*, Eur. Ct. H.R. 52207/99, 41 ILM 517 (2001), para. 71.

356 *Legal Consequences of the Construction of a Wall in the Occupied Palestinian Territory*, Advisory Opinion, ICJ Reports 2004, para. 109.

357 European Convention of Human Rights, Article 1.

358 *Sanum v. Laos* above (n 151).

359 An equivalent question arose in the *Tza Yap Shum* case, above (n 156), regarding the applicability of a Chinese BIT to the Hong Kong territory.

360 Under Article 29 VCLT and Article 15(b) of the Vienna Convention on Succession of States in respect of Treaties (neither State was party to the VCST, but the provision was deemed to reflect customary law).

extension.[361] One such circumstance was the apparent possibility that both China and Macao enter separate BITs with the same third State, with respect to the same territory.[362] The Respondent contended that the existence of a Macao BIT with a State implied the exclusion of Macao's territory from the application of a Chinese BIT with that same State.[363] The tribunal disagreed:

> The Tribunal does not accept this conclusion. It can indeed also mean, with as much if not more logic, that the PRC-BIT applies to the whole territory including the Macao SAR, while the Macao SAR-BIT is confined to the territory of Macao but cannot extend to Mainland China.... In the Tribunal's view, the superposition of instruments of protection does not bring about chaos, but rather better protection to foreign investors.[364]

Other instances of State succession concerned Kazakhstan and Serbia, which were sued in their alleged capacity as successors of the USSR and the State Union of Serbia and Montenegro. Kazakhstan was found to succeed in the obligations deriving from the 1991 Canada-USSR BIT, in a case relating to alleged breaches occurred after 1997.[365] In *Mytilineos*, the tribunal determined that Serbia was not bound by the obligations of the 1997 BIT between Greece and the Federal Republic of Yugoslavia. At the critical time of the seisin of the

361 The tribunal discarded the hypothesis that the BIT would impose '*communist*' values on Macao—hence considered it compatible with the 'one country, two systems' doctrine. See *Sanum v. Laos* above (n 151) para. 249. It also found that, under the *pacta tertiis* principle, Laos could not be bound by any arrangement between China and Macao (para. 267).

362 This possibility had indeed materialised with Portugal and the Netherlands.

363 Cases of explicit carve-outs are, obviously, easier to determine. In *Menzies* above (n 18) the tribunal noted that the investor, incorporated in the Virgin Islands, could not invoke the BIT between Senegal and UK, because Article 1(e)(i) of such treaty only includes Great Britain and Northern Ireland in the definition of '*territory*' applicable to the UK, see para. 154.

364 Ibid., para. 290, 292. See also para. 294: '*The Tribunal does not consider that the concomitant application of these two BITs would lead to "legal chaos". The more dispute settlement options an investor has, the better it is protected, and the more enhanced the economic cooperation will be between the concerned States.*' The same conclusion was reached by the tribunal in *Tza Yap Shum* above (n 156) para. 76. The Singapore Court of Appeal (competent because the seat of the investment arbitration was Singapore) confirmed the *Sanum* award, after the High Court had annulled it. See *Sanum Investments Ltd v Government of the Lao People's Democratic Republic* [2016] SGCA 57.

365 *World Wide Minerals* (Case 2) above (n 246). The case is not public, so it is not possible to elaborate on the tribunal's analysis.

tribunal, whereas the Union of Serbia and Montenegro was deemed to succeed the Yugoslav Federation, Serbia was only a constituent subdivision. As such, it could not have deemed to have consented to arbitration in its own right.[366]

5 Ratione Personae

An obvious jurisdictional issue *ratione personae* is the lack of standing of an investor that is not a party to the relevant arbitration clause. Whereas this circumstance is rare (most often investors accede an open-ended offer to arbitrate, proffered unilaterally in a treaty or a statute), it can arise when the arbitration clause is contained in a contract. In the case *Niko v. Bangladesh*,[367] the tribunal declined its jurisdiction over two of the three claimants, which were not parties to the applicable contract and, therefore, could not participate in the arbitration.[368] Likewise, tribunals do not have jurisdiction *ratione personae* over claimants who are unable to prove their relationship with the investment,[369] that have acquired a defective claim,[370] or that have not yet

366 *Mytilineos* above (n 238) para. 173–174. This conclusion was without prejudice to the possibility that Serbia's conduct might engage the responsibility of the Union, see para. 175.

367 *Niko Resources Ltd. v. Bangladesh Petroleum Exploration & Production Company Limited and Bangladesh Oil Gas and Mineral Corporation*, ICSID Case No. ARB/10/11, Decision on Jurisdiction of 19 August 2013.

368 Ibid., para. 515.

369 In *Ampal* above (n 22), an individual claiming to have a substantial interest in the investment failed to convince the tribunal that this was actually the case. See para. 218–223. The tribunal conceded that the absence of reliable evidence regarding the link between the individual and the investment might have been due to the former's attempt to avoid fiscal liability using an anonymous trust scheme. However, the evidence before the tribunal was considered insufficient to discharge the requisite burden of proof, see para. 226. In a couplet of twin cases, the tribunals concluded that the claimant had no relationship with the investor or the investment, see *Europe Cement Investment & Trade S.A. v. Turkey*, ICSID Case No. ARB(AF)/07/2, Award of 13 August 2009; *Cementownia* above (n 300). Likewise, the claimant must prove to have made a contribution to the investment (this requirement can be framed as one *ratione materiae*: insofar as an essential component of investments is the economic contribution, without it there is no investment, at least as far as claimant is concerned). See *Saba Fakes* above (n 45) para. 130–149; *KT Asia* above (n 48) para. 188–206 and *Gaëta* above (n 46) 222–223; *Flughafen Zürich A.G. et Gestión e Ingenería IDC S.A. v. Bolivarian Republic of Venezuela*, ICSID CASE No. ARB/10/19, Award of 18 November 2014, para. 254.

370 *Mihaly International Corporation v. Sri Lanka*, ICSID Case No. ARB/00/2, Award, 15 March 2002, para. 24. A Canadian company had transferred its claim against the host State to a US company, so as to enjoy protection under the US/Sri Lanka BIT. Because the transferring company enjoyed no protection under the treaty, the tribunal found that it could not

made an investment.[371] In *Nations Energy v. Panama*, interestingly enough, the tribunal took pains to re-characterise an objection *ratione personae* (the host State alleged that the claimant had transferred the investment and admitted its unlawfulness) as one of admissibility.[372] In *Tulip v. Turkey*, the tribunal rejected the claimant's attempt to act also on behalf and in representation of another investor who had not joined the claimant in the proceedings.[373]

An obverse and atypical issue of standing arose in *Cambodia Power v. Cambodia*[374] with respect to the respondent. Besides Cambodia, the claim was brought against a Cambodian State-owned company. The claimant asserted the *locus standi* of the latter as an agency '*designated*' to ICSID by the host State under Article 25(1) of the Convention, but the tribunal noted that the lack of a formal designation prevented it from establishing jurisdiction over the company as co-respondent.[375]

Claims by Shareholders and Indirect Investments

Shareholders typically qualify as investors with respect to their shares in a company incorporated in the host State;[376] they are entitled to bring claims for reflective loss.[377] Accordingly, they have *locus standi* in proceedings hinging

transfer a valid claim to the claimant (*nemo plus iuris ad alium transferre potest quam ipse habet*).

371 Whereas this is normally an issue *ratione materiae* (there is no investment yet), it might emerge also in the analysis of the autonomous protection granted to investors as such. In *Nordzucker* above (n 260), the treaty language allowed for the protection of pre-investment interests, since the Germany-Poland BIT requires investors to be '*entitled to engage in investments*' (and not to have made an investment) and future investments enjoy some minimal protection (namely, to be admitted in compliance with domestic law and enjoy FET, see Article 2(1) of the BIT).

372 *Nations Energy Corporation* above (n 224) para. 410–415.

373 *Tulip* above (n 129) para. 231.

374 *Cambodia Power Company v. Kingdom of Cambodia* above (n 55).

375 Ibid., para. 257–259. See also *Province of East Kalimantan v. PT Kaltim Prima Coal* above (n 14) para. 201.

376 Normally, shares in companies incorporated in the home State cannot be considered protected investments. See *Berschader* above (n 157) para. 121, and separate opinion by Todd Weiler (which concurs on this point), para. 9–10.

377 For an overview of the practice, see David Gaukrodger, 'Investment Treaties and Shareholder Claims: Analysis of Treaty Practice' (2014) OECD Working Papers on International Investment 2014/03, at http://dx.doi.org/10.1787/5jxvk6shpvs4-en. See also David Gaukrodger, 'Investment Treaties as Corporate Law: Shareholder Claims and Issues of Consistency' (2013) OECD Working Paper on Investment 2013/3, at http://dx.doi.org/10.1787/5k3w9t44mtov-en. See also Martin J Valasek and Patrick Dumberry, 'Developments

on the treatment granted to the company by the host State. Their right proceeds from a dedicated provision, like Article 1117(1) NAFTA[378] and Article 1(6)(b) ECT[379] or, more commonly, from the inclusion of shares in the definition of investment in treaties and statutes.[380] Claims based on shareholding in an investment and claims based on (indirect) investments are theoretically distinct, but not mutually exclusive:

> … under investment treaties, investments can just as well consist of a shareholding in a local company, as of the investments made by a local company, controlled by successive intermediate companies. The investor "steps into the shoes" of the local company and claims for damages suffered by the local company as if it had been inflicted, on a *pro rata* basis, on itself.… Each type of investment gives rise to specific legal questions: in the case of shares, whether the value of the shareholding is affected; in case of indirect investments, whether the rights of the local company have been violated.[381]

Since companies can be investors and bring a claim in their own right, the possibility of shareholders' claims is particularly relevant when the company is incorporated in the host State but the shareholders are foreign (of a treaty-protected nationality). This scenario, incidentally, is proximate to that contemplated by Article 25(2)(b) ICSID, which allows a local company to bring claims on *its own behalf* on grounds of foreign control. This possibility, which depends on State consent, is legally distinct from the standing rights of shareholders[382]: it does not rule out the right of foreign shareholders to bring a claim on their own behalf.[383] Moreover, shareholders claims and claims brought concurrent

in the Legal Standing of Shareholders and Holding Corporations in Investor-State Disputes' (2011) ICSID Review 73.

378 '*An investor of a Party, on behalf of an enterprise of another Party that is a juridical person* that the investor owns or controls directly or indirectly, *may submit to arbitration under this Section a claim* …' (emphasis added). Note however that: a) control is necessary to bring the claim and b) the claim is brought on behalf of the company.

379 According to which 'investment' includes '*a company or business enterprise, or shares, stock, or other forms of equity participation in a company or business enterprise.*'

380 See Gaukrodger (2013) above (n 377) 25 ff.

381 *Flemingo* above (n 332) para. 310.

382 *Vivendi I* annulment above (n 81) para. 50.

383 *Sempra Energy International v. The Argentine Republic*, ICSID Case No. ARB/02/16, Decision on Objections to Jurisdiction of 11 May 2005, para. 42; *CMS* above (n 86) para. 51.

by a local company under Article 25(2)(b) ICSID are subject to different conditions.[384] Primarily, while foreign shareholders can bring claim by virtue of their owning the local investment, the local company seeking to be treated as a foreign one under the exception of Article 25(2)(b) ICSID must base its claim on foreign control. Ownership and control can be related, but they are distinct: ownership is a formal requirement whereas the exercise of control must exist objectively to meet the '*foreign control*' requirement.[385]

For shareholders to qualify as investors there is no inherent requirement to control the company; minority shareholders are equally entitled,[386] and their claim is *pro quota* (that is, claims and remedies are measured upon the fraction of the company held by them[387]). Moreover, shareholders (including indirect ones[388]) can normally bring investment claims irrespective of company

384 *Copper Mesa v. Ecuador*, above (n 26) para. 5.53. Since the claimant companies could bring a claim on their own behalf as shareholders, they did not need to request the waivers of their subsidiaries as per the provision of Article XIII(12)(a)(iii) of the BIT between Canada and Ecuador.

385 *National Gas S.A.E v. Arab Republic of Egypt*, ICSID Case No. ARB/11/7, Award of 3 April 2014, para. 133, citing *Vacuum Salt* above (n 49); see also *Banro* above (n 295); *TSA Spectrum* above (n 42) para. 147, 153. See also *Plama* above (n 175) para. 170: '*control includes control in fact.*' *Guardian Fiduciary Trust, Ltd, f/k/a Capital Conservator Savings & Loan, Ltd v. Macedonia, former Yugoslav Republic of*, ICSID Case No. ARB/12/31, Award of 22 September 2015, para. 134: '*The issue of control is therefore ultimately a matter of evidence and cannot be determined solely on the basis of an analysis of* [*domestic*] *law.*'

386 *Lanco International Inc. v. The Argentine Republic*, ICSID Case No. ARB/97/6, Preliminary Decision on Jurisdiction of 8 December 1998, para. 10; *ST-AD* above (n 18) para. 275.

387 See for instance the dictum in *United Parcel Service of America Inc. v. Government of Canada*, Award on the Merits of 24 May 2007, para. 35: '*UPS is the sole owner of UPS Canada. As such, it is entitled to file a claim for its losses, including losses incurred by UPS Canada. If there were multiple owners and divided ownership shares for UPS Canada, the question of how much of UPS Canada's losses flow through to UPS—the question posed by Canada here—may have a very different purchase.*'

388 Whereas the precise legal standard might vary from treaty to treaty, indirect investments are routinely considered to qualify as investments. See for instance *Hesham T. M. Al Warraq v. Republic of Indonesia*, UNCITRAL, Final Award of 15 December 2014, para. 510–511. Other decisions in this sense, based on different investment treaties, are cited in support. See also *Berschader* above (n 157) para. 112, where the tribunal accepts that the protection of investments granted in the applicable treaty covers '*indirect investments made by investors of one of the Contracting Parties in the territory of the other Contracting Party by the intermediary of an investor of a third state.*' See *Ioannis Kardassopoulos v. Georgia*, ICSID Case No. ARB/05/18, Decision on Jurisdiction of 6 July 2007, para. 123–124; *Tza Yap Shum* above (n 156) para. 106–111; *Mobil* above (n 48) para. 162–166.

recourse[389] or of claims brought by shareholders at a different level of the corporate ladder.[390] In addition, shareholders at an intermediate position in the corporate structure can bring claims, without either directly owning the shares of the investment nor being the ultimate beneficiaries thereof.[391]

A case of lack of jurisdiction *ratione personae* (which could also be construed as a flaw *ratione materiae*) is the lack of standing of shareholders that seek to enforce treaty-based protection over the assets of their companies—which sometimes can be considered the investments of their investment.[392] The formal distinction between a company and its shareholders under international law[393] colours the applicable regime, and distinguishes the scenario from that of indirect control in the investment. The case *Poštová Banka v. Greece*[394] summarises the prevailing principle.[395] At stake was the claim brought by a Slovak bank holding Greek sovereign bonds. When Greece refused to repay the bonds in full, the Slovak bank brought an investment claim, accompanied by one of its shareholders, a Cypriot company. The latter, in particular, sought to bring a claim resting on the bonds held by the Slovak company, rather than on its own shares therein.[396] The claim was rejected: tribunals are competent to entertain shareholders' claims regarding their investment (for instance, allegations that the host State has breached the treaty and caused the loss of value of their shares) but have '*no jurisdiction to deal, in whatever manner, with property which does not belong to* [*the shareholders*]',[397] such as the assets of their company.

---

389 See *Eskosol S.p.A. in liquidazione v. Italian Republic*, ICSID Case No. ARB/15/50, Decision on Respondent's Application under Rule 41(5) of 20 March 2017, para. 170.

390 *Flemingo* above (n 332) para. 339.

391 Ibid., para. 325.

392 This is the position, incidentally, taken by the European Court of Human Rights, which normally rejects the applications brought under Article 1 of Protocol no. 1 (right to property) by the shareholders, with respect to the assets of the company, see for instance *Agrotexim v. Greece* (application 14807/89) (1995) 21 EHRR 250. For an overview on this point, see Ursula Kriebaum, 'The Nature of Investment Disciplines' in Zachary Douglas, Joost Pauwelyn and Jorge E Viñuales (eds), *The Foundations of International Investment Law* (OUP 2014) 45, 53–54.

393 *Barcelona Traction, Light and Power Company, Limited,* (Belgium v. Spain), Second Phase, Judgment, I.C.J. Reports 1970, 3, 32.

394 *Poštová Banka* above (n 225).

395 See also *ST-AD* above (n 18) para. 278; *CMS* above (n 86) para. 68; *Paushok* above (n 114) para. 202.

396 *Poštová Banka* above (n 225) para. 228.

397 *ST-AD* above (n 18) para. 284.

In the *Berschader* case, the majority of the tribunal reached a similar conclusion, when dealing with a case of compound indirectness of the investment: the claimants owned shares in a company incorporated in the home State, holding assets in the host State (contracts, property, credit rights). Their claims, ultimately, regarded assets in the host State held in turn by assets in the home State (the company) which could not qualify as foreign investments. In spite of the treaty's express coverage of indirect investments held through companies in *third* States,[398] the tribunal held that investments made through a corporate vehicle in the home State are not implitictly protected as indirect investments too.[399] The apparently odd result (vehicles in third parties can be used, whilst vehicles in the home State cannot) must be read in light of the obvious assumption that such vehicle could normally bring a treaty claim in its own right, as a home-State investor with investments in the host State.[400]

An apparently different conclusion was reached by the ad hoc Committee in the annulment proceedings of the *Azurix v. Argentina* award.[401] In the decision, the Committee noted that the '*legal and contractual rights*' of the company (ABA) could be regarded as investment of the shareholder (Azurix).[402] Possibly, the conclusion depended on the specific wording of the US/Argentina BIT, which qualified as 'investment' all '*interests ... in the assets [of a company]*',[403] and on the specific quality of the shareholder (which was controlling the company and had had an active role in the acquisition of the assets at stake).

---

398 Which led an arbitrator to reach a different conclusion, see Todd Weiler's separate opinion in *Berschader* above (n 157) para. 11–14.

399 *Berschader* above (n 157) para. 150.

400 This possibility was precluded in the *Berschader* case, because the vehicle had been declared bankrupt. See ibid., para. 149: '*The reason why the Claimants, and not BI [the Belgian vehicle], are bringing a claim under the Treaty is that the Claimants no longer control BI since that company has been declared bankrupt. The Tribunal does not believe that the purpose of the Treaty is to help shareholders overcome this kind of obstacle.*'

401 *Azurix Corp v. Argentina*, ICSID Case No ARB/01/12, Decision on the Application for Annulment of 1 September 2009.

402 Ibid., para. 94: '*... the wording of Article I(1)(a) of the BIT embraces that ABA itself would be an "investment" of Azurix for purposes of the BIT, since ABA is a company ... owned and controlled directly or indirectly by Azurix ... Although assets of ABA would as a matter of law belong to ABA and not to Azurix, Azurix nonetheless had, by virtue of its controlling shareholding in ABA, "interests in the assets" of ABA (Article I(1)(a)(ii)), ... Additionally,* the legal and contractual rights *of ABA (Article I(1)(a)(v)), including the rights of ABA under the Concession, being indirectly controlled by Azurix through its majority shareholding in ...,* would similarly be "investments" of Azurix *for the purposes of the BIT.*' (emphasis added).

403 Article I(1)(ii).

Nationality of Investors

Nationality is a critical element for jurisdiction, since investors which are nationals of the host State and/or do not possess the eligible nationality under an investment treaty are normally not entitled to bring an investment claim.

In the case of natural persons, the analysis is relatively straightforward. In *Soufraki v. UAE*, for example, the claimant's failure to prove his Italian citizenship in the face of the respondent's objections led the tribunal to decline jurisdiction to hear the claim.[404] In *Waguih Elie Siag v. Egypt*, the tribunal applied Egyptian law and rebutted the presumption of Egyptian nationality of the investor, based on the certificates of nationality relied upon by the respondent.[405] In *Burimi v. Albania*, the claimant was an Albanian company, relying on '*foreign control*' under Article 25(2)(b) ICSID and the applicable BIT[406] to establish the tribunal's jurisdiction. The company was indirectly owned, and controlled, by a dual national of Italy and Albania. The tribunal extended the principle against dual nationality of natural persons (when one is that of the host State)[407] to the evaluation of the nationality of control, and concluded that—since the controller had dual nationality—the claimant could not be treated as an Italian company because of '*foreign control*'.[408] The instrument establishing

404 *Hussein Nuaman Soufraki v. The United Arab Emirates*, ICSID Case No. ARB/02/7, Award of 7 July 2004, para. 84 (jurisdiction) para. 88. This decision was impugned in annulment for breach of Art. 52(1)(b) (manifest excess of powers), without success, see Decision of the ad hoc Committee on the Application for Annulment of Mr Soufraki of 5 June 2007.

405 *Waguih Elie George Siag and Clorinda Vecchi v. The Arab Republic of Egypt*, ICSID Case No. ARB/05/15, Decision on Jurisdiction, and Partial Dissenting Opinion of Professor Francisco Orrego Vicuña of 11 April 2007, para. 172 (because the investor had not made a request to retain Egyptian nationality upon obtaining Lebanese citizenship, he effectively lost Egyptian citizenship). In *Champion Trading Company, Ameritrade International, Inc. v. Arab Republic of Egypt*, ICSID Case No. ARB/02/9 (formerly *Champion Trading Company, Ameritrade International, Inc., James T. Wahba, John B. Wahba, Timothy T. Wahba v. Arab Republic of Egypt*), see Decision on Jurisdiction of 21 October 2003, at stake was a similar presumption of Egyptian nationality of individuals born in the US by a US naturalised father (Egyptian nationality is automatically transmitted to children of Egyptian nationals). The father was unable to prove that he had validly renounced his Egyptian citizenship. This conclusion seemed to rely on a different reading of Egyptian law from the *Waguih*'s one and/or on a different presumption (instead of presuming that Egyptian citizenship lapsed upon naturalisation, the tribunal relied on evidence of the claimants relying on Egyptian citizenship to presume that it had been maintained).

406 Namely, Article 8(3) of the Italy-Albania BIT.

407 In Article 25(2)(a) ICSID.

408 *Burimi SRL and Eagle Games SH.A v. Republic of Albania*, ICSID Case No. ARB/11/18, Award of 29 May 2013, para. 121.

the jurisdiction of the tribunal might require, *in lieu* of a specific nationality, residence in a specific country.[409] Whereas nationals who are (also) citizens of the host State cannot bring an ICSID claim,[410] the possibility is not precluded outside the ICSID framework proceedings if the applicable BIT allows it, as an UNCITRAL tribunal held in *García and García v. Venezuela*.[411] The tribunal in *Cem Cenzig Uzan v. Turkey* needed to determine whether a natural person satisfying the residency requirement at the time of the arbitration could qualify as investor even if, at the time of the investment, he was a national of, and resident in, the host State.[412] The tribunal found that the claimant was missing an '*essential transnational link*'[413]: the investment was made in Turkey, and Turkey committed the alleged breaches. Any subsequent change of residency would not suffice to make it an '*investor*' under the ECT.[414]

The analysis of the nationality of legal persons can be more complex. Layered corporate structures and restructuring operations might result in a claimant changing nationality and/or having a tenuous link with its formal State of nationality (or, better, in claimant's nationality having little to do with the investment).[415] In similar circumstances, the claimants' use of their new/formal nationality to derive benefits from a specific treaty—including access to arbitration—might appear inappropriate. However, the prevailing principle in general international law is that the nationality of corporations depends on their place of incorporation;[416] the formal *datum* prevails over the substantive

409 That is the case for the ECT, of which Article 1(7)(a)(i) defines '*investor*' as '[*A*] *natural person having the citizenship or nationality of or who is permanently residing in that Contracting Party in accordance with its applicable law*.'

410 See *Champion* above (n 405).

411 *García v. Venezuela* above (n 305) 197 ff.

412 *Cem Cengiz Uzan v. Republic of Turkey*, Award on Respondent's Bifurcated Preliminary Objection of 20 April 2016.

413 Ibid., para. 152.

414 Contrast this conclusion with the reasoning of the Decision of the Paris Court of Appeal above (n 305), 6 (the lack of a protected nationality at the moment of the making of the investment was not fatal, if it was subsequently acquired before the breach occurred, and maintained until the claim).

415 On the various strategies employed by multinational enterprises to benefit from treaties, and on how treaties could prevent abusive tactics, see Mark Feldman, 'Multinational Enterprises and Investment Treaties' (2017) Yearbook on International Investment Law and Policy (forthcoming).

416 Of course, international law might provide for specific criteria that would serve as *lex specialis* in specific cases, and domestic law might provide for a different rule, for instance the use of the *siége sociale* as decisive aspect. The applicable law will determine, in other words, whether the general principle of incorporation will apply. See, in general,

one when the two do not correspond.[417] Accordingly, investors are free to structure their business as they deem fit so as to enjoy treaty protection; for instance, they can establish a corporate vehicle in a specific jurisdiction covered by a BIT with the host State,[418] or choose a controller of a protected nationality when the exception under Article 25(2)(b) ICSID is available.[419] The principle of good faith patrols the fine line between legitimate corporate governance and malicious nationality-shopping:

> Such restructuring could be "legitimate corporate planning" as contended by the Claimants or an "abuse of right" as submitted by the Respondents. It depends upon the circumstances in which it happened.[420]

Manuel Casas, 'Nationalities of Convenience, Personal Jurisdiction, and Access to Investor-State Dispute Settlement' (2016) 49 NYUJ Int'l L. & Pol. 63, 68–80.

417 *Barcelona Traction* above (n 393) para. 56 ff (limiting the possibility of 'lifting the corporate veil' to exceptional cases). For instance, see *Gold Reserve* above (n 213) para. 252: '*where the test for nationality is "incorporation" as opposed to control or a "genuine connection", there is no need for the tribunal to enquire further unless some form of abuse has occurred.... It is irrelevant whether the company is headquartered at the location of incorporation or if it is the result of a corporate restructuring.*' The same conclusion was reached, for instance, in *Isolux* above (n 47) para. 668, 670 (the Respondent argued, unsuccessfully, that piercing the veil would be required, since the investor had no real presence in the Netherlands, and was controlled by Spanish and Canadian shareholders).

418 See *Saluka Investments B.V. v. Czech Republic*, UNCITRAL Partial Award of 17 March 2006, para. 229: '*The parties having agreed that any legal person constituted under their laws is entitled to invoke the protection of the Treaty, and having so agreed without reference to any question of their relationship to some other third State corporation, it is beyond the powers of this Tribunal to import into the definition of "investor" some requirement relating to such a relationship having the effect of excluding from the Treaty's protection a company which the language agreed by the parties included within it.*' See *Soufraki* above (n 404) 2004, para. 83; *ADC Affiliate Ltd. and ADC & ADMC Mgmt. Ltd v. Republic of Hungary*, ICSID Case No. ARB/03/16, Award of 2 October 2006, para. 357–359; *Mobil* above (n 48) para. 204; *Aguas del Tunari* (n 111) para. 330(d). An overview of the practice is available in Christoph Schreuer, 'Nationality Planning' in Arthur W Rovine (ed), *Contemporary Issues in International Arbitration and Mediation: The Fordham Papers* (Brill 2012) 15–27, 19 ff. Consider in particular *HICEE v. Slovakia*, above (n 166) para. 103.

419 In *Guardian Fiduciary* above (n 385), at stake was precisely the identity of the controlling investor. Whilst the putative controller had a Dutch nationality, the actual controller had not, which prevented the claimant from relying on the Dutch-FYROM treaty.

420 *Mobil v. Venezuela* (n 388) para. 191.

The award in the case *MNSS v. Montenegro*[421] supports this well-established view. A change of nationality will fail to provide treaty-protection only when the actual dispute has already arisen or a specific future dispute is foreseeable.[422] In rejecting the respondent's objection based on the nationality restructuring of claimant, the tribunal noted that it was an '*objection to its jurisdiction based on* ratione personae.'[423] This apparently innocuous remark could be taken to prove that similar objections relate to the jurisdiction of the tribunal rather than the admissibility of the claim—an arguably preferable characterisation, see the discussion below in respect of the *Philip Morris v. Australia* dispute.

Whilst ownership-engineering to accede a protected nationality is allowed in principle, the nationality of a trust or of its trustee might be insufficient to satisfy the requirements *ratione personae*. In *Blue Bank*, the claimant was a trustee from Barbados, acting on behalf of a trust established under the laws of Barbados. The applicable BIT defined investments as assets '*invested*' by '*companies*'.[424] On the one hand, Barbadian trusts do not have a corporate identity;[425] on the other, the trustee had very limited powers that could not establish ownership and, therefore, had not '*invested*' in the trust's assets.[426] Neither subject, therefore, met the basic requirements of the treaty; the tribunal declined jurisdiction.

The instrument recording the State's consent (whether domestic statute or investment treaty) can provide additional requirements *ratione personae*, for instance regulating the attribution of nationality to legal persons more strictly than does customary law. In *Ampal v. Egypt*,[427] for instance, the US/Egypt BIT provided that a company would be regarded as a US company only when, besides being incorporated there, US natural persons have a '*substantial interest*' in it.[428] The claimant showed the US residence of most shareholders, but was unable to prove that they were US citizens. The tribunal, however, relied on the

421 *MNSS v. Montenegro* above (n 37).

422 Ibid., para. 182.

423 Ibid., para. 183.

424 Article 8(1) of the Barbados-Venezuela BIT.

425 *Blue Bank* above (n 317) para. 165. See also *Renta 4* above (n 176) para. 122, 127. These cases are without prejudice to the possibility that the governing law—domestic or otherwise—provide differently. For instance, NAFTA expressly includes trusts among the entities that qualify as 'entreprise' under Article 201(1).

426 *Blue Bank* above (n 317) para. 168, 173.

427 *Ampal* above (n 22).

428 Article 1(1)(b).

presumption that at least some US residents are likely to be US citizens,[429] and rejected the objection of the respondent State.[430]

The host State was instead successful in the *Venoklim v. Venezuela*.[431] The claim was brought under the joint provisions of a BIT and of the national investment law,[432] which only applies to international investors, and requires international investors to own or control an international investment.[433] Since the parties did not discuss the criterion of ownership, the tribunal focussed on the control of the investment, piercing the veil of several ownership layers and finding that the ultimate owners were Venezuelan.[434] The tribunal's *dictum* that treating the investor as a foreign one under Article 25 ICSID would be tantamount '*to let formalism prevail over reality*'[435] is puzzling, because it seems to disregard the well-established view that incorporation—in the absence of specific safeguards resulting from different applicable rules—is the criterion for citizenship of corporations in international law. Moreover, it is doubtful whether the tribunal could simply disregard the possibility that the investor could in fact qualify as an international investor under the domestic law using the criterion of ownership (rather than control). Since this criterion is listed in the Venezuelan statute, the tribunal arguably had a duty to apply it, regardless of whether the parties discussed it (both because the tribunal should determine its jurisdiction *proprio motu* and under the principle *jura novit curia*). The *Thunderbird v. Mexico* case illustrates the interpretation of the specific NAFTA regime, which allows an investor that '*owns or control*' an enterprise in the host State to bring an investment claim against it.[436] The tribunal proceeded on the assumption that minority shareholding would not suffice to qualify as 'owner' and ascertained whether the claimants *de facto* controlled the enterprise.[437]

429 A similar presumption was used by the Iran-US Tribunal in the case *Flexi-Van v. Iran*, 82-0463 (D.D.C.), 2–3.

430 *Ampal* above (n 22) para. 121–123.

431 *Venoklim* above (n 321).

432 Ley de Promoción y Protección de Inversiones, promulgada mediante el Decreto No. 356 del 3 de octubre de 1999.

433 See Articles 3 and 22 of the Ley de Inversiones.

434 *Venoklim* above (n 321) para. 147–149.

435 Ibid., para. 156, my translation.

436 See Article 1117.1 NAFTA.

437 *International Thunderbird Gaming Corporation v. The United Mexican States*, UNCITRAL, Award of 26 January 2006, para. 105–106: '*The Tribunal does not follow Mexico's proposition that Article 1117 of the NAFTA requires a showing of legal control. The term "control" is not defined in the NAFTA. Interpreted in accordance with its ordinary meaning, control can*

In *Gaëta v. Guinea*,[438] consent to ICSID arbitration was recorded in a domestic statute which only applied to '*foreign claimants*.' Whereas the determination of the claimant's foreign-ness under Guinean law was ultimately not necessary in the specific case,[439] the requirement might have called for a different test than the customary one necessary to ascertain jurisdiction under Article 25(2)(b) ICSID.

2 *Inadmissibility Instances*

Arbitral practice with respect to admissibility is scarce, as the very notion of admissibility is far from established in this field.[440] Especially in the context of ICSID arbitration, objections alleging the inadmissibility of the claim must overcome the tribunal's reluctance to read admissibility into the Convention as an implicit notion.[441] The doctrinal reasons behind the dubious pedigree of this procedural institution are explained more fully below.[442] At this stage, suffice it to note that the procedural relevance of retaining admissibility as a separate grounds for preliminary objections is very limited, as these will be normally lumped together with the challenges to the jurisdiction of the tribunal, when bifurcation is granted.

References to admissibility in the practice are common but rarely respond to, or reflect, a systemic doctrine. In *BIVAC v. Paraguay* the tribunal cared to split the host State's objections regarding the umbrella clause claim in two. Paraguay's claim that the umbrella clause could not turn a contract claim into a treaty one was a jurisdictional objection (and it was rejected). Paraguay's claim that the exclusive forum-selection clause in the contract prevented the

---

be exercised in various manners. Therefore, a showing of effective or "de facto" control is, in the Tribunal's view, sufficient for the purposes of Article 1117 of the NAFTA. In the absence of legal control however, the Tribunal is of the opinion that de facto control must be established beyond any reasonable doubt.'

438 *Gaëta* above (n 46).

439 The tribunal determined that the claimant, in spite of French incorporation, lacked French nationality, in light of French law. The reasons why French law was applied, even if customary international law might have led to a different conclusion, might have to do with the Claimant's strategy to invoke it, see para. 128, 137, 139.

440 Andrew Newcombe, 'Investor Misconduct: Jurisdiction, Admissibility or Merits?' in Brown and Miles above (n 23) 187–200, 193, noting that it is not even accepted widely that tribunals have to power '*to dismiss a claim as inadmissible*.'

441 *Rompetrol* above (n 48) para. 115.

442 See Part B.

tribunal from hearing the umbrella clause claim, instead, was an objection to its admissibility (which was upheld).[443]

Coordination with parallel, potential or past proceedings (under the principles *res judicata, lis alibi pendens, electa una via, forum non conveniens*) is precisely a matter that often leads tribunals to declare the claim's inadmissibility, rather than their own lack of jurisdiction. The dispute falls under their institutional mandate, but there is an external reason (loosely concerned with the abuse of processes) why they should not exercise it in the specific instance.[444] Objections to parallel proceedings are not always successful, mainly due to the difficulty to prove the triple identity between them.[445]

Besides these instances of regulation of multiple proceedings, and a diverse set of other cases in which admissibility was used or at least invoked,[446] there are two issues which have arisen systematically and which tribunals tend to handle resorting to the category of inadmissibility. First, a claim can be inadmissible when it constitutes an abuse of process (1). Second, the investor's misconduct can lead to the tribunal's dismissal of the claim as inadmissible in accordance with the clean hands doctrine (2). Other instances where admissibility is used, but the practice is controversial, are discussed in the second half of the next Part of this essay.

---

443 *Bureau Veritas* above (n 31) para. 142.

444 For a discussion of some relevant cases, see Eric De Brabandere, "Good Faith', 'Abuse of Process' and the Initiation of Investment Treaty Claims' (2012) 3(3) Journal of International Dispute Settlement 609–636, 630–632. In *Hochtief* above (n 181) para. 90, the tribunal found that a claim might be inadmissible by virtue of *lis pendens* or *forum non conveniens*. Likewise, see *SGS v. Philippines* above (n 38) para. 170, footnote 95. Conversely, In *S.A.R.L. Benvenuti & Bonfant v. People's Republic of the Congo*, ICSID/ARB/77/2, Award of 8 August 1980 (not public), para. 1.13 and 1.14, the tribunal discussed *lis pendens* as a jurisdictional issue.

445 *Champion Trading International, Inc. v. Arab Republic of Egypt*, ICSID Case No. ARB/02/9, Award on Jurisdiction of 21 October 2003, para. 3.4.3 (because the claimants before ICSID and the claimant before the Egyptian Conseil d'Etat were not the same, there was no reason to reject the ICSID claim); *Alex Genin* above (n 89) para. 331.

446 See for instance *Occidental Exploration and Production Company v. The Republic of Ecuador*, LCIA Case No. UN3467, Award of 1 July 2004, para. 80 and 92 (the expropriation claim was manifestly groundless and was rejected as inadmissible); *H&H Enterprises Investments, Inc. v. Arab Republic of Egypt*, ICSID Case No. ARB 09/15, Decision on Objections to Jurisdiction of 5 June 2012, para. 86–88 (the objection based on an equitable principle of prescription—the claim was brought too late—is rejected because the respondent has not demonstrated its existence).

1 Abuse of Process

The *grand arrêt* for the doctrine of abuse of process in investment arbitration is the *Phoenix v. Czech Republic* case.[447] In that case, the host State argued that the claimant was a sham Israeli company, established by a Czech individual only to obtain the right to launch arbitration under the BIT. The tribunal concluded that the claimant, indeed, had engaged in bad faith conduct.[448] It ultimately declared its lack of jurisdiction *ratione materiae* (bad faith investments cannot be covered by the consent of the State parties, as codified in the applicable treaty) rather than inadmissibility of a claim on grounds of bad faith (abuse of process).[449] The decision of the *ST-AD* tribunal followed closely the reasoning in the *Phoenix* award and found a lack of jurisdiction.[450]

Some recent decisions, instead, construed abuse of process as grounds for inadmissibility or at least contemplated this legal characterisation.[451] In *Levy v. Peru*, the tribunal held that '*the characterization of the abuse of process objection as a jurisdictional or as an admissibility issue can be left open in the present case*'.[452] It recalled approvingly the dictum of the *Pac Rim* decision, that it was not worthy clinging on to '*a distinction without a difference*'.[453] However, the tribunal noted that the objection based on the abuse of process was not directed at the jurisdiction *ratione temporis* of the tribunal—which had been established—but to its exercise.[454] The claimant (Ms. Levy) appeared to satisfy the jurisdictional requirements *ratione personae* and *temporis*, after acquiring shareholding in the investment eight days before the challenged measures.[455] The tribunal correctly clarified that the acquisition of an investment after the challenged measures or after the dispute is squarely a problem of jurisdiction.[456] Beforehand, when no dispute is at the horizon, nationality and corporate

447 *Phoenix* above (n 254).

448 Ibid., para. 144: '*the claimant's initiation and pursuit of the arbitration* [*was*] *an abuse of the system of international ICSID investment arbitration*.'

449 On this approach, see the comments of Shany above (n 25) 142.

450 *ST-AD* above (n 18) para. 421–422.

451 An exception seems to be the reasoning of the tribunal in *Cervin* above (n 60) para. 287 ff, which refers to jurisdiction *ratione voluntatis*. However, resort to this catch-all category and reliance on the precedents using inadmissibility seem to suggest that the tribunal reasoned in terms of inadmissibility, as does the express attribution of the *onus probandi* to the respondent.

452 *Levy v. Peru* above (n 251) para. 181.

453 *Pac Rim v. El Salvador* above (n 302) para. 2.10.

454 *Levy v. Peru* above (n 251) para. 182. See also *Lao Holdings* above (n 247) para. 72–79.

455 *Levy v. Peru* above (n 251) para. 161.

456 Ibid., footnote 218.

restructuring is legitimate. Therefore, the temporal room available for abuse of process to occur is narrowly framed between the time when the dispute becomes foreseeable and the time when the challenged measures are actually passed and the dispute arises. The critical question, of course, is what counts as foreseeable. The threshold is high: the dispute must be highly probable and not just possible.[457] In the instant case, the sudden transfer of shares which qualified Ms. Levy as investor was clearly carried out with the sole purpose of bringing a claim taking avail of her nationality, at a time when she must have known about the forthcoming measure.[458]

In the *Philip Morris v. Australia* case, the tribunal rejected the claim as inadmissible, upon a finding that the claimant had artificially acquired Hong Kong nationality to launch abusively the arbitration. As noted above, the nationality was obtained in time for the tribunal to have jurisdiction over the claim (that is, before the adoption of the contentious measures). However, the tribunal surmised that the dispute with Australia was at least foreseeable at the time of the nationality restructuring,[459] and rejected the claim as inadmissible. In the *Lao Holding v. Laos*[460] case, the tribunal recalled the *Phoenix* doctrine[461] and aligned it with the later cases' distinction that hinges on the critical time at which the protected nationality is acquired (if before the breach/dispute, abuse of right can be invoked; if afterwards, lack of jurisdiction *ratione temporis*).[462] Whilst the tribunal did not go as far as explicitly ascribing to admissibility the objection relating to the abuse of right, it expressly contrasted it with the jurisdictional objection, and considered it waivable by the respondent.[463]

---

457 *Pac Rim v. El Salvador* above (n 302) para. 2.99; *Tidewater* above (n 137) para. 194; *Lao Holdings* above (n 247) para. 76.

458 Ibid., para. 195.

459 Arguably, the tribunal construed extensively a principle that was already established in the case-law, which concerned disputes that pre-dated the acquiring of nationality. See for instance *Aguas del Tunari* above (n 111) para. 330 and *Tidewater* above (n 137) para. 145–146 and 184. The 'foreseeability' criterion seems to derive only from the cases *Pac Rim v. El Salvador* above (n 302) para. 2.99 (where it is conceded that the distinction between is the 'very high probability' of a foreseeable dispute and an existing dispute is a 'thin red line') and *Levy v. Peru* above (n 251) para. 185.

460 *Lao Holdings* above (n 247).

461 Note that Brigitte Stern acted as chair in the *Phoenix* tribunal, and as respondent-appointee in the *Lao Holdings* one.

462 *Lao Holdings* above (n 247) para. 71, citing in *Mobil v. Venezuela* above (n 48) 205.

463 *Lao Holdings* above (n 247) para. 83. This approach would suggest that the objection did not go to the jurisdiction of the tribunal, otherwise it would have been expected to entertain it *proprio motu*. See in this respect the reasoning of the *Berkowitz* tribunal above (n 246)

In the case *Isolux v. Spain*, the investor acquired the protected nationality (Dutch) two months before the passing of the long-anticipated State measures later challenged in the claim. However, the tribunal characterised the move as '*legitimate corporate planning*',[464] simply noting that the corporate restructuring preceded the rising of the dispute.[465] The matter was clearly treated as one of jurisdiction *ratione temporis* rather than admissibility—a somewhat lamentable simplification since the objection had been expressly advanced as one based on abuse of process.[466] The *Cervin v. Costa Rica* tribunal focused the analysis differently; it held that what matters for jurisdiction *ratione temporis* is not so much whether a dispute was foreseeable at the critical time, but whether the investor acted in bad faith.[467] When it comes to jurisdiction *ratione voluntatis*, however, an objection can succeed if the respondent proves that the investor made the investment—and acquired a protected nationality—'*with the only purpose of benefitting abusively from a procedural advantage.*'[468]

In the TGGE case[469] the tribunal examined the preliminary objection alleging the investor's abuse of process. Whereas the tribunal did not expressly qualify abuse of process as a matter of admissibility, this characterisation would follow from the remark of the tribunal, noting that at stake was not its jurisdiction *tout court* but only its exercise:

> The Tribunal has chosen to consider this objection [relating to abuse of process] first, because the existence of abuse of process is a threshold issue that would bar the exercise of the Tribunal's jurisdiction even if jurisdiction existed.[470]

---

para. 225: '*the Tribunal notes that an assessment of whether jurisdiction exists in respect of a given dispute is required of all tribunals, whether a party raises the issue or not.*'

464 *Isolux v. Spain* above (n 47) para. 701, citing *Mobil* above (n 48).

465 *Isolux v. Spain* above (n 47) para. 704: '*el conflicto es posterior a la restructuración discutida y a la colocación de la inversión en una sociedad holandesa.*'

466 In other words, there was no issue in this case of a possible waiver of the abuse of right objection, as it was the case in the *Lao Holdings* proceedings, see above (n 247) and accompanying text.

467 *Cervin* above (n 60) para. 285.

468 Ibid., para. 292. My translation, the original reads: '*con el único propósito de lograr indebidamente una ventaja procesal.*'

469 TGGE *v. Panama* above (n 86).

470 Ibid., para. 100. See *Pac Rim v. El Salvador* above (n 302) para. 2.10.

The tribunal, indeed, noted that the Claimant had attempted to '*create artificial international jurisdiction over a pre-existing domestic dispute*.'[471] This attempt took the form of a contract whereby a local company was established, under the joint control of a Panama individual and a US company which held the majority of the shares. However, the tribunal held that, in spite of the ownership arrangements, the Panama individual retained *de facto* control of the company, while intending '*at the same time to benefit from the foreign nationality of TGGE for the purpose of pursuing this arbitration*.'[472] In other words, the entry on stage of the US company did not alter, in the facts, the nature of the claimant, which was a local individual managing a local company. The timing and circumstances of the corporate reconfiguration, moreover, were revealing. The US company only came into play after it appeared that Panama would not execute certain judicial decisions in favour of the Claimant—the circumstances might have warranted using the foreseeability criterion used in *Philip Morris v. Australia*. Moreover, the Claimant's manager repeatedly conceded that arbitral proceedings were a safety net, launched in case the host State did not comply with the domestic rulings.[473]

In *Ampal*, the host State argued that the claimant's alleged abuse of process resulted in four parallel arbitration proceedings (two sets of commercial arbitration, two investment disputes). The tribunal conceded that the dispute overlap might seem abusive, but that no problem emerged upon closer scrutiny. The commercial disputes were distinguishable from those based on treaty claims. The latter, in turn, were brought by separate investors (different shareholders in the investment) and their parallel development was not abusive *per se*.[474] However, the tribunal noted that the claimants in the two investment proceedings were seeking overlapping remedies from the same respondent, creating the risk of double recovery, an actual manifestation of abuse of process.[475] The tribunal noted that the abuse was not identifiable *a priori*: the attempt to bring different claims in different *fora* was legitimate and made

471 *TGGE v. Panama* (n 553) para. 118.

472 Ibid., para. 111.

473 So much so that, in a few occasions, Claimant requested the suspension of the arbitration proceedings when it seemed that Panama would comply with its domestic rulings without problems.

474 *Ampal* above (n 22) para. 329. The attempts to consolidate the investment claims into one set of proceedings failed because only one of the two could use the ICSID framework, and the parties disagreed, respectively, to have a consolidation under ICSID or under UNCITRAL rules.

475 The parallel investment dispute is the UNCITRAL case *Mr. Yosef Maiman and Others v. Egypt*, which is confidential.

in good faith. Nonetheless, since the tribunal in the parallel proceedings had upheld jurisdiction, the prospect of parallel proceedings reviewing the merits of partly overlapping claims had materialised.[476] To cure the resulting abuse of process, the tribunal invited the claimant to elect to pursue the relevant portion of the claim only in the ICSID proceedings before it, therefore forfeiting it in the parallel UNCITRAL proceedings.[477]

The *Orascom* case evinced another permutation of abuse of process, which resulted in the inadmissibility of the claim. At stake were parallel claims brought by entities in the same corporate structure—the claimant being one of the indirect shareholders of a local company affected by the State measures.[478] Because the applicable BIT protected shares as an investment, none of the claims fell outside the tribunal's jurisdiction,[479] no matter how indirect the shareholding. However, the tribunal framed the issue of multiple claims as one of admissibility:

> If the harm incurred by one entity in the chain is fully repaired in one arbitration, the claims brought by other members of the vertical chain in other arbitral proceedings may become inadmissible depending on the circumstances.[480]

It then examined whether the damages sought by the claimant, relating to the diminution of values of its shares in the local investment, had already formed the object of arbitral requests by the local company or by an intermediate holding company.[481] Moreover, the intermediate holding company had reached a settlement with the host State, which brought a PCA arbitration to an end. Insofar as the settlement agreement stood *in lieu* of an arbitral award, the *Orascom* tribunal found that it '*put*[]*an end to the dispute arising from*

476 *Ampal* above (n 22) para. 333: '*the abuse of process constituted by the double pursuit of the* [specific] *portion of the claim in both proceedings must now be treated as having crystallised*.'

477 Ibid., 339. The tribunal stressed the advantage of ICSID protection that would follow the election, and the mechanism of exclusive jurisdiction envisaged by Article 26 ICSID: '*Consent of the parties to arbitration under this Convention shall, unless otherwise stated, be deemed consent to such arbitration to the exclusion of any other remedy*.'

478 *Orascom* above (n 48) para. 495.

479 Ibid., footnote 764: '*The Tribunal may dispense with determining whether it is appropriate to fix a cut-off point beyond which an investor is "too far removed" to have a claim*.'

480 Ibid., para. 495.

481 Ibid., para. 518: '*the claims before the Tribunal in reality seek reparation for losses covered by the requests for relief raised in the OTH Arbitration* [involving an intermediate shareholder].'

Algeria's measures'[482] and, therefore, the claimant could not re-litigate claims that had thus ceased to exist.

The *Orascom* tribunal did not limit itself to find the claims inadmissible for these reasons. It noted '[i]*n addition*'[483] that the claimant also committed an abuse of rights by pursuing its claim. The tribunal referred to the doctrine's status as general principle to introduce its operation in a scenario hitherto unregulated.[484] It is doubtful whether the tribunal really pointed to a discrete ground for inadmissibility; the tribunal appeared rather to abstract from the specific conclusions of the case a more general framework for abuse of process in the case of multiple claims, applicable also to other scenarios. Citing the risk of multiple recoveries and conflicting decisions, in cases where a remedy has already been sought, the tribunal remarked:

> where multiple treaties offer entities in a vertical chain similar procedural rights of access to an arbitral forum and comparable substantive guarantees, the initiation of multiple proceedings to recover for essentially the same economic harm would entail the exercise of rights for purposes that are alien to those for which these rights were established.[485]

The tribunal unsurprisingly evoked the CME/*Lauder* precedent, less to distinguish it than to reject it, in light of a better and '*evolved*' case-law.[486] In light of such evolution, the tribunal felt confident to extend the notion of abuse of

482 Ibid., para. 524.

483 Ibid., para. 539.

484 All previous resort to abuse of process arguments concerned cases of abusive restructuring of the nationality of the investment or investor, see above.

485 *Orascom* above (n 48) para. 543. Note that whilst the tribunal in *Flemingo* seemed to endorse a different approach, the fact that one of the parallel claims was discontinued essentially defused the risk of conflicting decisions or double recovery, see *Flemingo* above (n 332) para. 339, 347.

486 Consolidation of virtually identical cases plays in favour of the Respondent, because it reduces the opportunity of adverse findings. In this light, it is fair to note that the Czech Republic refused consolidation of the CME and *Lauder* claims. A similar scenario occurred in the case of the *Lao Holdings* and *Sanum* claims against Laos. See *Lao Holdings* above (n 247) para. 367: '*Does the pursuit of overlapping claims in two different arbitral tribunals established under two different BITs by different parties constitute an abuse of process? As already observed above, it is undisputed that the Respondent refused to consolidate this proceeding and the Lao Holdings Arbitration. This fact is sufficient ground for the Tribunal to consider that there is no abuse of process.*'

process, to avoid frustrating the principles and '*the very purposes underlying the conclusion of* [investment] *treaties*.'[487]

This doctrine could apply in the pending *Eskosol v. Italy* case.[488] The claimant is a local company, owned at 80% by a Belgian investor, seeking to bring a claim because of foreign control. The Belgian investor had already brought an ICSID dispute against the same measures, and lost on the merits.[489] Italy brought proceedings under Rule 41.5 and alleged, among other things, that Eskosol's claim was duplicative and should have been barred by virtue of *res judicata* or *ne bis in idem*. The tribunal declined to throw out the claim, noting that claims brought by the investor and by its shareholders belonged to different subjects, hence presumptively failed the triple identity test—a conclusion redolent of that reached by the *Ampal* tribunal.[490] It also remarked that the shareholder only represented 80% of the claimant's shares, making the case distinguishable from *RSM v. Grenada* (see below).[491] Interestingly, the tribunal expressed sympathy at the position of the host State, forced to fend off repeatedly what essentially amounted to the same claims. However, it noted that the current design of ICSID and the applicable treaty allowed separate claims for corporations and shareholders:

> neither the ICSID system as presently designed, nor the ECT itself, incorporate clear avenues (much less a requirement) for joinder in a single proceeding of all stakeholders potentially affected by the outcome. Absent such a system—which States have the power to create if they so wish—it would not be appropriate for tribunals to preclude arbitration by qualified investors, simply because other qualified investors may have proceeded before them without their participation.[492]

This conclusion is in apparent tension with the doctrine of abuse of process formulated in *Orascom*. In that occasion, the tribunal considered that

487 *Orascom* above (n 48) para. 547: '*it cannot be denied that in the fifteen years that have followed those cases, the investment treaty jurisprudence has evolved, including on the application of the principle of abuse of rights (or abuse of process)*'.

488 *Eskosol* above (n 283).

489 *Blusun S.A., Jean-Pierre Lecorcier and Michael Stein v. Italian Republic*, ICSID Case No. ARB/14/3, Award of 27 December 2016.

490 *Eskosol* above (n 389) para. 166: '*A shareholder's claim for its reflective loss through an entity in which it holds shares cannot be equated automatically to that entity's claim for its direct losses.*'

491 Ibid., para. 168–169.

492 Ibid., para. 170.

'*preclud*[ing] *arbitration*' was indeed possible, even in the absence of an institutionalised system created by the parties. Whereas certain factual differences might be used to explain the different outcomes of the two cases (most importantly, the summary nature of all findings of Rule 41.5 proceedings), the statements of principle made by the tribunals point evidently in different directions, with regard to the management of corporate versus shareholders' claims.

The approach advocated by the *Orascom* tribunal had found an easy application in the *RSM v. Grenada* case.[493] In that case, the tribunal endorsed the parties' characterisation of the doctrine of collateral estoppel,[494] which bars re-litigation of a finding regarding matters that had already been discussed and determined in prior proceedings, and which were '*necessary to resolving the claims*'[495] put forward therein. Crucially, this doctrine refers to determinations already made ('issue preclusion') rather than legal claims: it does not mirror the *res judicata*, *lis pendens* and *ne bis in idem* claim-based doctrines. Therefore, certain matters of contracts law decided by a previous tribunal—including in commercial or domestic arbitration[496]—could not be re-opened,[497] and led to the tribunal's summary dismissal of the claims that hinged on their re-litigation. The conclusion was reached even if the claimants in the two cases were different: the prior one involved an investor, the subsequent one its 100% shareholders. The tribunal noted:

> The three individual Claimants collectively own 100% of RSM's stock and therefore entirely control the corporation. In these circumstances, we agree with Respondent, that there is nothing unfair in holding them to the results of RSM's Prior Arbitration.[498]

The doctrine of collateral estoppel—an atypical kind of estoppel, see below for other categories—seeks to curb abuse in parallel or multiple proceedings, but only operates on specific issues. It does not preclude the tribunal's exercise

493 *RSM v. Grenada* above (n 71).

494 For a seminal formulation of the principle, see *Amoco Asia Corporation v Republic of Indonesia*, ICSID Case No. ARB/81/1, Decision on Jurisdiction (Resubmitted Case) of 10 May 1988, para. 30.

495 *RSM v. Grenada* above (n 71) para. 7.11.

496 *Helnan International Hotels A/S v Egypt*, ICSID Case No. ARB/05/19, Award of 3 July 2008, para. 6.

497 *RSM Production Corporation v. Grenada*, ICSID Case No. ARB/05/14, Award of 13 March 2009.

498 *RSM v. Grenada* above (n 71) para. 7.1.6.

of jurisdiction of a claim, only its consideration of certain matters. Without triple identity, tribunals hesitate to decline jurisdiction, but collateral estoppel or simple persuasion by arguments might at least align the findings of separate tribunals.[499]

2 Investor's Clean Hands and Estoppel

Host States often invoke some form of misconduct allegedly committed by the investor to challenge the claim's admissibility. As will be explained below in relation to the allegations of corruption, the matter is often discussed as one of jurisdiction *ratione materiae*, or even merits.[500] The purpose of this section is to observe a set of instances in which the tribunals characterised the State objections as going to the admissibility of the claims (or, at least, not to the tribunal's jurisdiction) instead.

A straightforward application of the doctrine of clean hands occurred in *Hesham T.M. Al Warraq v. Indonesia*. The claimant had verifiably engaged in fraudulent tactics and was recklessly oblivious to his duties under local law.[501] The tribunal referred to a classic enunciation of the principle in common law, positing that '*[n]o court will lend its aid to a man who founds his cause of action upon an immoral or illegal act*.'[502] The claim was considered inadmissible and rejected. However, the tribunal did not apply a general principle of law alone, but relied on a specific and uncommon provision of the applicable

499 In this sense, see the tribunal's recommendation to the host State in the *Eskosol* case, following the rejection of the *res judicata* argument: '*Italy is free later in this case to argue, if it so wishes, that the conclusions of the* Blusun *tribunal were persuasive and should be followed by this Tribunal, exercising its independent judgment*.' See *Eskosol* supra (n 389) para. 172. Whilst in *Eskosol* the corporate claim followed the shareholders' one, it might be possible to apply the rationale of the *Grynberg* tribunal's dictum: '*It is true that shareholders, under many systems of law, may undertake litigation to pursue or defend rights belonging to the corporation. However, shareholders cannot use such opportunities as both sword and shield. If they wish to claim standing on the basis of their indirect interest in corporate assets, they must be subject to defences that would be available against the corporation—including collateral estoppel*.' RSM *v. Grenada* above (n 71) para. 7.1.7.

500 See also Jorge E. Viñuales, 'Investor Diligence in Investment Proceedings: Sources and Arguments' (2017) 32(2) ICSID Review 346–370.

501 *Hesham* above (n 388) para. 638–644.

502 Namely, Lord Mansfield in *Holman v. Johnson* (1775), 1 Cowp 341, an English contract law case decided by the Court of King's Bench. The court did not uphold the claimant's action for non-payment of a stock of tea, because he was aware that the purchaser intended to smuggle the tea from France into England.

investment treaty (the OIC Agreement[503]), imposing specific obligations on the investor. Specifically, investors are required to uphold '*the laws and regulations in force in the host state and … refrain from all acts that … may be prejudicial to the public interest* [and] *from trying to achieve gains through unlawful means*'.[504] Therefore the tribunal found that since he had '*breached the local laws and put the public interest at risk, he has deprived himself of the protection afforded by the OIC Agreement*'.[505]

The clean hands objection was discussed in detail in the *Hulley v. Russia* case.[506] The tribunal ultimately held that the irregularities attributable to the investor were negligible, and did not decide whether the objection would bar the jurisdiction of the tribunal or deprive the investment of the treaty protections (by making the claim inadmissible).[507] Crucially, whereas the tribunal was ready to construct the investment treaty so as to include a clean-hands requirement implicitly, it did not find the doctrine to exist under an autonomous rule of general international law.[508]

In *Awdi v. Romania* the State's assertion of the claim's inadmissibility (based on the investor's alleged misconduct) was countered by the claimant's invocation of *estoppel*, which required a special decision on the admissibility of the State's objection on admissibility.[509] Romania had stated before the tribunal that the arbitration was not about the criminal liability of the investor, hence in the investor's view it could not raise a clean-hands admissibility objection. The tribunal rejected the *estoppel* argument but reassured the claimant that, in assessing evidence drawn from the criminal proceedings, the tribunal should be guided by the presumption of innocence as a rule of public international law.[510] The admissibility objection was equally rejected: the State had not proved convincingly its allegations (that the claimants had looted the company's business and breached the rights of its employees), let alone provide '*evidence at a level required to meet the threshold of inadmissibility, be it on the*

503 The Agreement on Promotion, Protection and Guarantee of Investments among Member States of the Organisation of the Islamic Conference.

504 OIC Agreement, Article 9.

505 *Hesham* above (n 388) para. 645.

506 *Hulley Enterprises Limited (Cyprus) v. The Russian Federation*, UNCITRAL, PCA Case No. AA 226, Final Award of 18 July 2014, para. 1343 ff.

507 Ibid., para. 1353.

508 Ibid., para. 1363.

509 *Mr. Hassan Awdi, Enterprise Business Consultants, Inc. and Alfa El Corporation v. Romania*, ICSID Case No. ARB/10/13, Decision on the Admissibility of the Respondent's Third Objection to Jurisdiction and Admissibility of Claimant's Claims of 26 July 2013.

510 Ibid., para. 84.

ground of misrepresentation and/or the principle of good faith in an investment arbitration.'[511]

In *Chevron v. Ecuador*, the respondent claimed that the investor was estopped from bringing a denial of justice claim, since it had previously praised the work of the Ecuadorian judiciary in US domestic proceedings.[512] The tribunal appeared to accept in principle the respondent's objection, but held that it was not so strong, on the evidence, as to '*exclude*' the claimant's case *prima facie*.[513] At the stage of the merits the tribunal rejected the estoppel argument, finding that Ecuador had not '*overcome the presumption in favor of the Claimants' right to bring their claims under the BIT*.'[514]

In *Siag and Vecchi v. Egypt*, the respondent argued that since the claimants had previously maintained to have Egyptian nationality they were estopped from asserting the contrary in the proceedings. The tribunal cited the '*complete*[ness]' of the procedure set by Article 25 ICSID as reason to join the estoppel arguments to the phase of the merits.[515] Treated together with the merits, and in spite of the tribunal's refusal to consider it a preliminary issue in the merits phase, the matter of estoppel became an *exception préliminaire du fond*, akin to an objection of inadmissibility based on the investors' alleged misconduct. Indeed, the tribunal looked into the behaviour of the investors and held that although they had indeed represented themselves as Egyptian nationals when they were not, they were not aware of having lost Egyptian citizenship. In light of their good faith conduct, ultimately, they were not estopped from denying their Egyptian nationality in the arbitration.[516]

It is perhaps appropriate to end with the *Copper Mesa* tribunal, which characterised (illegality and clean hands) objections based on the post-establishment conduct of the investor as objections of inadmissibility.[517] The ensuing decision—in that case—to treat the objections jointly with the merits, instead, is not capable of generalisation and inevitably hinges on the facts of each dispute.

511 *Hassan Awdi* above (n 47) para. 212.

512 *Chevron Corporation (USA) and Texaco Petroleum Company (USA) v. The Republic of Ecuador*, UNCITRAL, PCA Case No. 34877, Interim Award of 1 December 2008, para. 128.

513 Ibid., para. 149.

514 *Chevron Corporation (USA) and Texaco Petroleum Company (USA) v. The Republic of Ecuador*, UNCITRAL, PCA Case No. 34877, Partial Award on the Merits of 30 March 2010, para. 354.

515 *Siag and Vecchi v. Egypt* above (n 405) para. 212.

516 *Waguih Elie George Siag and Clorinda Vecchi v. The Arab Republic of Egypt*, ICSID Case No. ARB/05/15, Award of 1 June 2009 para. 483.

517 *Copper Mesa v. Ecuador* above (n 26) para. 5.62.

3 *Conclusions of Part A*

This is the first part of a two-part essay. Its purpose is to survey the field, map the practice and support the largely theoretical analysis of Part B. However, it also retains a discrete function: it serves as an up-to-date representative selection of the practice of investment tribunals faced with questions of jurisdiction and admissibility. From this general look at the practice some general observations can be drawn:

- On several crucial matters *the arbitral practice has not reached consensus*. Among these are: the treatment of MFN-based jurisdiction, the survival of the State's offer to arbitrate after withdrawing from ICSID, the protection of indirect investments, the regime of denial of benefits clauses, the extent to which umbrella clauses apply *ratione materiae* (i.e., to which contractual or statutory obligations) and *ratione personae* (i.e., to obligations between entities other than the investor and the host State). Contradictions across awards are not rare, nor inherently worrisome. When inconsistency derives from the *ad hoc* nature of arbitration, it might be considered an inevitable side-effect of a system that ensure comparatively greater gains. However, the question might be asked whether at least part of this confusion is not ascribable to the uncoordinated work of the tribunals, but to the irreducible fuzziness of the notions used (jurisdiction and admissibility).
- Preliminary objections are predominantly treated as going to the jurisdiction of the tribunal rather than the admissibility of the claim. *Tribunals show a general reluctance to use the notion of admissibility*: the *Lao Holdings* tribunal's obstinate elusion of the word to characterise an objection based on abuse of right is revealing.
- Taking stock of the few instances in which admissibility is used, it is possible to identify a common feature. *All findings of inadmissibility have a retributory function*: they sanction some questionable aspect of the claim or the claimant. Inadmissibility thus is used to deter multiplication of claims, abusive tactics, shameless nationality-shopping, misconduct by the investor, lack of good faith. Inadmissibility considerations, moreover, are very likely to derive ultimate authority from general principles of law rather than treaty provisions.
- Conversely, *jurisdictional objections do not partake in direct or indirect value-judgment*. The alpha and omega of tribunals' determination of their own competence is the inquiry regarding the precise extent of the parties' consent. Of course, the distinction blurs when the parties stipulate (i.e., consent to) some explicit safeguard against misconduct—for instance, when they agree that compliance with domestic law is an essential aspect

of the investment. In that case, it is the parties' consent, as opposed to a general principle of procedural fairness, that entitles the tribunal to turn down a claim.

- *The practical difference between jurisdictional and admissibility objections does not emerge clearly* in the practice. From the awards, it is difficult to reverse-engineer a test to distinguish clearly jurisdiction from admissibility. At the same time, the tribunals' prevailing indifference towards the distinction might suggest that it is one ultimately not worth making.

These preliminary findings are statistically helpful but call for deeper scrutiny at the theoretical level. Part B will precisely question their root-causes and validity. It will explore whether the blurred distinction between jurisdiction and admissibility is inherited from the field of public international law litigation and analyse the import and implications of such elusive distinction. The study will reconsider and probe the received knowledge that purports to recognise one notion from the other, describe their respective distinctive features and their different legal effects.

Moreover, further examples in the practice of investment arbitration will be studied, which test the outer limits of the notions of jurisdiction and admissibility as commonly understood. These cases show that the conceptual lack of clarity can determine practical differences and unpredictable results.

PART B The Theory: An Inherited Confusion

After Part A illustrated the practice of investment tribunals dealing with jurisdiction and admissibility, this Part B turns to the theory behind these concepts. This Part is divided into two sections: Section 1 explores the theory of jurisdiction and admissibility in public international law, with the aim to expose its flaws and confusion. Section 2 returns to the investment arbitration practice and singles out specific cases in which this confusion emerged, accounting for the difficulty of tribunals called to handle it.

1 *Jurisdiction and Inadmissibility in International Law*

Investment arbitration is a *species* of international law litigation. Tribunals called upon to interpret and apply international norms draw from a shared set of concepts that pertain to the 'common law' of international law dispute settlement.[518] It is fair to assume that investment tribunals confronted with

518 Chester Brown, *A Common Law of International Adjudication* (OUP 2007).

the notions of jurisdiction and admissibility look back to the wider system and draw inspiration from the theory and the practice concerning international law adjudication and arbitration. This Section starts up by illustrating the public international law lineage of these doctrines. It will be shown that the lack of clarity is not a prerogative of investment arbitration, but a staple of these notions at the international level too.

1 Jurisdiction, Competence and Inadmissibility

Jurisdiction: A Concept Borrowed from Domestic Systems. The Role of Consent

In domestic systems, binding norms govern the allocation of jurisdiction to courts.[519] Moreover, the prescriptive reach of national law covers, in principle, all matters brought to litigation. Accordingly, by default there is a competent court and an applicable law for all claims with legal relevance. The law itself identifies both.[520]

Neither feature applies to international law.[521] There is no guarantee that international law regulate every instance of State conduct.[522] Even when an international norm exists, no tribunal possesses a jurisdiction of general scope (*juridiction de droit commun*) serving as a fall-back forum to hear any controversy regarding alleged breaches of such norm. The existence of several specialised jurisdictions does not guarantee that every case will fall under some tribunal's mandate: sometimes, no body is competent to hear a claim.[523]

State consent makes up, if partially, for the lack of a comprehensive system of compulsory international jurisdiction. States can bind themselves to

---

519 *Rights of Minorities in Upper Silesia (Minority Schools), Germany v. Poland,* Judgment of 26 April 1928, P.C.I.J. Series A, No 15, 23.

520 *Anglo-Iranian Oil Co. Case,* Order of July 5th, 1951: I.C.J. Reports 1951, 89, 96–97.

521 *Prosecutor v. Dusko Tadić a/k/a* 'Dule', decision on the defence motion for interlocutory appeal on jurisdiction, ICTY Appeals Chamber, 2 October 1995, para. 11.

522 *Case of the S.S. Lotus (France v. Turkey),* P.C.I.J. (ser. A) No. 10 (1927), para. 38.

523 Abi Saab hinted to this circumstance in the Dissenting Opinion in the case *Abaclat,* above (n 11). He rejected the claimants' argument that the tribunal's refusal to exercise jurisdiction would have amounted to denial of justice, see para. 257: '*international law, given its a-centralized character, has no system of courts or tribunals of plenary or general jurisdiction* (juridictions de droit commun) *covering all cases and litigants, barring a specific exception attributing jurisdiction over a particular type of matter or litigant to another specialized organ, and where every dispute or every claim can ultimately and necessarily find a competent forum to handle it. By contrast, as explained earlier …, all international courts and tribunals are tribunals of attributed jurisdiction* (juridictions d'attribution)*; a jurisdiction based on the consent of the parties or litigants and confined within the limits of this consent*'.

accept the authority and findings of an adjudicating body, whether permanent or established *ad hoc* (*juridiction attribuée*). States can be the parties to the dispute directly, or they can bear some connection—through consent—with the establishment of the tribunal and the formulation of its jurisdiction (for instance, when one party of the dispute is an individual).[524] Although expressed in various ways (even implicitly), consent underpins the activity of adjudicatory bodies of international law. Consent explains why international decisions have binding force and command compliance even by States that do not agree with them. In this sense, consent and willingness diverge; previous consent to unspecified future obligations—deriving from the judges' determinations—prevails over a lack of willingness to perform them when they arise.[525] In the field of international adjudication, the better comparator is not the system of domestic courts, but arbitration between private entities.[526] Consent must validate the *foundational* jurisdiction of a court (its establishment and general mandate) as well its *specific* jurisdiction (the authority to hear a specific dispute).[527]

A convincing demonstration of one State's consent to both is in principle sufficient to trump jurisdictional objections.[528] The elusive principle of *in dubio mitius*, hinting at a preference for the interpretation that least encroaches on

524 Note that even in the case of the establishment of the ICTY and the ICTR the former Yugoslavia and Rwanda, despite not having given their consent directly to the jurisdiction of such tribunals, had irrevocably consented, by signing the UN Charter, to be bound by the UN Security Resolutions that established them.

525 Alexander Orakhelashvili, 'The Concept of International Judicial Jurisdiction: A Reappraisal' (2003) 3 The Law and Practice of International Courts and Tribunals 501, 514: '*By giving consent to judicial jurisdiction a State merely performs an act the legal effects of which are pre-determined by a constituent instrument and not by the State itself*'.

526 A consequence of this setup is the parties' power to '*disseise*' the ICJ, which led Robert Kolb to comment that '[the ICJ's] *jurisdiction is probably a purely 'attributive' one, meaning that it is the parties who in this respect remain the sole* domini negotii'. See Robert Kolb, *The International Court of Justice* (Hart 2013) 197. For a recent study of the arbitration-like features of the ICJ's activity, see Serena Forlati, *The International Court of Justice—An Arbitral Tribunal or a Judicial Body?* (Springer 2014).

527 This distinction is made by Yuval Shany, 'Jurisdiction and Admissibility', in Cesare Romano, Karen Alter, and Yuval Shany, *Oxford Handbook of International Adjudication* (OUP 2014) 782. The two kinds of consent associated with each kind of jurisdiction are described in Abi Saab, dissent above (n 11), para. 162. Kolb above (n 526) 212, refers to a similar distinction, between general and specific jurisdiction (and uses a similar dichotomy with respect to admissibility).

528 *Factory at Chorzów*, Jurisdiction, Judgment No. 8, 1927, P.C.I. J., Series A, No. 9, 32.

sovereignty,[529] cannot upset the expression of the State's consent. To identify State consent as expressed in the relevant instruments, courts and tribunals tend to use the ordinary principles of interpretation rather than a deferential bias against obligations.[530]

In the *Delimitation of the Continental Shelf Case* the arbitral panel held that '*the Court necessarily derives its competence from the consent of both the parties to the present arbitration*.'[531] Consent founds the jurisdiction of permanent bodies too: both the PCIJ and ICJ repeatedly clarified that the Court's jurisdiction depends on the will of the Parties,[532] and that '*it cannot decide a dispute between States without the consent of those States to its jurisdiction*.'[533] One obvious implication of this approach is the principle developed in the *Monetary Gold Case*, typically referred to as the principle of the indispensable third party.[534] The Court refused to establish its jurisdiction on the dispute because a decision would have been tantamount to determining the international responsibility of a State that did not partake in the proceedings and, therefore,

529 SS *Louts above* (n 522) 18. The WTO Appellate Body mentioned this principle in the case *EC—Measures Concerning Meat and Meat Products*, WT/DS26/AB/R, WT/DS48/AB/R, report of 16 January 1998 (para. 165, footnote 154). However, its operation is unclear, at least when it should entail the displacement of legal commitments. See Christopher J Larouer, 'In the Name of Sovereignty? The Battle over *In Dubio Mitius* Inside and Outside the Courts' (2009) Cornell Law School Inter-University Graduate Student Conference Papers 22; Luigi Crema, 'Disappearance and New Sightings of Restrictive Interpretation(s)' (2010) 21(3) European Journal of International Law 681.

530 Indeed, although the role of consent has been central in the emersion of the international judicial systems, the practice has significantly evolved since then, and there have been cases where the principle of consent was invoked by certain States to escape the jurisdiction of a tribunal, but was dismissed by the latter. See generally Orakhelashvili above (n 525) 501–502, referring to the case *LaGrand (Germany v. United States of America)*, Judgment, I.C.J. Reports 2001, p. 466; the ECHR cases *Chrysostomos v. Turkey* (App. Nos. 15299/89, 15300/89 and 15318/89, 68 Eur. Comm'n H.R. Dec. & Rep. 216, 245 (1991)) and *Loizidou v. Turkey*, preliminary objections (App. No. 25781/94, Ser. A, No. 310) and the Inter-American Court of Human Rights' cases *Ivcher Bronstein*, Competence, Judgment of September 24, 1999 (Ser. C) No. 54 (1999) and *Constitutional Court*, Competence, Judgment of September 24, 1999 (Ser. C) No. 55 (1999).

531 See 1977, 18 UNRIAA at 24.

532 *Status of Eastern Carelia*, Advisory Opinion of 23 July 1923, P.C.I.J. Series B, No. 527, 22; *Minority Schools above* (n 519) 22; *Corfu Channel case*, Judgment on Preliminary Objection: I.C.J. Reports 1948, 15, 27; *Anglo-Iranian Oil Co.* above (n 520) 103.

533 *East Timor (Portugal v. Australia)*, Judgment, I.C.J. Reports 1995, 90, 101.

534 *Case of the monetary gold removed from Rome in 1943* (Preliminary Question), Judgment of June 15th, 1954: I.C.J. Reports 1954, 19.

had not given consent thereto (nor, by extension, had entered an obligation to comply with the judgment).[535]

The search for an intention to confer jurisdiction informs the assessment of any procedural objection. The PCIJ clarified as much in the *Chorzów Factory* judgment:

> [t]he Court will, in the event of an objection—or when it has automatically to consider the question—only affirm its jurisdiction provided that the force of the arguments militating in favour of it is preponderant. The fact that weighty arguments can be advanced to support the contention that it has no jurisdiction cannot of itself create a doubt calculated to upset its jurisdiction. 'When considering whether it has jurisdiction or not, the Court's aim is always to ascertain whether an intention on the part of the Parties exists to confer jurisdiction upon it.'[536]

In sum, the element of consent is critical to distinguish the international system from the national one[537] and to justify the establishment of certain obligations, but cannot go much further. Once consent is established as a gateway requirement, the operation of international jurisdiction is redolent of that of national jurisdictions (*mutatis mutandis*). As Madame Rosalyn Higgins said, speculating on the scholarly tendency to overrate the importance of sovereignty and the deference it should elicit,

> once [consent to jurisdiction] has been given—and, if necessary, the Court has determined that it *has* been given—States become normal litigants before a court.[538]

535 For a recent appraisal of the principle, and an analysis of its use by the ICJ and ITLOS, see Filippo Fontanelli, 'Reflections on the indispensable party principle in the wake of the judgment on preliminary objections in the *Norstar* case' [2017] 1 Rivista di Diritto Internazionale 163–183.

536 *Factory at Chorzów* above (n 528) 32.

537 Cesare PR Romano, 'The Shift from the Consensual to the Compulsory Paradigm in International Adjudication: Elements for a Theory of Consent' (2006) 39 New York University Journal of International Law & Policy 791, 793–794.

538 Rosalyn Higgins, 'Respecting Sovereign States and Running a Tight Courtroom' (2001) 50 International and Comparative Law Quarterly 121–132. (emphasis in the original) For a slightly different view, see Romano above (n 537) 801: '*international courts should tend to err on the side of declining jurisdiction whenever jurisdiction is contested rather than on the side of exercising jurisdiction, as they currently do*'.

This analogy accounts for the vast set of terminology and conceptual categories that domestic and international jurisdictions have in common.[539] However, it is precisely the search for consent that informs the powers of international judicial actors.[540] In this sense, all reference to the general principles of competence, jurisdiction and admissibility in international law requires a *caveat.* These general principles cannot have a precise correspondent in domestic law. In other words, they are general principles that, in spite of the terminological overlap, are relevant only under *international* law.[541] They flow from the States' recognition of their validity as expressed in international practice, as they ensure the viability of international proceedings; they do not arise from States' practice *in foro domestico*.[542] If anything, the principles relating to jurisdiction in international proceedings find the closest parallel to the corresponding rules governing the jurisdiction of arbitral tribunals, in view of the (still) prevailing consensual paradigm that both share.

The Notions of Jurisdiction, Competence and Admissibility in International Law

The terms 'jurisdiction' and 'competence' are commonly used as synonyms,[543] even if their etymon suggests a distinction. 'Jurisdiction' (from *jus dicere*) refers

539 Orakhelashvili, above (n 525) 514, quoting Hugh Thirlway, 'The Law and Procedure of the International Court of Justice' (1998) British Yearbook of International Law 4.

540 Abi Saab, above (n 11), para. 17: '*As with jurisdiction, the concept of admissibility in international law partakes of its generic meaning in the general theory of law, but is further particularized in function of the specificities of international adjudication, including its consensual basis*'.

541 For a brief overview of this category of principles, which is not expressly mentioned in Article 38 of the ICJ Statute, see Giorgio Gaja, 'General Principles of Law' (2013) Oxford Encyclopedia of Public International Law, para. 17–20. See also Oscar Schachter, *International Law in Theory and Practice* (Martinus Nijhoff 1991) 50–54 and the short discussion in Neha Jain, 'Judicial Lawmaking and General Principles of Law in International Criminal Law' (2016) 57(1) Harvard Journal of International Law 119: '[this] *category of general principles that stem from the specific characteristics of the international community is the only conception where municipal laws appear to play little to no role*.'

542 Whether the general principles operating in the international legal order are capable of application as such in the field of investment arbitration is another issue. Section 2, below, accounts for the peculiarities of investment arbitration in this respect.

543 Shabtai Rosenne and Yael Ronen, *The Law and Practice of the International Court, 1920–2005* (Brill 2006) 524, try to infer a doctrinal distinction: "[j]*urisdiction' is a stricter concept than 'competence'. Jurisdiction relates to the capacity of the Court to decide a concrete case with a binding force. 'Competence', on the other hand, is more subjective, including both jurisdiction and the element of the propriety of the Court's exercising its jurisdiction*.' Although

to the activity and power of declaring what the law is;[544] 'competence' (from *cum petere*) implies a notion of physical pertinence: a specific matter is naturally falling within the sphere of action of the (competent) subject. Yet, this terminological distinction is virtually irrelevant in judicial practice; since there is no added value to retaining it, jurisdiction and competence are hereafter used interchangeably.[545] Jurisdictional powers are scrutinised when their limits are at stake: jurisdiction is exercised unless a procedural hurdle is raised and not overcome. Determining the jurisdiction of a tribunal encompasses a variety of matters that, normally, are determined at the preliminary stage of the proceedings and before the review of the merits,[546] for reasons of judicial economy.

This section analyses the practice of international courts and tribunals other than investment tribunals. Undoubtedly, this practice informs the work

---

this distinction is plausible, it blurs the boundaries between jurisdiction and admissibility, see discussion below.

544 See Abi Saab's Dissenting Opinion above (n 11), para. 10: '*The term 'jurisdiction' (from the latin 'jurisdictio', literally to 'pronounce' or 'enunciate the law', dire le droit), when used in the judicial or adjudicative context, denotes 'the legal power of an organ to decide cases (in general) or a case (in particular) by application of law'. In other words, it is the empowerment to exercise the judicial function. Thus, jurisdiction refers first and foremost to a legal power to exercise a certain type of activity, the judicial function*'.

545 Kolb above (n 526) 211–212. Heiskanen's proposal (Veijo Heiskanen, 'Jurisdiction v. Competence: Revisiting a frequently neglected distinction (1994) 5 Finnish Yearbook of International Law 1) deserves special attention for attempting to square the circle by considering competence as the institutional side of admissibility. His proposal, therefore distinguishes between jurisdiction and competence/admissibility, differently from most other authors.

546 Such distinction between the jurisdictional phase and the merits is commonly referred to by the ICJ, see *Legality of Use of Force (Yugoslavia v. United States of America)*, Provisional Measures, Order of 2 June 1999, I.C.J. Reports 1999, 916, 925: '*there is a fundamental distinction between the question of acceptance by a state of the Court's jurisdiction and the compatibility of particular acts with international law; the former requires consent; the latter question can only be reached when the Court deals with the merits after having established its jurisdiction.*' See also the dissenting opinion of judge Ndiaye in case *The M/V 'SAIGA'* (No 2), Saint Vincent and the Grenadines v. Guinea, Merits, Judgment, ITLOS Case No. 2, ICGJ 336 (ITLOS 1999), 1st July 1999, para. 5: '*Il ne faut pas se méprendre sur «un principe universel du droit de la procédure» indiquant qu'il faut distinguer entre, d'une part, le droit de saisir un tribunal et le droit du tribunal de connaître du fond de la demande et, d'autre part, le droit au regard de l'objet de la demande que le demandeur doit établir à la satisfaction du tribunal (voir Affaire du Sud-Ouest-Africain, C.I.J. Recueil 1966, paragraphe 64).*'

of investment tribunals, as it clearly emerges, for instance, from the ubiquitous use of public international law authorities in arbitral awards.[547]

In *Tadić*, the ICTY's Appeal Chamber embarked on an accurate appraisal of the concept of jurisdiction. It concluded that a challenge to its own establishment was, too, a jurisdictional matter. The Chamber recalled a significant quote, pointing at the original and most basic meaning of jurisdiction:

> '[Jurisdiction] is the power of a court to decide a matter in controversy and presupposes the existence of a duly constituted court with control over the subject matter and the parties.' Black's Law Dictionary, 712 (6th ed. 1990) (citing Pinner v. Pinner, 33 N.C. App. 204, 234 S.E.2d 633).)[548]

The Chamber correctly remarked that jurisdiction does not simply indicate an ambit, shaped by the combination of the qualifying features—dimensions, or *rationes*—for a dispute to be heard (*ratione temporis, loci, personae* and *materiae*). The jurisdiction of a court constitutes '*a legal power, hence necessarily a legitimate power, «to state the law»* (dire le droit) *within this ambit, in an authoritative and final manner*.'[549] If a court has jurisdiction, it is entitled and required to make the necessary legal determinations to process the claim:

> once a case is duly referred to it, [a tribunal] is endowed with full jurisdiction and may take cognisance of all questions of fact or of law arising in the course of the proceedings, including questions which may have been raised before the Commission under the head of admissibility.[550]

Indeed, the admissibility of a claim (or *recevabilité*) is a separate matter, which falls to be considered and reviewed only when the jurisdiction is not contested or is positively established. Impediments that do not ensue from a lack of consent to its primary jurisdiction may nonetheless prevent a tribunal from decide a case on the merits. In other words,

547 For instance, see a study of the impact of the ICJs' case law over arbitral decisions relating to the preliminary objections: Alain Pellet, 'The Case Law of the ICJ in Investment Arbitration' (2013) 28 ICSID Review 223, especially at 231–232 and cases referred to therein.

548 See *Tadić* above (n 521), para. 10.

549 Ibid.

550 See ECHR case *Klass and Others v. Germany*, App. No. 5029/71, Series A no. 28, para. 32.

> an unsuccessful jurisdictional plea leaves open the possibility that a finding on the ultimate merits may still be excluded through a decision given against the substantive admissibility of the claim.[551]

A widespread—but ultimately unsatisfactory—understanding is that these defects of the claim relating to admissibility are less fundamental or immutable than those tainting the primary jurisdiction of the tribunal.[552] Labelling is not inconsequential. Grounds for inadmissibility might be subject to different rules of invocability (the tribunal might have no obligation to raise them *proprio motu*,[553] or the parties could lose the right to invoke them after a certain phase of the proceedings).[554] Moreover, whereas the jurisdiction of a tribunal

---

551 Gerald G Fitzmaurice, *The Law and Procedure of the International Court of Justice* (Grotius 1986) Vol. 2, 439.

552 Amerasinghe above (n 35) 71.

553 The seemingly unusual case of *Larsen/Hawaii* (*Lance Larsen v. the Hawaiian Kingdom*, PCA, case no. 99–001, under the UNCITRAL 1976 Rules, Award of 5 February 2001 (2001) 119 ILR 566; (2001) 95 AJIL 927–933), in which the Tribunal appeared to analyse admissibility *proprio motu*, is exceptional because it deals with a fabricated claim in which both parties had no interest in raising procedural objections. An obverse exception might be found in *Transglobal Green Energy, LLC and Transglobal Green Energy de Panama, S.A. v. The Republic of Panama*, ICSID Case No. ARB/13/28, Award of 2 June 2016, where the tribunal noted that the Respondent had failed to pursue a jurisdictional objection *ratione materiae*, and that a decision on it was unnecessary (para. 96). Since the claim failed on other preliminary objections, this remark might have been just a signal of judicial economy rather than a refusal to observe jurisdictional objections *proprio motu*. See also ibid., para. 100: '*The Tribunal may choose to consider the objections to its jurisdiction in any particular order*.' On the impossibility to examine admissibility flaws *proprio motu*, see the characterisation of the ICJ's approach in *Hochtief AG v. Argentina*, ICSID Case no. ARB/07/31, Decision on Jurisdiction of 24 October 2011, para. 5: '[i]*n the ICJ, for example, rules on admissibility include such matters as the rules on the nationality of claims and the exhaustion of local remedies. The ICJ may have jurisdiction to decide whether State A had injured corporation B in violation of international law; but it may be that the claim actually filed is inadmissible because it has been brought by the wrong State, or because local remedies have not yet been exhausted. But if no objection is raised on such grounds, the Court will not raise the matter* proprio motu.' An interesting case, explored below, is that of the objection to the jurisdiction *ratione loci* of a Tribunal seised by the claim against Russia of an Ukranian investor relating to measures in Crimea. The Respondent having no interest in pointing out that Crimea had been illegally occupied, it was for the Tribunal to raise the concern *proprio motu*. See case *PJSC Ukrnafta v. The Russian Federation*, UNCITRAL, PCA Case No. 2015–34, Award on Jurisdiction of 4 July 2017 (confidential).

554 Amerasinghe above (n 35) 71: '*an objection relating to* recevabilité *may be waived or the opportunity to raise it lost, whereas a defect in jurisdiction can technically never be cured*'.

is fixed, the inadmissibility of a claim can sometimes be cured (for instance, when brought again after the local remedies are exhausted or the waiting period expires). A crucial difference concerns the possibility of review.[555] Findings on jurisdiction might be subject to the review of a controlling body entitled to ascertain that the decision-maker did not exceed its powers, but determinations on the admissibility of a claim are normally final, or at least as final as the findings on the merits.[556] Characterising a matter as pertaining to competence rather than inadmissibility might affect the logical sequencing of the analysis carried out by the tribunal, as well as the allocation of the evidentiary *onus* between the parties.[557]

The ICJ cared to distinguish between matters of competence and admissibility. In *Interhandel*[558] it specified that the claimant's failure to exhaust local remedies tainted the admissibility of the application, not the Court's jurisdiction. Likewise, in *Nottebohm*,[559] the Court treated the failure to negotiate and exhaust local remedies, as well as the nationality of the claimant, as matters of *recevabilité*. The ICJ also underlined that the jurisdiction of the tribunal is directly linked with the consent of the parties, whereas the admissibility of the claim is not: '*in determining the scope of the consent expressed by one of the parties, the Court pronounces on its jurisdiction and not on the admissibility of the application*'.[560] Normally, the fact that jurisdictional and admissibility objections are raised together and pursue the same goal (preventing the tribunal

555 This distinction is used by Jan Paulsson (see the article 'Jurisdiction and Admissibility' in Gerald Aksen et al. (eds), *Global Reflections on International Law, Commerce and Dispute Resolution: Liber Amicorum in Honour of Robert Briner* (International Chamber of Commerce 2005) 601) to highlight the importance of the distinction between jurisdiction and admissibility.

556 This distinction is crucial in the field of international arbitration, where annulment or setting aside of awards is typically possible only on narrow grounds which do not include a review of the merits.

557 Yuval Shany, *Questions of Jurisdiction and Admissibility before International Courts* (CUP 2015) 130, accompanies the list of these practical consequences with a careful assessment of the 'analytical reasons' which depend on the correct distinction between jurisdiction and admissibility, that is, '*the distinction may help us better understand the way courts exercise judicial power and the legal interests of relevant constituencies affected as they do so.*' The present study will not focus on this illuminating aspect of the distinction and will only focus on its practical applications.

558 *Interhandel* (Switzerland v. USA), Judgment, Preliminary Objections, I.C.J. Reports 1959, 6, 26.

559 *Nottebohm* (Liechtenstein v. Guatemala), Preliminary Objections, I.C.J. Reports 1955, 26.

560 *Certain Questions of Mutual Assistance in Criminal Matters* (Djibouti v. France), Judgment, I.C.J. Reports 2008, para. 48.

from entering the merits of a controversy) makes it unnecessary to distinguish the latter from the former. As the PCIJ noted in the *Mavrommatis* case:

> The Court has not to ascertain what are, in the various codes of procedure and in the various legal terminologies, the specific characteristics of … an objection [to the effect that the Court cannot entertain the proceedings]; in particular it need not consider whether "competence" and "jurisdiction", *incompétence* and *fins de non-recevoir* should invariably and in every connection be regarded as synonymous expressions.… [Ultimately, the Court should not just assess] whether the nature and subject of the dispute laid before the Court are such that the Court derives from them jurisdiction to entertain it, but also whether the conditions upon which the exercise of this jurisdiction is dependent are all fulfilled in the present case.[561]

Critically, only the constitutive instrument of a judicial body can define the grounds for inadmissibility of a claim brought before it. However, these grounds being directly or indirectly inspired by general principles of international adjudication and arbitration, it is possible to spot recurring solutions across the different judicial frameworks, which sometimes emerge in the absence of express rules and fill the gaps. To better explain the distinction between jurisdiction and inadmissibility in the practice, two lists of typical instances are provided below, categorising jurisdictional and inadmissibility issues, respectively. As it will be explained below, one element's belonging to either list is often contestable: the classification is not normative but descriptive. It primary collates the patterns and the outliers emerged in the practice. When inconsistencies and overlaps exist between the categories, they will be pointed out.

2 Issues of Competence

This classification starts from very preliminary and abstract questions and progressively advances towards the merits of a case. It is implied in the following that a claim has already been brought to litigation, in compliance with the applicable procedural rules for the submission of a claim (*seisin*). The question is not perfunctory, insofar as matters of inadmissibility could result in the invalidity of the seisin and halt the procedure before the proceedings

561 *Mavrommatis Palestine Concessions*, Greece v. United Kingdom, Objection to the Jurisdiction of the Court, Judgment, P.C.I.J. 1924 Series A, No 2, 10.

come into existence and the tribunal is even empowered to review its own competence.[562]

The Correct Establishment and Functioning of the Tribunal

The most preliminary notion of jurisdiction regards whether an international court or tribunal is lawfully established. This aspect necessarily '*goes beyond and subsumes*' any other issue regarding the scope of its judicial activity.[563] This element is not likely to be scrutinized with respect to long-established permanent bodies.[564] Questions of original legitimacy, however, can be relevant for the activity of arbitral tribunals, which are often appointed *ad hoc* to resolve a specific dispute or class of disputes. Any matters that may concern the legal and proper functioning of the tribunal and affect its ability to act judicially, as constituted in the particular proceedings, may be relevant to this scrutiny of competence. These include the conditions of establishment of the judicial body, the constitution of its bench and the profile of the judges, and instances of conflict of interest or impartiality which pre-date the establishment.[565]

562 Juan Pablo Hugues Arthur, 'The legal value of prior steps to arbitration in international law of foreign investment: Two (different?) approaches, one outcome' (2015) 15 Anuario Mexicano de Derecho Internacional 449, 459 and literature cited therein. See for instance in *Bosca v. Lithuania* how the respondent argued that the claimant's failure to include his address in the Statement of Claim rendered the claim inadmissible, in light of the applicable UNCITRAL rules. *Luigiterzo Bosca v. Lithuania*, PCA Case No. 2011-05, Award of 17 May 2013, para. 109 and 119.

563 See *Tadić*, above (n 521), para. 12: '*In sum, if the International Tribunal were not validly constituted, it would lack the legitimate power to decide in time or space or over any person or subject-matter. The plea based on the invalidity of constitution of the International Tribunal goes to the very essence of jurisdiction as a power to exercise the judicial function within any ambit. It is more radical than, in the sense that it goes beyond and subsumes, all the other pleas concerning the scope of jurisdiction. This issue is a preliminary to and conditions all other aspects of jurisdiction.*'

564 Unsurprisingly, it was raised with respect to the (then) newly created ICTY in the *Tadić* judgment, above (n 521).

565 Subsequent questions, that arise or are known after the start of the proceedings, can be used by the parties or the arbitrators to denounce or terminate the proceedings, see for instance the case of the arbitration between Croatia and Slovenia administered by the PCA. See Arman Sarvarian and Rudy Baker, 'Arbitration between Croatia and Slovenia: Leaks, Wiretaps, Scandal' (2015) EJIL: Talk! of 28 July 2015, at http://www.ejiltalk.org/arbitration-between-croatia-and-slovenia-leaks-wiretaps-scandal/.

The Tribunal's Competence to Assess Its Own Jurisdiction

Next to that of lawful establishment, the most preliminary question is whether a certain tribunal can determine its own power to hear a particular legal claim. This scrutiny is typically devolved to the tribunal itself, pursuant to the principle of *Kompetenz-Kompetenz*. This formula indicates the competence of every international tribunal to assess, in addition to any challenge aimed at the tribunal *per se*, its own competence to hear a legal claim considered in the abstract, including any preliminary objections thereto.

Again, the Appeals Chamber in *Tadić* provided an exhaustive account of this principle:

> This is not merely a power in the hands of the tribunal. In international law, where there is no integrated judicial system and where every judicial or arbitral organ needs a specific constitutive instrument defining its jurisdiction, 'the first obligation of the Court—as of any other judicial body—is to ascertain its own competence.'[566]

The standing of this general principle is such that it is rarely challenged, and it has also been codified in many instruments, like the statute of the ICJ (Art. 36(6)), the statute of the UN Adminstrative Tribunal (Art. 2(3)), the European Convention Human Rights (Art. 49), the statute of the ILO Adminstrative Tribunal (Art. II(7)), or the ICSID Rules (Art 41). This is, perhaps, the only general principle of international procedure that applies without questions in the field of investment arbitration.[567]

There can be also cases where findings on jurisdiction of a tribunal, originally devolved to the tribunal itself, can be challenged and brought before a second forum for review.[568] Note that the competence to determine the lawful

566 See *Tadić* above (n 521) para. 18, quoting from Judge Cordova's dissenting opinion in *Advisory Opinion on Judgements of the Administrative Tribunal of the I.L.O. upon complaints made against the U.N.E.S.C.O.*, 1956 I.C.J. Reports, 77, 163.

567 Jorge E. Viñuales, 'International Investment Proceedings: Converging Principles?' in Enzo Cannizzaro (ed), *International Procedural Law: Common Principles or General Principles?* (Sapienza Universita Editrice 2017).

568 This is the case, for instance, of Art. XII of the ILOAT statute and the corresponding provision of a former version of the UN Administrative Tribunal Statute (in force between 1955 and 1996), entrusting the ICJ with the task of reviewing the correctness of a finding of jurisdiction. More generally, arbitral awards are typically subject to second level review on matters of jurisdiction (through setting aside proceedings in domestic courts, or annulment in the ICSID framework). This is an important point: the principle of *Kompetenz-Kompetenz* does not rule out the possibility that another body is ultimately entrusted with

establishment and the competence of a tribunal, discussed above, is of inherent nature, and does not need an express consent to be established.[569] This does not mean that the requisite of consent is overlooked; in fact, once the tribunal has found the lawfulness of its own establishment or its own competence to decide on jurisdictional issues, the next step is precisely the scrutiny of procedural objections, if any arise, based on an alleged defect of consent.

Requirements of Primary Jurisdiction

A tribunal's power to proceed judicially in a particular case and reach the merits (i.e., its primary jurisdiction[570]) flows from its constitutive instruments. These might be a statute, an international convention, a *compromis* concluded by the parties, and/or any other instrument governing its activity. This power results from the combination of foundational and specific jurisdiction. Matters of jurisdiction can only be determined with reference to an actual dispute. To ascertain the existence of foundational jurisdiction, the dispute is broken down into a set of essential components. *Foundational* jurisdiction can be construed as a check-list exercise, which notes the essential features of a dispute, as opposed to a review of admissibility, which is normally understood to hinge on the circumstantial or accidental aspects of a claim or a claimant. *Specific* jurisdiction, relating to the parties' consent that the tribunal entertain the specific claim, is an intermediate notion—the existence of which reveals the difficulty to draw a line between jurisdiction and admissibility.

General rules with respect to the establishment of primary jurisdiction concern the existence and continuing presence of a dispute,[571] which

---

the power to review the initial decision on jurisdiction. See William W Park, Determining an Arbitrator's Jurisdiction: Timing and Finality in American Law (2007) 8 Nev. LJ 135, 136: '*the principle that arbitrators may decide jurisdictional questions says nothing about who (judge or arbitrator) will ultimately decide any particular case*'.

569 The expression 'inherent jurisdiction' usually refer to the set of powers implicitly entrusted to a tribunal in order for it to discharge its mandate, see e.g. Human Rights Committee *Kennedy v. Trinidad and Tobago* Communication No. 845/1998 26 March 2002 CCPR/C/74/D/845/1998, par. 6.4. For further details, see Chester Brown, 'The Inherent Powers of International Courts and Tribunals' (2005) 76 BYIL 195, and Filippo Fontanelli and Paolo Busco, 'The function of procedural justice in international adjudication' (2016) 15(1) The Law and Practice of International Courts and Tribunals 1–23.

570 This power is often termed 'primary jurisdiction,' in contrast with other jurisdictional powers relating, for instance, to the management of the proceedings or the issuing of remedies and interim measures.

571 *Mavrommatis* above (n 561) para. 164–166; *Territorial and Maritime Dispute* (Nicaragua v. Colombia), Preliminary Objections, Judgment, I.C.J. Reports 2007, 832. Shany above

presupposes that the claim is genuine and is not moot for lack of object, or merely hypothetical.[572] Outside these general principles, the scope of jurisdiction of one tribunal is to be identified interpreting its constitutive instrument(s), with the auxiliary help of general principles of law when necessary. Jurisdiction may be delimited *ratione personae* (e.g., the Iran—US Tribunal can only hear cases against a government or a government-controlled entity; only States can appear before the ICJ in contentious proceedings), *ratione materiae* (e.g., the ICTY has jurisdiction only over crimes committed in the context of an international armed conflict; many compromissory clauses expressly confer jurisdiction only over disputes arising from, or related to, the obligations created by a specific instrument, some compromissory clauses are defined by reference to their limits[573]), *ratione loci* and *temporis* (e.g., the ECCC only have jurisdiction over crimes committed in Cambodia between 17 April 1975 and 6 January 1979). All these dimensions of jurisdiction have a direct connection with consent: when the dispute lacks one of the qualifying features, the defendant State has not consented to its resolution in the forum seised by the claimant (better: the instrument registering the defendant's consent to jurisdiction does not extend to such a dispute).

Requisites which make access to a court contingent on the exhaustion of some previous procedure (negotiation, quasi-judicial settlement, domestic proceedings) are harder to categorise. They can be used as instance of the grey area in which (specific) jurisdiction and admissibility are difficult to tell apart

(n 557) 69 refers to a set of cases in which the ICJ derived from Article 36 ICJ the conclusions that only 'legal disputes' fall under its jurisdiction, and therefore characterised the absence of a legal dispute as a jurisdictional flaw. See in particular *South West Africa* (*Ethiopia v. South Africa*), 1962 ICJ 319, 328; *Aegean Sea* (*Greece v. Turkey*), 1978 ICJ 3, 13; *East Timor* (*Portugal v. Australia*), 1995 ICJ 90, 99–100. However, this requirement is sometimes described as one of admissibility, due to its threshold character.

572 Note, however, that the similar conclusion in *Case concerning the Northern Cameroons* (Cameroon v. United Kingdom), Preliminary Objections, Judgment of 2 December 1963: I.C.J. Reports 1963, 15, at 33–34, appears to be reached on the basis of inadmissibility. In the arbitration *Pan American Energy LLC and BP Argentina Exploration Company v. The Argentine Republic*, ICSID Case No. ARB/03/13, Decision on Preliminary Objections of 27 July 2006, the tribunal held in passing that it had no jurisdiction over hypothetical claims, see para. 169.

573 See Article 282 UNCLOS, which restricts the reach of the methods of dispute settlement of Part XV of UNCLOS when the parties have agreed to an alternative method of compulsory dispute settlement.

in the practice.[574] Although procedural in nature, these requirements speak directly to consent, as they are normally contained precisely in the compromissory clauses establishing the court's jurisdiction. The fact that the defect might not be fatal (a fresh claim can be brought in the future, upon compliance with the precondition) would suggest qualifying it as a matter of inadmissibility, but the weight of State consent prevails and militates in favour of a different conclusion when they are registered in treaty language. Along these lines, the ICJ has prevalently[575] treated similar requirements as matter of competence, stating clearly that

> its jurisdiction is based on the consent of the parties and is confined to the extent accepted by them ... When that consent is expressed in a compromissory clause in an international agreement, any conditions to which such consent is subject must be regarded as constituting the limits thereon. The Court accordingly considers that *the examination of such conditions relates to its jurisdiction and not to the admissibility of the application.*[576]

It can be tentatively suggested that the subsumption of the consent's '*limits*' under the rubric of jurisdiction flows from their form (i.e., their being recorded '*in an international agreement*') rather than from the quality of the substantive

574 See Arthur above (n 562); Gary Born and Marija Šćekić, 'Pre-Arbitration Procedural Requirements 'A Dismal Swamp'' in David D Caron et al. (eds), *Practising Virtue, Inside International Arbitration* (OUP 2015) 227–263.

575 One exception being *Border and Transborder Armed Actions* (Nicaragua v. Honduras), Jurisdiction and Admissibility, Judgment, I.C.J. Reports 1988, 69, where the Court treats interchangeably competence/jurisdiction and admissibility, treating in turn the preliminary objections raised by Honduras.

576 *Armed Activities on the Territory of the Congo* (*New Application: 2002*) (Democratic Republic of the Congo v. Rwanda), I.C.J. Reports 2006, 39, para. 88 (emphasis added); *Case Concerning mutual assistance in criminal matters* (Djibouti v. France), I.C.J. Reports 2008, 204, para. 62. The Court, in the 2002 order, mentioned his previous case law to support this view, for instance *South West Africa* (Ethiopia v. South Africa; Liberia v. South Africa), Preliminary Objections, Judgment, I.C.J. Reports 1962, 344–346; *Military and Paramilitary Activities in and against Nicaragua* (Nicaragua v. United States of America), Jurisdiction and Admissibility, Judgment, I.C.J. Reports 1984, 427–429, para. 81–83; *Border and Transborder Armed Actions* (Nicaragua v. Honduras), Jurisdiction and Admissibility, Judgment, I.C.J. Reports 1988, 88–90, para. 42–48; *Questions of Interpretation and Application of the 1971 Montreal Convention arising from the Aerial Incident at Lockerbie* (Libyan Arab Jamahiriya v. United Kingdom), Preliminary Objections, Judgment, I.C.J. Reports 1998, 16, para. 16–19; 24, para. 39–40.

or procedural requirements. This could be the conclusion reached through adding a catch-all dimension to the four classic jurisdictional elements: the category of jurisdiction *ratione voluntatis*.[577] As such, one could conceive a formalistic policing of the blurry line between jurisdiction and admissibility: States are allowed to elevate any matter to a condition of jurisdiction, if they so will. This additional category is redundant: it simply serves as reminder that the parties can shape their consent to be subject to a court's jurisdiction by common agreement, but has no pre-determined or inherent content. As a separate *ratio* of jurisdiction is unspecific (all jurisdictional *rationes* flow from and codify the parties' consent); as a catch-all category covering all conditions to the exercise of jurisdiction it appears over-inclusive (as discussed, it is not difficult to tuck admissibility requirements into this fifth *genus*). If the parties do not agree on express qualifiers in the applicable instruments, the distinction between jurisdiction and admissibility defects falls to be determined by general principles of law.

3 Other Procedural Impediments *Matters of Inadmissibility*

The following list is merely illustrative, but gathers the most common reasons for a court or tribunal to reject a claim on grounds of inadmissibility.[578] *Indeterminacy of the claim's object*: the tribunal is unable to recognize a discrete claim or the remedy sought (and consequently to assess its merits under the relevant applicable law), or the claim litigated is a different one from the one presented in the seisin.[579] *Absence of a genuine legal dispute*: there is no dispute,[580] or the claim refers nominally to norms falling within the

---

577 Because of its apparent self-reference, the category is not employed in this study. However, it might simply indicate all other conditions precedent for the operation of consent, codified in international instruments.

578 Reasons for inadmissibility are not organised in a conceptual taxonomy and might be difficult to predict. See *Application of the Convention on the Prevention and Punishment of the Crime of Genocide* (*Croatia v. Serbia*), Preliminary Objections, Judgment, I.C.J. Reports 2008, 412, 456: '*If the objection is a jurisdictional objection, then since the jurisdiction of the Court derives from the consent of the parties, this will most usually be because it has been shown that no such consent has been given by the objecting State to the settlement by the Court of the particular dispute. A preliminary objection to admissibility covers a more disparate range of possibilities.*'

579 *Certain Phosphate Lands in Nauru* (*Nauru v. Australia*), Preliminary Objections, Judgment, I.C.J. Reports 1992, 240, para. 62–67.

580 In the *Northern Cameroon* case, *above* (n 572), it is unclear whether the Court treated this matter as one of jurisdiction or admissibility. See para. 38: '*Whether or not at the*

jurisdiction of the tribunal, but the question submitted hinges on purely political matters and exceeds the boundaries of adjudication.[581] *Lack of legal interest or mootness*: the claimant bears no legal interest in the dispute,[582] or the case has become moot during the proceedings.[583] *Coordination with connected proceedings*: when there is triple identity between two disputes, *lis pendens* or *res judicata* could arise in international adjudication.[584] Alternatively,

---

moment the Application was filed there was jurisdiction in the Court to adjudicate upon the dispute submitted to it, circumstances that have since arisen render any adjudication devoid of purpose. Under these conditions, for the Court to proceed further in the case would not, in its opinion, be a proper discharge of its duties ... The Court finds that the proper limits of its judicial function do not permit it to entertain the claims submitted'. Waibel above (n 27) 1212 lists this requirement among those of jurisdiction, but also noted the decision in *Larsen v. Hawaiian Kingdom*, above (n 553), in which the tribunal declared itself obliged to consider (*proprio motu*) the absence of a legal dispute and—crucially—the fact that a third country was a necessary third party in the case, as '*objections to the admissibility of arbitral proceedings*' (para. 13.2). *Contra*, see Amerasinghe above (n 552); Shany above (n 557) 69 (see above, where the requirement of existence of a dispute is also listed as a possible obstacle for jurisdiction).

581 *Northern Cameroon* above (n 672) 37.

582 *South West Africa*, Second Phase, Judgment, I.C.J. Reports 1966, 6, para. 44.

583 *Lockerbie*, Preliminary Objections above (n 576) 129, para. 37. This requirement, which in fact is seldom applied in the practice, has been sometimes considered one of jurisdiction, see above (n 572). One case that is arguably treated as one of admissibility is the *Nuclear Tests* (*Australia v. France*), Judgment, I.C.J. Reports 1974, 475–476: '*there is no occasion for a pronouncement in respect of rights and obligations of the Parties concerning the past ...* [the Court] *must not fail to take cognizance of a situation in which* the dispute has disappeared *because the final objective which the Applicant has maintained throughout has been achieved by other means*' (*emphasis added*). *Whereas the Court avoided referring to either category in the judgment, in the earlier Order on preliminary measures it had assessed its own jurisdiction* prima facie, *noting that 'it cannot be assumed a priori ... that the Government of Australia may not be able to establish a legal interest in respect of* [its] *claims entitling the Court* to admit the Application' (emphases added), see *Nuclear Tests* (*Australia v. France*), Interim Protection, Order of 22 June 1973, I.C.J. Reports 1973, 99, para. 23. But see the declaration attached by Judge Jiménez de Aréchaga (ibid., 108), who argued that the existence of a legal interest was a question of merits unfit for determination *prima facie*, and that the applicable test at the stage of the interim measures was one of jurisdiction, i.e. '*whether the parties are in conflict as to their respective rights*'.

584 This is a rare occurrence, as the triple identity test requires the two disputes to share same parties, same object and same legal cause of action. See Anzilotti's dissent in the case *Interpretation of Judgments Nos. 7 and 8* (*Factory at Chorzów*) 1927 PCIJ Series, No. 13, 23, commenting on Article 59 of the Statute of the PCIJ: '*we have here the three traditional elements for identification,* persona, petitum, causa petendi'. The *res judicata* objection was confirmed to concern admissibility by the International Court of Justice in *Question of the*

a court could decide—exercising comity[585]—to refrain from exercising jurisdiction or suspend proceedings if a connected dispute is pending elsewhere, if another forum is fitter for the case (*forum non conveniens*),[586] or if the parties agreed '*to use another method of pacific settlement*'.[587] *Non-exhaustion of local remedies*: the defendant has consented to the use of the international tribunal by a foreigner only as a subsequent and subsidiary forum to its domestic judicial system, not as an alternative.[588] *Procedural irregularities*: the claimant has not complied with the applicable procedure (for instance, it has not respected a deadline for the seisin).[589] Note, however, that the PCIJ declared that it would

Delimitation of the Continental Shelf between Nicaragua and Colombia beyond 200 Nautical Miles from the Nicaraguan Coast (*Nicaragua v. Colombia*), Judgment on the Preliminary Objections of 16 March 2016, para. 53.

585 Luiz Eduardo Salles, *Forum Shopping in International Adjudication: The Role of Preliminary Objections* (CUP 2014) 217. See also Filippo Fontanelli, *Comity* (2015) Westlaw UK Insight.

586 UN Convention on the Law of the Sea, *MOX Plant* (Ireland v. UK), Order No. 3, 42 ILM 1187, 1190 (2003) (PCA, 24 June 24), para. 26; in the case *Arbitral Tribunal Southern Bluefin Tuna Case* (Australia and New Zealand v. Japan) Award on Jurisdiction and Admissibility of 4 August 2000, para. 54 and 65, the tribunal held that it '*lacked jurisdiction*' but also expressly refrained from assessing the matters of admissibility, exercising judicial economy. Moreover, the conclusion of the tribunal was based on Article 281(1) UNCLOS which limits the scope of application of the UNCLOS dispute settlement procedures when an alternative means of dispute resolution has been agreed and has been attempted. In other words, the conclusion relied on a finding of lack of jurisdiction *ratione materiae*.

587 *Application of the Convention on the Prevention and Punishment of the Crime of Genocide* (Croatia v. Serbia), Preliminary Objections, Judgment, I.C.J. Reports 2008, 412, 456. This instance of inadmissibility, perhaps, is better characterised as one of jurisdiction *ratione materiae*, at least when the priority for the alternative forum is expressly envisaged in the instrument establishing the jurisdiction of the tribunal (the parties have consented not to extend the foundational jurisdiction of the court to a category of cases). See for instance Article 282 UNCLOS.

588 Article 42 of the ECHR; Article 5(2)(b) of the ICCPR first Optional Protocol; Article 14 of the ILC Articles on Diplomatic Protection (UN Doc. A/61/10), see for instance *Case concerning Elettronica Sicula* (United States of America v. Italy), Judgment, I.C.J. Reports 1989, 15, para. 59. But consider the ICJ's more recent view, mentioned above, that the previous exhaustion on alternative dispute resolution *fora* required in the compromissory clause is a matter of jurisdiction/competence. See *Application of the International Convention on the Elimination of All Forms of Racial Discrimination* (Georgia v. Russian Federation), Preliminary Objections, Judgment, I.C.J. Reports 2011, 70, 125 (para. 131) and 140 (para. 184).

589 For the practice of the PCIJ and the ICJ, see Kolb (n 446), 165 ff. In particular, it is important to note that '*the Court rejects the idea that defects of form are a fatal bar to its jurisdiction or to the admissibility of a document*' (ibid., 166).

not '*attach to matters of form the same degree of importance which they might possess in municipal law*'.[590] The ICJ has been flexible with formal defects, to the point of implying that it would not refuse to proceed if a procedural flaw were the only reason not to.[591] *Nationality of the claim*: this requisite is critical in the field of diplomatic protection and investor-State disputes. A State cannot espouse a foreign citizen's claim in diplomatic protection; to invoke a protection treaty an investment/investor must have the nationality of a State party to it (other than the host State), at the time of the claim.[592] This requisite can alternatively be considered as one of *recevabilité* or of primary jurisdiction, depending on whether customary law applies or treaty rules, respectively.[593] The constitutive instrument of a tribunal might treat nationality as a matter of jurisdiction, to highlight its fundamental importance in the specific *régime* (for instance, under the ICSID Convention, or the Claims Settlement Declaration establishing the Iran—US Tribunal). This oscillation, similar to that highlighted above related to the procedural preconditions of alternative dispute procedures, revolves perhaps around the relative fixity of the nationality condition (the claim cannot change nationality, but it can be espoused by the right State).

Interestingly enough, the *Monetary Gold* principle is difficult to categorise despite its direct bearing on consent.[594] That a court is unable to hear a dispute entailing the determination of a third party's responsibility seems to flow from the limits of its foundational jurisdiction and the *pacta tertiis* rule.[595] The fact that the parties cannot seek a binding decision on the rights of a third

590 *Mavrommatis* above (n 561).

591 Such as the failure to indicate the precise norms invoked in the application, as required under Art. 32(2) of the Rules of Court, see *Northern Cameroon* (n 572) 27–28.

592 See *Barcelona Traction, Light and Power Company, Limited*, (Belgium v. Spain), Second Phase, Judgment, I.C.J. Reports 1970, 3, 32, para. 32–33 (consider, however, how the Court treated the question of nationality as a matter of *jus standi* rather than mere admissibility; i.e., it looked at whether Belgium was owed any obligations by Spain). An odd case is the investment case *Loewen Group, Inc. and Raymond L. Loewen v. United States of America*, ICSID Case No. ARB(AF)/98/3, Award of 26 June 2003, in which the tribunal decided to dismiss the claim because the investor, which met the nationality requirement at the moment of seisin, had lost the qualifying nationality during the proceedings. The requirement is listed among the instances of inadmissibility in the Croatia v. Serbia Judgment on Preliminary Objections above (n 587) 456.

593 *Nottebohm*, above (n 559), 16, 20; Iran—US Claims Tribunal, *Iran and United States*, Case No. A/18, Decision No. DEC 32-A18-FT (6 April 1984), 5 Iran-US Cl. Trib. Rep. 251.

594 On the difficult classification of this principle, Fontanelli above (n 535) 120–125.

595 See Amerasinghe above (n 35) 90–91.

State suggests a lack of *locus standi*, i.e., a matter of specific jurisdiction.[596] Alternatively, the principle can be regarded as one of admissibility, designed to ensure the propriety of the judicial function: a tribunal can refrain from exercising its (otherwise existing) jurisdiction on the claim if its judgment could undermine the fundamental rule of consent to international obligations and international adjudication.[597] See how the ambiguity of the 'indispensable third party' principle emerged in the characterisation of the doctrine provided by the tribunal of the *Chevron v. Ecuador* arbitration tribunal.[598] At first, the tribunal noted that the principle prevents a court from exercising its validly established jurisdiction (pointing to an objection relating to admissibility):

> although a tribunal *may have jurisdiction* over a dispute it must not or should not exercise that jurisdiction if the very subject-matter of the decision would determine the rights and obligations of a State which is not a party to the proceedings.[599]

In the next paragraph, however, the tribunal considered the *Monetary Gold* principle as one flowing from consent, and accordingly (but contradictorily) situated it among the requirements of jurisdiction:

> no arbitration tribunal *has jurisdiction* over any person unless they have consented. That may be called the 'consent' principle, and *it goes to the question of the tribunal's jurisdiction*.[600]

---

596 Ibid., 77: '*matters of standing* (locus standi) *are concerned with jurisdiction* (compétence) *and not receivability*'. *Contra*, see *Elettronica Sicula SpA* (*ELSI*) (USA v. Italy), I.C.J. Reports 1989, 15; Campbell McLachlan, Laurence Shore and Matthew Weiniger, *International investment arbitration: substantive principles* (OUP 2007) para. 6.93; likewise Wehland above (n 39) 239. It is however possible to consider the *ELSI* case as one hinging on a *question préliminaire du fond*. In *Pan American Energy LLC and BP Argentina Exploration Company v. The Argentine Republic*, ICSID Case No. ARB/03/13, Decision on Preliminary Objections of 27 July 2006 the tribunal rejected the claimant's submissions that objections to the investor's *jus standi* be joined with the merits, and agreed to examine them '*when dealing with jurisdiction*', see para. 209.

597 Shany above (n 527) 798; id. above (n 557) 49; Waibel above (n 27); Arthur above (n 562) 458. *Contra*, see Amerasinghe above (n 35) 93.

598 *Chevron Corporation and Texaco Petroleum Corporation v. The Republic of Ecuador*, UNCITRAL, PCA Case No. 2009–23, Third Interim Award on Jurisdiction and Admissibility of 27 February 2012.

599 Ibid., Part IV, para. 4.60 (emphasis added).

600 Ibid., para. 4.61 (emphases added).

This example unveils another complication: the tribunal, in any specific instance, might find a problem that appears to affect, at the same time, its jurisdiction and the claim's admissibility both. The application of the *Monetary Gold* principle might just be one such instance.[601] Moreover, if one accepts that matters of jurisdiction are simply determined by their inclusion in a binding instrument, it is easy to anticipate instances where the parties chose to elevate a matter of inadmissibility (actionable under the general principles of law, or customary law, or the inherent powers of the tribunal) to a jurisdictional requirement. When that is the case, the court's power to declare a case inadmissible as a matter of judicial propriety is codified and, for this reason alone, turned into a limit to its jurisdiction.

Excéptions préliminaires du fond

At times, a preliminary objection is such that the tribunal is not able to address it conclusively without considering the merits of the case. In this scenario, tribunals can proceed to the examination of the merits suspending the decision on competence.[602]

In light of the generalization mentioned above (all preliminary objections are gathered under the 'jurisdictional' umbrella), these particular objections, whose treatment is non-preliminary by definition, end up having a '*secondary impact*'[603] on the judgment (that is, they are tackled at the stage of the merits).

Already did the PCIJ find little interest in treating this category as a discrete one, noting that the correspondent distinction in domestic procedural laws had little bearing on the functioning of the Court, and that the ultimate purpose of objections purportedly linked with the merits was in any event to stop the Court from ruling on the merits (if after having looked into them).[604] In two cases (*South West Africa* and *Barcelona Traction* (*new application*)), the Court upheld one jurisdictional objection that it had previously joined to

601 See, for another example relating to the finality of judgments challenged for denial of justice, below (n 721).

602 See Dissenting Opinion of Judge Ndiaye in the case *M/V 'SAIGA'* above (n 546) para. 29: '*Autrement dit, la jonction au fond s'impose dans la mesure où une décision sur lesdites exceptions exige un examen de l'intégralité ou de la quasi-intégralité du fond … Car ce que conteste le défendeur, ce n'est pas la recevabilité de la demande au regard de la procédure, mais le droit qui sert de fondement à cette demande. Ce sont des exceptions préliminaires de fond.*'

603 Rosenne and Ronen above (n 543) 820.

604 *German Interests in Upper Silesia* (Germany v. Poland), Judgment of 25 August 1925, P.C.I.J. Series A, No. 6. See also *Panevezys-Saldutiskis Railway* (Estonia v. Lithuania), Preliminary objections, Order of 30 June 1938, P.C.I.J. Series A/B, No. 75, 16.

the merits, therefore pronouncing on it only at the second phase (that usually deals with the merits).

Generally, this category of jurisdictional issues is not a separate one from the ones described above, it just differs from them for not being preliminary in practice.

Applicable Norms and Oil Platforms*—a species of the* excéptions préliminaires du fond

A question on the merits might be framed as an *excéption préliminaire du fond*, if the subject matter of the claim lies outwith the tribunal's jurisdiction.[605] When the claim is based on an erroneous legal characterisation of the facts, the respondent can successfully claim that the norms invoked cannot apply, even taking the factual allegations of the claimants at face value. This scenario, in turn, would determine a lack of jurisdiction *ratione materiae* or of inadmissibility (the claim could theoretically proceed to the merits, but the outcome being pre-determined the tribunal would better decline to entertain it).

When the tribunal is competent only to hear disputes arising from the interpretation and application of a specific instrument, the impossibility of that instrument applying would be fatal to the claim. This is why, as Sperduti noted,

> il arrive assez fréquemment qu'un Etat défendeur, qui se considérait en mesure d'introduire une exception préliminaire de fond s'il la considérait recevable, s'applique à transformer une exception de cette nature en une exception formelle, notamment en une exception d'incompétence.[606]

In this sense, every question of competence *ratione materiae* of a tribunal (in the sense of the power to solve a dispute applying the rules of a certain legal regime) is necessary intertwined with the analysis of the merits. This is because

---

605 Veijo Heiskanen, 'Dealing with Pandora: The Concept of 'Merits' in International Commercial Arbitration' (2006) 22 Arbitration International 597, 603: '*a defence which challenges the admissibility of the claimant's claims on the basis that the subject matter of the dispute is elsewhere can never be considered as possessing 'an exclusively preliminary character.*'

606 Giuseppe Sperduti, 'La recevabilité des exceptions préliminaires de fond dans le procès international' (1970) 53 Rivista di Diritto Internazionale 461, 465; see also Roberto Ago, 'Eccezioni 'non esclusivamente preliminari'' in *Il Processo internzionale, Studi in onore di Gaetano Morelli, Comunicazioni e Studi, vol. XIV* (Giuffré 1975) 1.

the question of the norms applicable to a dispute can only be conclusively defined in light of the facts submitted.[607] As it has been authoritatively noted,

> the issue concerning the competence of an international court or tribunal is precisely [an issue that can never be decided independently of the merits], because it relates to the question of applicable law … and thus raises, in a very specific and concrete way, the question of the competence not only of the court or of the tribunal, but also of the judge or of the arbitrator, in terms of education and otherwise, to deal with the claim.[608]

The divergence between the claim's subject matter and the ICJ's competence *ratione materiae* arose specifically in the case *Oil Platforms*.[609] Whereas the US's objection failed, Judge Higgins cared to elucidate '*the methodology for determining whether a particular claim falls within the compromissory clause of a specific treaty*.'[610] She concluded that

> The Court should thus see if, on the facts as alleged by Iran, the United States actions complained of might violate the Treaty articles.[611]

This test established itself in the practice. A successful *Oil Platforms* objection will result in the dismissal of the claim for inadmissibility, but it would be equally plausible to speak of a lack of jurisdiction *ratione materiae* or, more simply, of an issue of the merits.[612] The hybrid categorisation of this objection derives from its pedigree: it essentially emerged as a gateway objection, so it shares in the preliminary character of other procedural objections, but concerns in fact the merits of the dispute.[613]

607 A learned analysis of what 'merits' means in the arbitration field is Heiskanen above (n 605).

608 Heiskanen above (n 545) 31.

609 *Oil Platforms* (Islamic Republic of Iran v. United States of America), Preliminary Objection, Judgment, I.C.J. Reports 1996, p. 803.

610 Ibid., Separate Opinion of Judge Higgins, 847, para. 2.

611 Ibid., 856, para. 33.

612 I.e., the breach alleged falls under the jurisdiction of the tribunal, but the conduct is *not precluded* but the applicable norms.

613 The preliminary character of any objection is a matter to determine with a view to '*ensure the administration of justice*', see *Mavrommatis* above (n 561) p. 16.

4 Conceptual Difficulties

One common characterisation of the divide between jurisdiction and admissibility refers to the distinction between fundamental and less fundamental procedural impediments. Fundamental flaws would affect the competence of the tribunal to hear the case, whereas other impediments would only prejudice the admissibility of the specific claim.[614] Accordingly, the former would be irremissible whereas reasons for inadmissibility could be either cured or waived by the parties, implicitly by failing to raise them timely or expressly.[615] Generally, flaws pertaining to the foundational jurisdiction can be raised by the tribunal *motu proprio* (or should even be raised *ex officio*), and the parties cannot agree to waive them.[616] This distinction also accounts for the regime of finality mentioned earlier: jurisdictional decisions are more likely to be reviewable because they speak to the delegation of State powers to international courts,[617] whereas admissibility decisions are by definition taken within the remit of the court's delegated powers and are ill-fitted for external review.[618]

These distinctions are either porous (they tolerate overlaps) or inessential (they speak to the effects of the distinction, but do not clarify how to draw it in the first place).[619] Take the case of a failure to exhaust local remedies. This

614 See for instance Douglas above (n 77) 148.

615 Amerasinghe above (n 35) 192. For an example, see HRC, *Husseini v. Denmark*, Communication No. 2243/2013, U.N. Doc. CCPR/C/112/D/2243/2013 (2014), para. 8.3: the Committee does not ascertain whether the author of the communication has exhausted domestic remedies under Article 5(2)(b) of the ICCPR Optional Protocol, noting that the State has not raised a preliminary objection to this effect. Shany and Seetulsingh, in a joint dissenting opinion, objected to the finding of the majority, implicitly considering the State's conduct as a waiver regarding an admissibility flaw. They noted that the HRC should have examined this requirement *proprio motu*, therefore characterising it as a jurisdictional threshold (see on this Shany above (n 557) 136).

616 This common view is expounded for instance in Andrea Marco Steingruber, 'Some remarks on Veijo Heiskanen's Note 'Ménage à trois? Jurisdiction, Admissibility and Competence in Investment Treaty Arbitration' (2014) 29 ICSID Review 675, 681–682.

617 Shany above (n 527).

618 Paulsson above (n 555) 601.

619 Classification can be an arduous task. Cfr the dispirited words of Herman Melville, who advised against using specific elements upon which to build a classification of whales (*Moby Dick; or, The Whale* (1851, ed. Simonds 1922), Chapter 32, 133): '*it may possibly be conceived that, in the internal parts of the whale, in his anatomy—there, at least, we shall be able to hit the right classification. Nay; what thing, for example, is there in the Greenland whale's anatomy more striking than his baleen? Yet we have seen that by his baleen it is impossible correctly to classify the Greenland whale. And if you descend into the bowels of the various leviathans, why there you will not find distinctions a fiftieth part as available*

impediment can be characterised both ways. 1) The parties have agreed that a specific tribunal only hear cases that have been tried domestically (an issue of consent, a fixed delimitation of the tribunal's authority); 2) the claim is not ripe for adjudication (a procedural accident, a curable defect of the claim). Insofar as the conceptual definitions of jurisdiction and admissibility are supposed to exclude each other, but do not, overlaps will occur and render the two categories normatively useless or, worse still, capricious. A pragmatic approach would suggest considering all conditions agreed by the parties as jurisdictional:[620] States confer authority on a court through consent, and by consent can they remove it. Distinctions based on the possibility to waive the requirement, the *ex parte* or *proprio motu* nature of the objections, the allocation of evidentiary burdens, and the possibility of review are not real distinctions: they might specify what follows from, but not what constitutes, the doctrinal division between jurisdiction and admissibility.

Moreover, it is difficult to agree that admissibility requirements can be always waived, or never raised *proprio motu*,[621] that jurisdictional requirements can never be waived and must be reviewed *ex officio*,[622] that a mistaken finding of admissibility is always immune from review,[623] that an admissibility defect

---

to the systematizer as those external ones already enumerated. What then remains? nothing but to take hold of the whales bodily, in their entire liberal volume, and boldly sort them that way. And this is the Bibliographical system here adopted; and it is the only one that can possibly succeed, for it alone is practicable.'

620 Thirlway above (n 539) 114–115.

621 Especially when they constitute safeguards to the propriety of the judicial mandate. See Shany above (n 557) 51, referring to *Northern Cameroons*, 1963 I.C.J. Reports 15, 29: '*The Court itself, and not the parties, must be the guardian of the Court's judicial integrity*'.

622 Suffice it here to recall the *forum prorogatum* doctrine, with respect to ICJ practice. In arbitration, consider *Waguih Elie George Siag and Clorinda Vecchi v. The Arab Republic of Egypt*, ICSID Case No. ARB/05/15, Award of 1 June 2009, para. 189: '*Egypt was able to waive its objections to jurisdiction based on Mr Siag's claimed bankruptcy*' (note that in this case the tribunal characterised all preliminary objections as jurisdictional).

623 See for instance the case *Tahsin Acar v. Turkey*, App. No. 26307/95, Eur. Ct. H.R. 8 (2004). After a first decision of admissibility by the Commission, a Chamber of Court of Human Rights agreed to strike out the case after the unilateral settlement offer made by Turkey (under Article 37 ECHR, allowing the Court to strike out an application from its list of cases, *inter alia*, when '... (*b*) *the matter has been resolved; or* (*c*) *for any other reason established by the Court, it is no longer justified to continue the examination of the application*'). The Grand Chamber, seised by the applicant, reversed the strike out decision, see *Tahsin Acar v. Turkey* (preliminary objection) [GC], no. 26308/95, 6 May 2003, para. 84–85. See Gregory S Weber, 'Who Killed the Friendly Settlement? The Decline of Negotiated Resolutions at the European Court of Human Rights' (2007) 7(2) Pepp. Disp. Resol. L.J. 1, 20 ff.

is always curable,[624] that a jurisdictional requirement can never lapse after the *seisine* of the tribunal,[625] that a jurisdictional flaw cannot be remedied in fresh proceedings.[626]

A line of distinction is difficult to draw in the practice, when procedural objections based on either category are often collapsed and raised by the defendant at the same stage.[627] The case law of the ICJ in this respect is particularly unhelpful, as intimated above. All findings of the ICJ are final and the Court's

624 Think of all the irreversible causes of inadmissibility relating, for instance, to the mootness of the claim, the lack of interest, arguments of *res judicata* or *forum non conveniens*, the claimant's prior behaviour (estoppel, clean hands).

625 According to a well-established principle, jurisdictional requirement are only assessed at the moment of seisin. See for instance *Ampal-American Israel Corporation and others v. Arab Republic of Egypt*, ICSID Case No. ARB/12/11, Award of 1 February 2016, para. 136–137. The tribunal took issue with the fact that the denial of benefits declaration was issued 8 months after the claim was registered by ICSID (the host State should have issued it during the pre-litigation negotiations, to delimit the tribunal's jurisdiction *ex ante*). However, see *Loewen* above (n 592) (the tribunal declined jurisdiction because the claimant had lost the qualifying nationality during the arbitration). It is also possible to hypothesise that the ICJ would not refrain from re-assessing its jurisdiction should one of the States be extinguished during the proceedings. A suggestion in this sense can be read in the dictum of the ICJ in the *Croatia v. Serbia* case, judgment of 3 February 2015, para. 116, relating to the application of the Monetary Gold principle to an extinguished third necessary party: '*That rationale has no application to a State which no longer exists, as is the case with the SFRY, since such a State no longer possesses any rights and is incapable of giving or withholding consent to the jurisdiction of the Court.*' A tribunal dealing with the less radical issue of succession between States noted, however, that '*... jurisdiction is to be determined in light of the situation as it exists on the date the judicial proceedings are instituted.... Though changes in the "identity" of States occur less frequently than changes of the nationality of natural or legal persons, there is no reason why the two should not be treated in the same way.*' See *Mytilineos* above (n 238) para. 159, 162.

626 Consider for instance the ICJ cases *Application of the International Convention on the Elimination of All Forms of Racial Discrimination* (*Georgia v. Russian Federation*) and *Obligations concerning Negotiations relating to Cessation of the Nuclear Arms Race and to Nuclear Disarmament* (*Marshall Islands v. United Kingdom*). In each case, the Court declined jurisdiction because the applicant had failed to carry out certain compulsory procedural steps (consultation, negotiation, exhaustion of alternative means of dispute resolution). It stands to reason that, in spite of the Court's dismissal of the cases for want of jurisdiction, the applicants could comply with these requirements and bring fresh applications. See, on this point, *Urbaser* jurisdiction (n 576) para. 118, which is discussed more in detail below.

627 The ICJ has repeatedly noticed this confusion when analysing the grounds for objection raised by the defendant, see *Nicaragua* (*Jurisdiction and Admissibility*) above (n 572) 429; *Northern Cameroon* (*Preliminary Objections*) above (n 492) 26.

foundational jurisdiction is not limited *ratione materiae*, hence an erroneous labelling of a procedural objection as relating to jurisdiction as opposed to admissibility (or *vice versa*) has no practical consequence. A mislabelled finding of lack of jurisdiction will not be reviewable, just like it would not be if it were correctly characterised as one of inadmissibility. A failure to raise *proprio motu* an objection relating to the specific jurisdiction will often result in the claim falling nevertheless under the Court's subject-matter fundamental competence. For instance, the ICJ has never asked the parties to tackle a jurisdictional issue that they had not raised, possibly due to the application of the principle of *forum prorogatum*, whereby the parties can heal a defect of specific jurisdiction displaying their consent to the continuation of the proceeding after its institution.[628]

To illustrate how consent operates differently on matters of specific and foundational jurisdictions, consider the following examples. The Court could exercise jurisdiction if the defending State failed to invoke a procedural objection (for instance, a reservation *ratione materiae* to the declaration under Article 36 ICJ, or a failure to exhaust local remedies contained in the treaty conferring jurisdiction), but would have to decline a claim brought by an individual, even if the defendant had not raised a procedural objection.[629] Likewise, no jurisdiction can operate when there appears to be no dispute underlying the claim[630]: the existence of a legal dispute is a primary requisite for the institution of any judicial procedure, and the seised tribunal has the competence

628 *Land and Maritime Boundary between Cameroon and Nigeria*, Preliminary Objections, Judgment, I.C.J. Reports 1998, 275, Sep. Opinion Higgins, 345: '*it is in principle for a respondent State to decide what points of jurisdiction and inadmissibility it wishes to advance. If a State is willing to accept the Court's jurisdiction in regard to a matter, it is generally not for the Court—its entitlement to raise points* proprio motu *notwithstanding—to raise further jurisdictional objections.*' A general description of *forum prorogatum* is provided by Judge Lauterpacht in *Application of the Convention on the Prevention and Punishment of the Crime of Genocide* (Bosnia and Herzegovina v. Serbia and Montenegro), Order of 13 September 1993 (Further Requests for the Indication of Provisional Measures), Separate opinion of Judge ad hoc Lauterpacht, 416, para. 24: '[Forum prorogatum] *is the possibility that if State A commences proceedings against State B on a non-existent or defective jurisdictional basis, State B can remedy the situation by conduct amounting to an acceptance of the jurisdiction of the Court*'.

629 Shany above (n 527) 784, frames this remark distinguishing between foundational jurisdiction (on which the parties have no control) and specific jurisdiction (whose lacks can be healed through *forum prorogatum*).

630 *South-West Africa Case* (*Preliminary Objections*) above (n 576) 328.

and the duty to ascertain the presence of this element.[631] The ICJ, for instance, '*must always ... itself be satisfied that a dispute exists*.'[632]

Accordingly, the analysis of each procedural objection has to be performed on a case by case basis, looking at the governing instruments of the tribunal at stake.[633] For example, consider the World Bank Administrative Tribunal. A claim relating to facts occurred before the entry into force of its Statute would be rejected for lack of jurisdiction *ratione temporis*.[634] Article II of the Statute, in turn, provides that applications '*shall be admissible ... if filed within one hundred and twenty days after* [the occurrence of certain qualifying events]'. In this case, the requirement is expressly one of admissibility *ratione temporis*.[635] Whereas the former element is surely jurisdictional (it pertains to the foundational jurisdiction of the Tribunal) the latter is labelled as pertaining to admissibility but could just as well be characterised as a matter of specific jurisdiction *ratione temporis*, relating to the competence of the Tribunal over the specific dispute.[636] In this case, the Treaty language is dispositive of the issue, rather than the substance of the requirement.[637]

631 *South-West Africa Case (Second Phase)* above (n 582) 33; *East Timor Case* above (n 533) 100.

632 *Land and Maritime Boundary*, Sep. Opinion Higgins above (n 628) 347; *Mavrommatis* above (n 561).

633 For instance, issues of nationality of the parties, that are customarily deemed to be relevant for the *recevabilité* of the claim (see *Nottebohm*, above (n 559)), are instead treated as a requisite of primary jurisdiction by the Iran—US Tribunal. Another example might be the competence *ratione temporis*, which bears a more fundamental character before tribunals like the ICTY, the jurisdiction of which is defined precisely in connection to a fixed period.

634 *George Kavoukas et al. v. International Bank for Reconstruction and Development*, Decision No. 3 of 5 June 1981.

635 It was indeed treated as a matter of admissibility in *Elizabeth Tweddle v. International Bank for Reconstruction and Development*, Decision No. 508 of 29 May 2015 (Preliminary Objection), para. 25–31.

636 For a similar requirement *ratione temporis*, see NAFTA, Articles 1116(2) and 1117(2).

637 See also the example of the European Commission of Human Rights, case *Macit and 53 others v. Turkey* decision on admissibility of 31 March 1993, App. No. 19934/92 (Sperduti was sitting on the bench). After noting that the facts alleged by the claimants had taken place before the cut-off date after which Turkey accepted the Commission's competence over individual applications. The Commission on one hand noted that '*la requête échappe à la compétence* ratione temporis *de la Commission*,' but concluded on the other hand that the application was inadmissible ('*irrecevable*').

Yuval Shany advanced a proposal to sketch a principled taxonomy—less reliant on language conventions or analogical patterns.[638] Shany conceded that the interchangeable labelling of the same factors indicates their essential similarity: saying that a procedural impediment entails a lack of jurisdiction *ratione personae*, instead of inadmissibility *ratione personae*, is sometimes a matter of convention. As such, the current understanding is unsatisfactory because it has no normative value. Shany suggested arranging the distinction between jurisdiction and admissibility along the critical criteria of discretion and propriety. Whenever the claim is dismissed for breach of an objective rule regarding the dimensions (the *rationes*) or conditions of the court's powers (e.g., for lack of qualifying nationality, failure to comply with a precondition, inapplicability *ratione temporis* of the rule invoked) the problem is one of jurisdiction.[639]

Conversely, inadmissibility would operate whenever tribunals exercise judicial discretion and refrain from entertaining a claim based on considerations of propriety.[640] For example, the tribunal could opt for inadmissibility when an essentially but not formally identical claim is pending elsewhere, there is abuse of process, the object of the dispute is not arbitrable or susceptible to adjudication, there is no legal interest at stake, the claimant did not come to court with clean hands or is otherwise estopped from bringing the claim.[641]

---

638 The proposal is briefly but clearly articulated in his Chapter of the *Handbook* above (n 527).

639 Shany above (n 527) 785: '*The scope of jurisdiction conferred upon international courts thus consists of the intersection between the different jurisdictional dimensions (often phrased in positive terms) and the jurisdictional conditions (often phrased in negative terms) found in the relevant jurisdiction-creating instruments.*'

640 The reasoning seems to be foreshadowed *Waste Management, Inc. v. United Mexican States*, ICSID Case No. ARB(AF)/98/2, Dissenting Opinion of Keith Highet, of 8 May 2000, see para. 58: '*admissibility is whether the case itself is defective—whether it is appropriate for the tribunal to hear it.*' However, it is doubtful whether the thrust of Highet's reasoning was in the remark matter about appropriateness. His reasoning seemed to inscribe itself in the mainstream view that admissibility depends on the features of the claim. Another precursor of Shany's approach is the view of Rosenne, see Shabtai Rosenne, 'International Courts and Tribunals, Jurisdiction and Admissibility of Inter-State Applications' (2006) Max Planck Encyclopaedia of Public International Law, para. 2: admissibility '*may import an element of discretion that has to be exercised not whimsically but strictly in accordance with legal criteria.*'

641 The gist of Shany's proposal seems to be in line with Judge Fitzmaurice's separate opinion in *Northern Cameroons (Cameroon v. UK)*, 1963 ICJ 15, 101: '*… the real distinction and test would seem to be whether or not the objection is based on, or arises from, the jurisdictional clause or clauses under which the jurisdiction of the tribunal is said to exist. If so, the objection is basically one of jurisdiction. If it is founded on considerations lying outside the ambit*

2 *The Implications of This Blur for Investment Arbitration*

One of the main claims of this study is that there is no reliable line between jurisdiction and admissibility, either in the practice of international law proceedings or in investment arbitration. This Section zooms in on the practice of investment disputes: whereas Part A was devoted to the practice *tout court*, this section will examine a selection of hard cases, in which the blur affects the reasoning of the tribunals and the outcome of the disputes.

By way of introduction, note the dispirited words of the tribunal in *Apotex v. US* (UNCITRAL), referring to the requirement of finality of judicial acts in connection with denial of justice claims and the futility exception:

> The Parties have differed … on the precise calibration of the "obviously futile" exception. At the outset of the oral hearing, the Tribunal questioned the proper characterisation of this objection, and in particular whether it raised an issue of jurisdiction or admissibility, or whether it might also be viewed as a preliminary substantive objection. This is a debate with a long heritage as a matter of international law, and long-divided views.… In line with both Parties' approach, the Tribunal proceeds on the basis that this objection concerns the Tribunal's jurisdiction *ratione materiae*. In the alternative, the Tribunal has also considered the matter in terms of the admissibility of claims.[642]

Whereas the tribunal's approach is commendable for acknowledging the debate,[643] the arbitrators avoided to take a position and relied on the parties' characterisation. When the distinction entails no practical difference, doctrinal precision is not necessary. However, there are cases in which the difference matters. In investment arbitration, the practice is still confused about, or uninterested in, the distinction. The scholarship has diligently borrowed from

---

of any jurisdictional clause, and not involving the interpretation or application of such a provision, then it will normally be an objection to the recevability of the claim.'

642 *Apotex* UNCITRAL above (n 246).

643 However, it is important to note that the exhaustion of local remedies in a denial of justice claim is perhaps better characterised as a '*substantive law requirement*' (see Shany above (n 557) 100) rather than a procedural issue. As such, it should be reviewed at the merits stage, or at most at the *Oil Platforms* stage of the jurisdictional stage. See, for instance, *Pantechniki* above (n 90) para. 102. A similar characterisation appears in *Mytilineos* above (n 238) para. 212: '*In the final award the* Loewen *tribunal did not entertain any jurisdictional challenge to the claim brought against the United States. Rather, it found that there was a substantive obligation incumbent upon claimants to challenge lower court judgments in order to invoke the international responsibility of the forum State for a denial of justice.*'

the field of international law the alleged hallmarks of each category, and some authors have accepted that a distinction exists and is positively identifiable. Typically, they explain how jurisdiction and admissibility differ in relation to reviewability of the determination; allocation of the pertaining evidentiary burdens; invocability *ex officio*, waivability and timeliness of the respective objections; curability of the underlying flaws; essential characters (tribunal's power versus claim's defects).[644]

Section (1), below, accounts for the difficulty to tell jurisdiction from admissibility in investment arbitration, in light of the remarks made above (in **Part A**) about the corresponding difficulty in international legal proceedings at large. The main take-away of this section is that the prevailing taxonomies are unsatisfactory. Section (2) zooms in and tackles selected scenarios in which these doctrinal shortcomings affect the outcome of the proceedings, or simply undermine the principle of legal certainty. These, as will be shown, are the cases where the elusive line of distinction is critical, and clarity more urgently needed.

1 The Line between Jurisdiction and Admissibility in Investment Arbitration

When it comes to assess the host State's consent and its jurisdictional implications, it is impossible to find a consistent use of the concepts of jurisdiction and admissibility in investment arbitration. The ICSID Convention and most investment treaties do not differentiate between jurisdictional, admissibility and procedural requirements, nor do they specify which are mandatory and which are not.[645] Moreover, the investment arbitration practice is influenced by the cognate practice in international commercial arbitration, in which a similar confusion exists regarding procedural requirements.[646] As a result, the distinction between jurisdiction and admissibility, tentatively outlined above in the field of public international law litigation, is all the more difficult to trace in the practice of investment arbitration.[647]

644 See in particular Waibel above (n 27) and Wehland above (n 39) 232–234.

645 *Ambiente Ufficio S.p.A. and others v. Argentine Republic*, ICSID Case No. ARB/08/9 (formerly *Giordano Alpi and others v. Argentine Republic*) Decision on Jurisdiction and Admissibility of 8 February 2013, para. 572.

646 For an exhaustive overview of pre-arbitration requirements in the practice of commercial and investment tribunals, see Born and Šćekić above (n 574) 227.

647 The difference between jurisdiction and competence is largely ignored.

A Confused Practice: The Example of the Investor's Misconduct

There are several reasons why, arguably, the conceptual essence of these two notions is blurred almost insolubly and, at any rate, a normative classification is elusive. First, matters of jurisdiction and admissibility are conflated in the phase of the procedural objections.[648] In this sense, the pragmatic stance of several tribunals is not to fixate on a distinction that might not reflect a difference: if upheld, a preliminary objection will prevent the review of the merits, whatever its label.[649] Second, specific investment agreements, the ICSID Convention (when applicable) and other procedural instruments like the UNCITRAL Convention contain different language concerning the powers of the tribunal. It is therefore possible that a matter of admissibility under the practice governed by general international law is considered one of jurisdiction under the applicable treaty rules (the most common examples being the requirements of nationality and local exhaustion[650]). Third, when a tribunal is established *ad hoc* to hear a specific claim the conceptual distinction between competence (the power to hear a category of disputes, and a specific dispute in particular) and admissibility (the specific claim's capability to be heard by that tribunal) is very porous.

A good example in point is the arbitral practice relating to the allegations of corruption, or illegality *lato sensu*, on the part of the investor.[651] If a tribunal upholds these assertions, what are the consequences? In the abstract, it is possible to anticipate:

---

648 Which often, but not always, are treated in a different stage of the proceedings. On bifurcation, see Lucy Greenwood, 'Does Bifurcation Really Promote Efficiency?' (2011) 28 Journal of International Arbitration 105.

649 Ian Laird, 'A Distinction without a Difference? An Examination of the Concepts of Admissibility and Jurisdiction in Salini v. Jordan and Methanex v. USA' in Todd Weiler (ed), *International Investment law and Arbitration: Leading Cases from ICSID, NAFTA and Customary International Law* (Cameron May 2005) 201.

650 Whereas exhaustion of local remedies in normally inapplicable in the field of investment arbitration, States can make it a pre-arbitration requirement. See Christoph Schreuer, *The ICSID Convention: A Commentary* (CUP 2001) 392.

651 These cases are to be distinguished from the scenario in which the investor is not implicated (for instance, when the State is alleged to have attempted extortion). A perceptive commentary of this set of cases in contained in Aloysius P Llamzon, *Corruption in International Investment Arbitration* (OUP 2014) and in the book review Joan E Donoghue, 'The Corruption Trump in Investment Arbitration' (2015) 30(3) ICSID Review 756–761. See also Attila Tanzi, 'The Relevance of the Foreign Investor's Good Faith' in Attila Tanzi, Andrea Gattini, Filippo Fontanelli (eds), *General Principles of Law and International Investment Arbitration* (Brill 2018) 193.

a) a lack of jurisdiction[652] of the tribunal *ratione materiae* (particularly if there is a treaty[653] or statutory[654] clause requiring the investment's legality under domestic law but, arguably, also when there is none[655]); and/or

652 *Fraport AG Frankfurt Airport Services Worldwide v. The Republic of the Philippines* (Fraport I), ICSID Case No. ARB/03/25, Award of 16 August 2007, para 396–404. *Fraport AG Frankfurt Airport Services Worldwide v. Republic of the Philippines*, ICSID Case No. ARB/11/12, Award of 10 December 2014, para. 467–468; *Alasdair Ross Anderson and ors v. Costa Rica*, ICSID Case No. ARB(AF)/07/3, Award of 19 May 2010, para. 59; *Inceysa Vallisoletana S.L. v. Republic of El Salvador*, ICSID Case No. ARB/03/26, Award of 2 August 2006, para. 207. See also, for a discussion of the applicable law to this kind of illegality objections, *Oxus* above (n 140) para. 705 ff.

653 *Metal-Tech Ltd v. Republic of Uzbekistan*, ICSID Case No ARB/10/3, Award of 4 October 2013. An accurate analysis of the possible effects of domestic legality clauses is found in Cameron A Miles, 'Corruption, Jurisdiction and Admissibility in International Investment Claims' (2012) 3(2) Journal of International Dispute Settlement 329, 343 ff. A straightforward case of application of a specific domestic legality clause is the dispute *Yaung Chi Oo Trading Pte Ltd v Government of the Union of Myanmar*, ASEAN Case No ARB/01/1, Award of 31 March 2003, see para. 62. In this case, the applicable investment treaty (the ASEAN Investment Agreement) contained an explicit requirement that investments be approved and registered by the host State. The tribunal thus declined jurisdiction *ratione materiae*. Lack of approval of the investment determined also the lapse of the tribunal's jurisdiction in the case *Gruslin v. Malaysia*, ICSID Case No. ARB/99/3, Award of 27 November 2000, para. 25.5.

654 See for instance *Gaëta* above (n 46) para. 232–233. The Guinean statute providing for the right to launch ICSID arbitration required that foreign investments be approved and comply with domestic laws.

655 *Plama Consortium Limited v. Republic of Bulgaria*, ICSID Case No ARB/03/24, Award of 27 August 2008, para. 138: '*Unlike a number of Bilateral Investment Treaties, the* [Energy Charter Treaty] *does not contain a provision requiring the conformity of the Investment with a particular law. This does not mean, however, that the protections provided for by the ECT cover all kinds of investments, including those contrary to domestic or international law.... The Tribunal concludes that the substantive protections of the ECT cannot apply to investments that are made contrary to law*'. According to Miles above (n 653) 338, this passage would suggest that corruption would entail the inadmissibility of the claim: '*where a tribunal simply refers to the dismissal of a claim or a general refusal to extend the protections of an IIA to a particular investment, the tribunal is generally holding the claim in question inadmissible*'; the same view is shared by Newcombe above (n 440) 197. *Ampal* above (n 625) para. 301: '*It is a well-established principle of international law that a tribunal constituted on the basis of an investment treaty has no jurisdiction over a claimant's investment which was made illegally in violation of the laws and regulations of the Contracting State*'; see also *Getma International and others v. Republic of Guinea*, ICSID Case No. ARB/11/29, Award of 16 August 2016, para. 174. See also *David Minnotte and Robert Lewis v. Republic of Poland*, ICSID Case No. ARB(AF)/10/1, Award of 16 May 2014, para. 131 (corruption

b) the inadmissibility of the claim under the doctrines of *ordre public international*,[656] clean hands,[657] estoppel, abuse of rights/process[658] or *ex injuria jus non oritur*; and/or
c) a finding on the merits against the investor;[659] and/or, possibly,
d) a finding on the merits that might ultimately favour the investor but takes the illegality into account in the calculation of damages owed by the State,[660] or even just in the allocation of legal costs.

---

disqualifies the investment from treaty protection). It is however doubtful whether legality could be an implicit requirement of investments or whether an *'illegal or bad-faith investment remains an investment*', see Cyrus Benson, Penny Madden and Ceyda Knoebel, 'Covered investment' in Barton Legum (ed), *The Investment Treaty Arbitration Review* (Law Business Research 2016) 15, citing *Quiborax S.A., Non Metallic Minerals S.A. and Allan Fosk Kaplún v. Plurinational State of Bolivia*, ICSID Case No. ARB/06/2, Decision on Jurisdiction of 27 September 2012, para. 226; *Metal-Tech Ltd. v. Republic of Uzbekistan*, ICSID Case No. ARB/10/3, Award of 4 October 2013, para. 127; *Liman Caspian Oil BV and NCL Dutch Investment BV v. Republic of Kazakhstan*, ICSID Case No. ARB/07/14, Excerpts of Award of 22 June 2010, para. 187; *Saba Fakes v. Republic of Turkey*, ICSID Case No. ARB/07/20, Award of 14 July 2010, para. 114, 119; *Oostergetel* above (n 28) para. 176, 178 (the tribunal's jurisdiction requires the legality of the investment's making even in the silence of the treaty).

656 *World Duty Free* above (n 29) para. 157, 188. See Newcombe above (n 440) 196–197.

657 Patrick Dumberry and Gabrielle Dumas-Aubin, 'The Doctrine of "Clean Hands" and the Inadmissibility of Claims by Investors Breaching International Human Rights Law' (2013) 10(1) Transnational Dispute Management.

658 *Phoenix* above (n 254) para. 100.

659 *Plama* above (n 655) para. 112 and 135. It is however not too clear from this award whether the matter is one of merits or it is just joined to the merits phase. Para. 138 is particularly ambiguous, see above (n 655). A good instance of this approach is the *Oxus* case above (n 140). For instance, the investor's irregularities contributed to the tribunal's determination that a governmental audit was not arbitrary or unfair—and therefore did not breach the FET standard, para. 799. Likewise, the tribunal concluded that the non-renewal or non-extension of certain licenses did not breach the FET obligation, since the investor had failed to comply with the applicable regulations, see para. 802–803 ('*the Complex State Audit ... identified serious non compliances with various regulations, including on the operational level ...* [thus] *Respondent had sufficient justifiable reasons not to renew or issue such licenses.*' Likewise, see *Minnotte* above (n 655) para. 163: '*It is ... entirely possible that the conduct of a third party, or a claimant's negligence, may justify specific conduct of a respondent that could in other circumstances amount to a violation of the BIT.*'

660 *MTD Equity Sdn. Bhd. & MTD Chile SA v. Chile*, ICSID Case No. ARB/01/7, Award of 25 May 2004, para. 242–243.

These consequences are radically different, but they do not necessarily exclude each other and it is not possible to maintain with any precision, at the state, which is normatively correct.[661]

A plausible rule of thumb relates to the time of the wrongdoing: if it is committed before the investment is established, or in connection with its establishment, there is a lack of jurisdiction.[662] If the misconduct arises subsequently, the problem is one of admissibility or merits.[663] For an example of this approach, consider the reasoning of the *Oxus* tribunal:

> ... the Arbitral Tribunal finds that only this argument [i.e., the claimant's misrepresentation allegedly occurred before or during the making of the investment] is relevant to determine whether Claimant's investment qualifies for protection under the BIT. As concerns Respondent's contentions regarding allegedly ill-gotten profits through the unlawful operation of AGF and the violation of currency regulations, they are irrelevant for the issue of jurisdiction or admissibility. They may nevertheless be relevant when assessing the justifiable character of certain of Respondent's actions, which Claimant claims are in breach of the BIT protection standards or as an element of the evaluation of damages and will thus, to the extent necessary, be examined in such contexts.[664]

661 A recent critique of the current situation is contained in Miles above (n 653) and Newcombe above (n 440).

662 This practice mirrors that relating to the requirement that the investment be 'admitted' by the host State, which stands to apply only '*at the time of entry into the country and not during the entire operation of the project.*' See *Churchill* above (n 13) para. 290; see also *Minnotte v. Poland* above (n 655) para. 132: there are cases in which '*fraud is so manifest, and so closely connected to facts (such as the making of an investment) which form the basis of a tribunal's jurisdiction as to warrant a dismissal of claims in limine for want of jurisdiction.*'

663 Miles above (n 663) 339–340. This approach is pragmatic but ultimately stands on the assumption that there is a legality clause (not a given) and that is refers to investments 'made' in accordance with domestic law. See *Copper Mesa v. Ecuador* above (n 26), para. 5.54–5.55. See also *Teinver* above (n 190) para. 344 (note that the applicable BIT, between Argentina and Spain, includes a domestic legality clause at Article 1(2)); *Oostergetel* above (n 28) para. 176 (issues of management of the investment pertains to the merits); *Anatolie Stati et al. v. Republic of Kazakhstan*, Arbitration SCC V (116/2010), Award of 19 December 2013, para. 812.

664 *Oxus* above (n 140) para. 709.

The *Copper Mesa* tribunal also relied on this distinction, when interpreting a legality clause of the applicable investment treaty. It noted that elevating post-establishment wrongdoing as a jurisdictional barrier would be an excessive aggravation on the investor and would raise the question as to the required seriousness of the wrongdoing. The better solution, in the tribunal's view, was to deal with subsequent illegality at the stage of the merits.[665]

The tribunal, however, did not exclude the possibility that a clean hands objection regarding post-establishment misconduct could pertain to the admissibility of the claim (rather than the merits). Whilst it accepted this characterisation in principle,[666] it also noted that in the instant case the host State's failure to react to the alleged misconduct under international norms estopped it from challenging the admissibility of the claim.[667] As for the separate allegations of misconduct under domestic law, the tribunal explained that they should be dealt with at the merits stage. Interestingly, the tribunal did not simply join the analysis of this preliminary objection to the merits, in light of the factual determinations required to assess it. Instead, it re-framed the objection as a plea of defense on the merits:

> the Tribunal there prefers to take into account the Claimant [sic: presumably Respondent]'s case not in the form of the doctrine of unclean hands as such, but rather under analogous doctrines of causation and contributory fault applying to the merits of the Claimant's claims arising from events subsequent to the acquisition of its investment. That result, based on the Respondent's case on the merits, strikes the Tribunal as more legally appropriate to this case than an outright dismissal of the Claimant's claims (in regard to the Junín concessions) on the ground of inadmissibility.[668]

Whereas the finding is plausible, it shows the difficulty of the tribunal in the characterisation of the host State's objection. The language (*'prefers'*; *'more ...*

665 Ibid., para. 5.56: '*the jurisdictional significance of the requirement of legality was exhausted once the investment was made.*'

666 Ibid., 5.61 (emphasis added).

667 Ibid., 5.63–5.64: '*... as regards international law, international public policy and human rights, not a single complaint was made by the Respondent against the Claimant at the time. Such a complaint surfaced for the first time after the commencement of this arbitration.... In these circumstances, the Tribunal considers that it is far too late for the Respondent to raise such objections to the Tribunal's exercise of jurisdiction in this arbitration.*'

668 Ibid., para. 5.65.

appropriate') is tentative and the reasoning is not cogent ('*the outright dismissal*' of a claim being indeed the correct consequence of its inadmissibility, it cannot be portrayed as an absurd occurrence, such as to require re-framing the objection as a matter of merits). The tribunal used the doctrine of contributory loss, coloured by the 'unclean hands' allegations, to determine that the claimant was responsible for 30% of the injury suffered.[669] In this dispute case it is possible to see how the same allegations were raised, considered, partly upheld and ultimately applied in relation to all possible stages of the proceedings: jurisdiction, admissibility, liability, compensation.

This variety of legal consequences was noted by the *Churchill* tribunal. In the dispute, it was found that the mining licenses on which the claim was based were forged by an associate of the claimant.[670] After reviewing the diverse characterisations made in the case-law, the tribunal simply noted that the claims, vitiated by a large-scale fraudulent scheme, could not '*benefit from investment protection*' and were inadmissible.[671] The tribunal quoted approvingly the *Minnotte v. Poland* award, and the test developed therein to decide cases of alleged fraud which were not clearly attributed to the claimant, but from which the claimant's claim sought to benefit. The *Minnotte* tribunal considered that a deliberate failure '*to make inquiries which might ... have unearthed evidence of fraud*'[672] could '*vitiate a claim*'[673] on the merits, but could not affect the tribunal's jurisdiction, or render the claim inadmissible. This barely sketched test to assess the merits was used by the *Churchill* tribunal in flagrant disregards of the *Minnotte* tribunal's instructions, that is, precisely to determine inadmissibility of the claim. The juxtaposed awards in the *Minnotte* and *Churchill* cases display, again, the permeability of the prevailing legal categories when at stake are the legal consequences of misconduct related to the investment or the investor.

An Irrelevant Distinction?

The doctrinal hesitations of the *Copper Mesa* tribunal are not surprising, giving that a clear distinction between jurisdiction and admissibility does not

669 Ibid., 6.102.

670 *Churchill* above (n 13) Award of 6 December 2016, para. 494: '*A review of international cases shows that fraudulent conduct can affect the jurisdiction of the tribunal, or the admissibility of (all or some) claims, or the merits of a dispute.*'

671 Ibid., para. 528.

672 *Minnotte* above (n 655) para. 139.

673 Ibid., para. 163.

exist in the practice.[674] The conceptual overlap is often irrelevant for practical purposes[675] and tribunals are used to pointing that out.[676] Consider for instance the forceful remarks of the tribunal in the *L.E.S.I. v. Algeria* case:

> dans les procédures CIRDI, la distinction est sans portée pratique, à la différence de ce qui peut valoir dans d'autres procédures arbitrales; en effet, les recours à l'encontre des décisions rendues à propos de l'une ou de l'autre question ne sont pas différents, dans le système de la Convention, qu'il s'agisse de compétence ou de fins de non-recevoir.[677]

A similar approach has prevailed in NAFTA arbitration. The *Mondev* tribunal pointed to a common distinction between '*issues going to their jurisdiction and questions of procedure in relation to a claim which is within jurisdiction*'.[678] Nevertheless, it noted that NAFTA '*elides that distinction*'[679] and therefore all procedural conditions really go to the extent of the parties' consent to

674 In *Enron Corporation and Ponderosa Assets, LP v Argentine Republic*, ICSID Case No ARB/01/3, Decision on Jurisdiction of 14 January 2004, para. 33, the tribunal noted that the ICSID framework only contemplates jurisdiction and competence, therefore the category of admissibility does not appear necessary.

675 See for instance *Corona Materials LLC v. Dominican Republic*, ICSID Case No. ARB(AF)/14/3, Award on Preliminary Objections of 31 May 2016, para. 191. The tribunal, commenting on a three-year limitation period for the launching of arbitration, did not qualify it as a limit of jurisdiction or admissibility, and simply made the pragmatic point that the '*Parties have plainly conditioned their consents to arbitration. If a claimant does not comply with the [time-limit], its claim cannot be submitted to arbitration.*' In para. 280 the tribunal, however, noted specifically that since the Claimant's request for arbitration had been filed too late, the tribunal had '*no jurisdiction over the claims.*'

676 See for instance *Bayindir* above (n 38) para. 87: '*The Tribunal will examine Pakistan's objections in turn, without distinguishing between objections to the jurisdiction of the Tribunal and objections to the admissibility of the claims.*' This approach was followed in several disputes, see for instance Heiskanen above (n 38) 232–233, and cases mentioned in the footnotes accompanying the text.

677 *Consortium Groupement L.E.S.I.-DIPENTA v. République algérienne démocratique et populaire*, ICSID Case No. ARB/03/08, Award of 10 January 2005, Part II, para. 2. The ICSID translation reads: '*It is true that, in ICSID proceedings, the distinction is without practical consequences, in contrast to what may be the case in other arbitration procedures: indeed, recourse against decisions rendered on one question or the other does not differ in the system instituted by the Convention, whether they relate to jurisdiction or to admissibility.*'

678 *Mondev* above (n 13) para. 42.

679 Ibid.

arbitration,[680] save for procedural requirements of minor scope which would not be read '*in an excessively technical way*'.[681]

Even when the distinction surfaces in the practice, sometimes it is for the sake of doctrinal accuracy rather than to support a critical passage of the reasoning. An example is found in the award of the *S.G.S. v. Philippines* case. The dispute hinged on the respondent's invocation of a forum-selection clause in the contract with the claimant, which indicated domestic courts for the resolution of disputes. Pursuant to this clause, the tribunal ultimately declined to entertain the claim—which was reserved to the local judiciary. However, the tribunal took pains to characterise the issue as one of admissibility rather than jurisdiction, observing that the jurisdiction of the tribunal, as determined by treaty law, could not be curtailed by the stipulations contained in a private contract. The contractual forum selection clause did not affect the tribunal's jurisdiction, but entailed the inadmissibility of the claim.[682]

In *Micula*, the tribunal echoed some of the commonly cited differences between jurisdiction and admissibility: reasons for inadmissibility can arise or be removed after the seisin[683] and must be raised by the parties—as opposed to reasons for lack of jurisdiction which the tribunal can raise *motu proprio*.[684] However, the distinction played little role in the judgment and the tribunal was ready to concede that the labelling depends on the context and that the utility of the notion of admissibility in ICSID proceedings is dubious.[685] The *Supervision v. Costa Rica* tribunal took pains to expound the distinction between jurisdiction and admissibility and its implications.[686] However, the resulting remarks are uncharacteristically superficial and rehash the

680 See Article 1122.

681 *Mondev* above (n 13) para. 44.

682 *SGS v. Philippines* above (n 38) para. 154.

683 *Joan Micula, Viorel Micula, S.C. European Food S.A., S.C. Starmii S.R.L. and S.C. Multipack S.R.L. v. Romania*, ICSID Case No. ARB/05/20, Decision on Jurisdiction and Admissibility of 24 September 2008, para. 64: '[W]*hen an objection relates to a requirement contained in the text on which consent is based, it remains a jurisdictional objection. If such a requirement is not satisfied, the Tribunal may not examine the case at all for lack of jurisdiction. By contrast, an objection relating to admissibility will not necessarily bar the Tribunal from examining the case if the reasons for the inadmissibility of the claim are capable of being removed and are indeed removed at a subsequent stage. In other words, consent is a prerequisite for the jurisdiction of the Tribunal*'.

684 Ibid., para. 65: '*a tribunal can rule on and decline its jurisdiction even where no objection to jurisdiction is raised if there are sufficient grounds to do so on the basis of the record.*'

685 Ibid., para. 63.

686 *Supervision v. Costa Rica* above (n 90) para. 268–276.

usual distinction (limits of the tribunal's powers *versus* defects of the claim) and the obvious conclusion that admissibility must be examined after jurisdiction.[687] In the application of these principles, the distinction proved largely irrelevant: the tribunal qualified as matters of inadmissibility issues that could as well be read to delimit the tribunal's jurisdiction. It rejected some of the investor's claims because the claimant had breached an express fork-in-the road requirement, by failing to discontinue court proceedings relating to the same claims;[688] other claims were rejected for failure to provide notice before launching arbitration. As regards the second grounds for inadmissibility, a couple of hints suggest that the tribunal was less clear about the distinction between jurisdiction and admissibility than it declared to be. First, it introduced the notice requirement as an '*important element of the State's consent to arbitration*',[689] using language typically associated to the tribunal's jurisdiction. Second, it quoted approvingly the *Burlington v. Ecuador* tribunal, which also considered a failure to notify a dispute to be grounds for inadmissibility. In that case, the tribunal appeared comfortable to conflate inadmissibility and lack of jurisdiction, as this short quote illustrates:

> Claimant failed to abide by the conditions for acceptance of the offer of ICSID arbitration contained in Article VI(3)(a) of the Treaty ... and *this claim is therefore inadmissible*.... As a result, the Tribunal upholds Respondent's objection and declares that *it lacks jurisdiction* over Claimant's Treaty claim.[690]

The *Achmea* tribunal[691] recited the canon endorsed in *Micula* and *Supervision* but somewhat revealed its contradictions. First, it set a deadline to the respondent for the submission of procedural objections pertaining also to the jurisdiction of the tribunal,[692] warning that further objections would be

687 For a critical reading of the award, see Filippo Fontanelli and Attila Tanzi, 'Jurisdiction and Admissibility in Investment Arbitration. A View from the Bridge at the Practice' (2017) 16(1) The Law and Practice of International Courts and Tribunals 3, 10–11.

688 Ibid., para. 330–331.

689 Ibid., para. 339.

690 *Burlington v. Ecuador* on Jurisdiction 2010 above (n 161) para. 317–318.

691 *Achmea* above (n 60).

692 See the letter to the parties dated 31 March 2013, quoted in footnote 147 of the award: '*the Respondent shall file a statement containing all and any of its objections to the jurisdiction of this Tribunal and to the admissibility of Claimant's claims to be submitted on or before 14 June 2013, failing which the Respondent will have waived the possibility to raise any further objections thereafter*'.

regarded as waived; then it proclaimed that jurisdictional objections must be considered by the tribunal irrespective of the parties' invoking them, implicating that no waiver is possible and, it would follow logically, no deadline appropriate.[693] The distinction in any event played no apparent role in the decision. It only allowed the tribunal to announce its right to rebrand some of the respondent's jurisdictional objections as relating in fact to admissibility.[694] This was ultimately unnecessary; the claim was dismissed over a finding of lack of jurisdiction *ratione materiae* (the claimant had failed to show a *prima facie* case under the *Oil Platforms* test). In *Isolux*, the tribunal noted that the characterisation of an objection affected the sequencing of the decision: admissibility objections must be examined '*at the outset of the merits review*'.[695]

In *Abaclat*, the tribunal noted that whereas the existence and validity of the claimant's consent was a precondition to the tribunal's jurisdiction, the validity of the power of attorney which expressed such consent and empowered the legal representative was an issue of admissibility.[696] The distinction entailed a different applicable law: whereas general international law regulates the existence of consent, the instruments of representation are governed by the ICSID Rules (Rule 18), possibly in light of domestic law.[697] The distinction did not seem to matter to the outcome.

The *Urbaser* tribunal took issues with some of these common-place views regarding the distinction between admissibility and jurisdiction, noting they might have '*theoretical appeal but add*[] *nothing*' to the task of interpreting BITs.[698] It contested the view that non-compliance with admissibility criteria might be agreed or acquiesced to.[699] It also rejected the ideas that admissibility

---

693 *Achmea* above (n 60) para. 120.

694 Ibid. On this point see Amerasinghe above (n 35) 78–79. The Author observes that, as a matter of principle, rules requiring that jurisdictional pleas be made early in the procedure (see for instance Rule 21(3) of the Iran-US Claims Tribunal) are unable to '*affect or change the jurisdictional authority of the tribunal' and must be intended solely to facilitate 'the orderly conduct of business*'.

695 Courtesy translation, see *Isolux* above (n 47) para. 709: '*Si fuera una excepción de admisibilidad y no de jurisdicción, tendría que ser examinada al principio del examen del fondo del litigio, toda vez que el Tribunal no decline su jurisdicción por otros motivo.*'

696 *Abaclat* above (n 11) para. 448.

697 On the application of domestic law to the validity of the claimant's power of attorney, see *Teinver* above (n 190) para. 203.

698 *Urbaser S.A. and Consorcio de Aguas Bilbao Bizkaia, Bilbao Biskaia Ur Partzuergoa v. The Argentine Republic*, ICSID Case No. ARB/07/26, Decision on Jurisdiction of 12 December 2012, para. 113.

699 Ibid., para. 114.

determinations are not annullable[700] and that jurisdictional defects cannot be cured.[701] Interestingly for the present study, it debunked the *Abaclat* majority's attempt to find an essential distinction between the categories, and exposed its fuzziness:

> The *Abaclat* Tribunal observes that a salient feature of admissibility demonstrates that a lack of admissibility means that the claim was neither fit nor mature for judicial treatment, while a lack of jurisdiction strict [sic] sensu means that the claim could not at all have been brought before the body called upon. *Such a distinction contributes more to the confusion than to any elicitation of the issue.* If the claim is not mature for judicial treatment it cannot be brought before the designated judicial body either, which means that it satisfies both requirements of unavailability and irredeemably dilutes the suggested distinction.[702]

Under UNCITRAL rules,[703] the case has been made that admissibility problems, although normally treated in conjunction with jurisdictional ones, are essentially matters of merits.[704] The *Chevron* tribunal motivated as follows:

> An objection to the admissibility of a claim does not, of course, impugn the jurisdiction of a tribunal over the disputing parties and their dispute; to the contrary, it necessarily assumes the existence of such jurisdiction; and it only objects to the tribunal's exercise of such jurisdiction in deciding the merits of a claim beyond a preliminary objection. Under the UNCITRAL Arbitration Rules, that is an exercise belonging to the merits phase of the arbitration, to be decided by one or more awards on the merits.[705]

700 Ibid., para. 117. On this aspect, see below, section 2.2.

701 Ibid., para. 118.

702 Ibid., para. 116. Footnotes omitted, emphasis added.

703 Which contain no reference to admissibility. The relevant provision is Article 21(1), which reads: '*The arbitral tribunal shall have the power to rule on objections that it has no jurisdiction, including any objections with respect to the existence or validity of the arbitration clause or of the separate arbitration agreement.*' Note also that the UNCITRAL Rules contain no equivalent to ICSID Rule 41(5).

704 Gerold Zeiler, 'Jurisdiction, Competence and Admissibility of Claims in ICSID Arbitration Proceedings' in Christina Binder et al. (eds), *International Investment Law for the 21st Century: Essays in Honour of Christoph Schreuer* (OUP 2009) 76.

705 *Chevron v. Ecuador* above (n 598) para. 4.91. See also *Methanex v. USA*, UNCITRAL (NAFTA), First Partial Award, 7 August 2002, para. 107, 123–126. In *Methanex*, the tribunal dismissed

This conclusion is reached through a reasoning of elimination. Given the letter of the UNCITRAL Rules, all non-jurisdictional aspects pertain to the merits. This view is pragmatic, but it overlooks the relevance of general principles and the inherent jurisdiction that international courts have to preserve the integrity of their judicial function by declining to exercise an existing jurisdiction in specific circumstances.[706] Whereas clearly admissibility review presupposes a positive finding of jurisdiction, it does not follow necessarily that it belongs to the merits. The conflation is ultimately justifiable, since there is no reliable and accepted notion of admissibility: each tribunal is forced to investigate its relevance, and it might as well conclude that it has no practical value as an autonomous legal category, like the *Chevron* tribunal did. No single tribunal is responsible for the doctrinal blur, but many of them are forced to handle it *ad hoc*.

The Relevance of the Distinction for the Burden of Proof

It is sometimes argued that the distinction between jurisdiction and admissibility has repercussions on the burden of proof of the parties. Whereas this is technically true (the investor must prove the existence of the jurisdictional requirements;[707] the State must prove that a claim on which jurisdiction exists is inadmissible) the practice is more nuanced and rarely would a difference affect the outcome. See how the tribunal in *Philip Morris v. Australia* articulated the evidentiary principles regarding jurisdiction:

the admissibility objection based on the impossibility that the alleged conduct, even if factually corroborated, could amount to a breach of NAFTA (an objection based on the so-called *Oil Platforms* test).

706 See *Nuclear Tests (Australia v. France)*, 1974 I.C.J. Rep. 253, 259–260.

707 *Phoenix* above (n 254) para. 58–64: '*if jurisdiction rests on the existence of certain facts, they have to be proven* [not just established *prima facie*] *at the jurisdictional phase*'; *Pac Rim v. El Salvador* above (n 302) para. 2.9–2.11. *Blue Bank* above (n 317) para. 66. A similar statement was made by Franklin Berman in a Dissenting Opinion attached to *Lucchetti* above (n 273) para. 17: '*It is one thing to say that factual matters can or should be provisionally accepted at the preliminary phase, because there will be a full opportunity to put them to the test definitively later on. But if particular facts are a critical element in the establishment of jurisdiction itself, so that the decision to accept or to deny jurisdiction disposes of them once and for all for this purpose, how can it be seriously claimed that those facts should be assumed rather than proved?*'. See also *Gaëta* above (n 46) para. 135: '[le Tribunal] *est habilité à se livrer à un examen approfondi du droit national applicable; … Cette manière de procéder est en effet indispensable, dès lors que c'est la compétence du Tribunal arbitral qui en dépend*'.

> The Tribunal finds that there is no general disagreement between the Parties as to the principles governing burden of proof, although the application of these principles to certain preliminary objections requires further discussion. Specifically, it is for the Claimant to allege and prove facts establishing the conditions for jurisdiction under the Treaty; for the Respondent to allege and prove the facts on which its objections are based; and, to the extent that the Respondent has established a prima facie case, for the Claimant to rebut this evidence.[708]

Similarly to positive objections to the tribunal's jurisdiction, objections alleging the claim's inadmissibility are for the State to raise and support with evidence.[709] Whether the specific issue is one of jurisdiction or admissibility is virtually irrelevant if one takes the view that the party which wants to rely on certain facts must prove them.[710] Consider for instance a scenario in which at stake is the alleged misconduct of the investor. If the allegation seeks to found an objection to the tribunal's *competence* (which is normally the case if corruption is invoked), the respondent must prove[711] the facts supporting it[712]—the investor is not supposed to provide evidence of lack of

708 *Philip Morris* above (n 301) para. 459.

709 See for instance *Flemingo* above (n 332) para. 345 (the State was unable to prove that the acquisition of the investment was made in bad faith and the subsequent claim constituted abuse of process). See also *ABCI* above (n 19) para. 195 (the State did not prove the investor's bad faith in changing the investment nationality). A different view is asserted in *Tulip Real Estate and Development Netherlands B.V. v. Republic of Turkey*, ICSID Case No. ARB/11/28, Decision on Bifurcated Jurisdictional Issue of 5 March 2013, para. 48: '*As a party bears the burden of proving the facts it asserts, it is for Claimant to satisfy the burden of proof required at the jurisdictional phase. Here, the Parties agree that whilst the Article 8(2) Objection* [on a one-year compulsory consultation period] *was raised by Respondent, the onus remains on Claimant to establish that the requirements of Article 8(2) have been satisfied, and that the Tribunal has jurisdiction.*' It is, however, possible to distinguish between negative and positive objections to jurisdiction, and consider the failure to comply with the waiting period a negative one, which the respondent cannot be expected to prove. See *Pac Rim v. El Salvador* above (n 302) para. 2.11.

710 See the discussion in *Siag and Vecchi v. Egypt* above (n 405) para. 138 ff (it was not for the claimant to prove that he was not Egyptian, but for the State to support with evidence the relative jurisdictional objection).

711 *Getma International and others v. Republic of Guinea*, ICSID Case No. ARB/11/29, Award of 16 August 2016, para. 181.

712 A similar conclusion was reached in *Fraport II* above (n 576), see for instance para. 481 and 519. See also, with respect to jurisdiction *ratione temporis*, the concession of the respondent in *Lao v. Lao* above (n 213) para. 66–67.

corruption at the outset of the case.[713] When the allegations against the investors are raised to challenge the *admissibility* of their claims (on grounds of bad faith, or lack of clean hands) the burden of proving them, in spite of the change in legal characterisation, stays with the host State.[714] For instance, the host State's allegations that the claims were inadmissible because the investor '*did not pursue its investments in good faith*' were rejected in *Rusoro v. Venezuela*[715] because the State failed to provide any evidence to support them. In the context of an objection based on estoppel or abuse of process, the tribunal conceded its doubts whether it would be one of jurisdiction or admissibility, but found that either way the burden of submitting the decisive evidence would be on the State.[716]

A critical scenario where the difference would matter is one in which jurisdiction depends on a positive fact (for instance, a specific nationality, or the existence of the investment) rather than a negative one (the absence of corruption, the absence of the nationality of the host State, the absence of duplicative proceedings pending in domestic courts in breach of fork-in-the-road clause). In such cases, if the investor is unable to prove convincingly an essential element for its claim,[717] jurisdiction cannot be established, even in the absence of convincing contestation:

---

713 On the germane case of forged documents, see *Churchill* above (n 670), para. 238: '*It is a well-established rule in international law that each Party bears the burden of proving the facts which it alleges* (actori incumbit onus probandi). *Since the Respondent alleges that the Survey and Exploration Licenses and related documents are forged and that the Exploitation Licenses were obtained through deception, the Respondent bears the burden of proving its allegations of forgery and deception.*' Footnote omitted.

714 *Copper Mesa v. Ecuador* above (n 26) para. 5.59.

715 *Rusoro* above (n 246) para. 350 ff.

716 *Chevron v. Ecuador* above (n 512), paras 138–142. See also *Cervin v. Costa Rica* above (n 60) para. 292 (the State must prove that the only purpose of corporate restructuring was to acquire abusively the right to start arbitration).

717 Like the link between the claimant and the investment, see *Ampal* above (n 625) para. 119; or the existence and location of an investment, see *Apotex* UNCITRAL above (n 246) para. 150. See also *Mohammad Ammar Al-Bahloul v. The Republic of Tajikistan*, SCC Case No. V (064/2008), Partial Award of 2 September 2009, para. 145 (noting that the uncontested evidence provided by the Claimant is sufficient to prove that he owned the investment). It is important to note that the Respondent's contestation determines the width of the Claimant's burden to prove the facts that establish jurisdiction, see *Blue Bank* above (n 317) para. 66: '*the Claimant bears the burden of proving the facts required to establish jurisdiction, insofar as they are contested by the Respondent.*' This suggestion minimises the gulf between the regime of evidence applicable to jurisdiction and admissibility, as

> the burden of establishing jurisdiction, including consent, lies primarily upon the Claimant. Although it is the Respondent which has here raised specific jurisdictional objections, it is not for the Respondent to disprove this Tribunal's jurisdiction. Under international law, as a matter of legal logic and the application of the principle traditionally expressed by the Latin maxim "actori incumbit probatio", it is for the Claimant to discharge the burden of proving all essential facts required to establish jurisdiction for its claims.[718]

More commonly, however, the jurisdictional objection will rely on a positive contestation of the facts presented by the Claimant, rather than on their insufficiency. In *Oostergetel*, for instance, the State failed to demonstrate that the claimants had lost their Dutch nationality as a result of their permanent residency abroad.[719]

Similarly, consider the requirement of futility of any foregone domestic remedy, when exhaustion of local remedies applies, but was not observed the investor.[720] It is unsettled whether this requirement pertains to jurisdiction, admissibility, merits, or more than one of these categories at once.[721] If exhaustion is a matter of jurisdiction and the investor fails to prove futility, the claim is rejected for lack of competence *ratione materiae*. If exhaustion is framed as

---

in both cases the respondent must act to promote its position (contesting the Claimant's evidence on jurisdiction, or proving the facts entailing the inadmissibility of the claim).

718 *National Gas S.A.E. v. Arab Republic of Egypt*, ICSID Case No. ARB/11/7, Award of 3 April 2014, para. 118. See also *Emmis* above (n 158) para. 171: '*The Tribunal must decide* [the question of whether the Claimant owned an investment capable of expropriation] *finally at the jurisdictional stage on the balance of probabilities. The Claimants bear the burden of proof. If the Claimants' burden of proving ownership of the claim is not met, the Respondent has no burden to establish the validity of its jurisdictional defences.*'

719 *Oostergetel* above (n 28) para. 124, 129.

720 When required by the parties, for instance under the power granted in Article 26 of the ICSID Convention, or in the context of a denial of justice claim, see for instance the provision of Article 10(1) of the Spain-Colombia BIT. As noted above (n 568), it is perhaps better to characterise exhaustion in the context of denial of justice as a question for the merits.

721 See, for instance, the reasoning of an investment arbitration tribunal concerning the finality of court decisions connected to the claim brought in arbitration, and the requirement to exhaust local remedies: the investor's claim '*would fall to be dismissed in any event, on the additional basis that Apotex has failed to exhaust all local judicial remedies, and the Tribunal therefore lacks jurisdiction* ratione materiae.... *In the alternative,* and for the same reasons, *all such claims would be inadmissible in any event*'. See *Apotex* UNCITRAL above (n 246) para. 258 and 298–299 (emphasis added).

an admissibility requirement, futility would constitute an exception in favour of the claimant. Normally, the claimant would then be expected to provide the supporting evidence—not differently from the jurisdictional scenario. It is fair to say that, in most cases, the characterisation of a matter as regarding jurisdiction of admissibility would not change the burden of proof dynamics in the facts.[722]

Some Proposals to Solve the Confusion

Regrettably, the haphazard treatment of the category of admissibility, taken alone or in relation to the category of jurisdiction, has generated an inconsistent practice that resists any attempt of normalisation or theorisation by inference. The widely espoused distinctions are, as demonstrated so far, porous and/or contestable. It is therefore wiser to discuss a principled theory that is preferable to the current practice, rather than attempting to extract one from it.

Veijo Heiskanen has shown the permeability between matters of jurisdiction and admissibility in the reasoning of investment treaty tribunals. Questions relating to the steps that the investor must take before requesting arbitration are interchangeably treated as jurisdictional or admissibility issues.[723] These include the ripeness of the claim for exhaustion of specified procedures like negotiations, attempted resolution in alternative *fora*, respect of waiting periods and deadlines. See for instance how a NAFTA tribunal treated an objection based on the non-finality of the State measure challenged (i.e., that the claimant had failed to pursue all available domestic judicial avenues, and was therefore attacking a non-final judicial act):

722 There are, of course, cases in which the allocation of burden of proof is critical, but they do not concern cases in which it is unclear whether a requirement is of jurisdiction or admissibility. An obvious case is OPIC *Karimum Corporation v. The Bolivarian Republic of Venezuela*, ICSID Case No. ARB/10/14, Award of 28 May 2013, in which the tribunal rejected the claim because the investor was unable to prove that the Venezuelan investment law constituted the State's consent to ICSID arbitration, see para. 179.

723 Heiskanen above (n 38) 238 ff, and cases cited therein. To consider just two examples, just compare *Burlington* above (n 161) para. 336 (failure to comply with the 6-month waiting period renders the claim inadmissible) with *Enron* above (n 674) para. 88 (the six-month waiting period is '*very much a jurisdictional one*'). See also, for instance, the different characterisation of the requirement of domestic litigation for 18 months in *Hochtief* above (n 181) para. 96 and *Urbaser* above (n 14) para. 114.

> the Tribunal proceeds on the basis that this objection concerns the Tribunal's jurisdiction *ratione materiae*. In the alternative, the Tribunal has also considered the matter in terms of the admissibility of claims.[724]

This sentence betrays the non-contradiction between the received definitions of jurisdiction and admissibility. The impediment arises because 1) the parties have not conferred on the tribunal the power to adjudicate non-exhausted claims, and/or because 2) the claim is defective—it is not ripe for arbitration.[725]

Various scholars have suggested some ordering criteria to support a principled taxonomy. Abi Saab weighed in favour of the formal criterion: any condition included in the jurisdictional instrument would become jurisdictional, even those normally considered as conditions of admissibility under customary law.[726] Heiskanen proposed to consider competence and admissibility as one thing (a tribunal is competent to entertain only admissible claims), and suggested that claims are inadmissible when they are essentially domestic rather than international.[727] Paulsson elaborated on the notion of arbitrability, concluding that claims are inadmissible when they are not capable of, or essentially intended for, resolution through arbitration.[728] Born and Šćekić, whose analysis is focused only on pre-arbitration requirements but spans across the investment and commercial fields, elaborate on Paulsson's and Heiskanen's proposals. They suggest that the jurisdiction/admissibility dichotomy is unhelpful, and the guiding criterion should be whether the parties intended to submit the issue of non-compliance with a preliminary requirement to arbitral or judicial determination.[729]

724 *Apotex* UNCITRAL above (n 246) para. 260.

725 A similar confusion is admitted with respect to a 12-month negotiation requirement in *Tulip* above (n 709) para. 57: '*the jurisprudence is very much* non constante.' See ibid. the list of cases which constitute this contradictory case-law. For a similar remark regarding cooling-off periods, see *Al-Bahloul v. Tajikistan*, above (n 717) para. 154.

726 Abi Saab, dissenting opinion above (n 11) para. 23: '*these conditions become conventionally jurisdictional, in addition to being admissibility conditions by their legal nature*'. The tribunal in *ST-AD* seemed to adopt this view, noting that any pre-condition to arbitration is a limit to consent, and '*if these conditions are not fulfilled, there is indeed no consent*'. See *ST-AD* above (n 18) para. 336.

727 Heiskanen above (n 38).

728 Paulsson above (n 554).

729 Born and Šćekić above (n 574) 259, fn 132. This suggestion, obviously, is much more practicable in the field of international commercial arbitration, where judicial review of awards is a default option. In the field of investment arbitration, it is difficult to believe that BIT

The most unhinging proposal to date is perhaps Shany's one, discussed above and developed with reference to public international law adjudication. This theory uses judicial discretion as the controlling element for the distinction. It builds on Abi Saab's conclusion that '[a]*ny limits to* [the legal power to exercise the judicial or arbitral function], *whether inherent or consensual, i.e. stipulated in the jurisdictional title ... are jurisdictional by essence.*'[730] What is more, Shany provides a normative definition of admissibility, something on which Abi Saab's theorisation did not elaborate.

All these proposals have the advantage of identifying a normative principle that should govern the distinction (the source of the condition, the domestic essence of the dispute, the arbitrability, the appropriateness). Shany's proposal reaches further because it deeply reshapes the concepts and disrupts the received understanding that the division has something to do with the dichotomy *the authority of the court* versus *the features of the claim*. His proposal relies on a different dichotomy, between *the power/duty to exercise powers* and *the discretionary right to refrain from such exercise*. The tribunal in *Unglaube v. Costa Rica* seemingly hinted to a similar approach:

> ... objections on the ground of admissibility are different in nature from objections to jurisdiction. Respondent has not maintained that the Tribunal <u>may</u> not properly rule on these matters, but that, it <u>should</u> not—both as a matter of prudence and in consideration of the ongoing deliberations of courts and administrative bodies in Costa Rica, which should be permitted to complete their functions without interference or interruption.[731]

The distinction begs the question to an extent: what criteria guide a tribunal's discretion (in this case: '*prudence*' and '*consideration*' for domestic courts)? Yet, it is a workable distinction. It poses difficult questions, but relies on falsifiable answers.

2 Selected Cases

Besides the cases discussed above, in which the distinction did not ultimately matter for the dispute, there are other cases in which it proved crucial. Some are reported here by way of example.

---

parties—which are not the parties of the arbitration—thought of post-award review of compliance with pre-arbitration requirements.

730 *Abaclat* dissent above (n 11) para. 126.

731 *Marion Unglaube v. Republic of Costa Rica*, ICSID Case No. ARB/08/1, Award of 16 May 2012, para. 293, emphasis in the original.

Change of Nationality during Proceedings

In the case of *Loewen*, the requirement of nationality was treated as a jurisdictional condition. One of the claimants—the corporation—had the requisite Canadian nationality at the date of the claim, but was restructured into a US company during the proceedings. The tribunal decided that this occurrence might affect its jurisdiction,[732] and decided the issue applying general international law. The tribunal held that—by virtue of the customary requirement of continuous nationality—after the claimant's restructuring '*a NAFTA claim cannot exist or cannot any longer exist … so that the Tribunal cannot continue with the resolution of the original dispute, there being no dispute left to resolve*'.[733] In the reasoning, the tribunal seemed to conflate the jurisdictional requirement of nationality (which could have been assessed only at the moment of seisin[734]) and the admissibility requirement of the continuing existence of a legal dispute (which can be reviewed during the proceedings, to terminate disputes that have become moot).[735] This decision cannot be explained by

---

732 *Loewen* above (n 592) para. 226.

733 Ibid., para. 236. See Maurice Mendelson, 'Runaway Train: The 'Continuous Nationality' Rule from the Panavezys-Saldutiskis Railway case to Loewen' in Todd Weiler (ed), *International Investment Law and Arbitration* (Cameron May 2005) 97.

734 Waibel above (n 27). The doctrine was spelled out by the ICJ in *Case Concerning the Arrest Warrant of 11 April 2000* (Democratic Republic of Congo v. Belgium), Judgment, 14 February 2002, I.C.J. Reports 2002, para. 26: '*The Court recalls that, according to its settled jurisprudence, its jurisdiction must be determined at the time that the act instituting proceedings was filed. Thus, if the Court has jurisdiction on the date the case is referred to it, it continues to do so regardless of subsequent events*'. Note that in *Philip Morris* above (n 301) the tribunal has highlighted that an exception to this principle can be made in the interest of the sound administration of justice (para. 148), and to avoid unnecessary '*waste of time and resources*'. It cited in support *Mavrommatis* above (n 571) and *Case Concerning Application of the Convention on the Prevention and Punishment of the Crime of Genocide* (Croatia v. Serbia), Preliminary Objections, Judgment, 18 November 2008, I.C.J. Reports 2008, pp. 441–442, para. 87, as well as the investment award in *Teinver* above (n 14), para. 135. However, this exception seems to apply only to cure defective jurisdiction, and in the interest of justice. In the *Loewen* case, instead, the reconsideration led to the relinquishment of jurisdiction during the proceedings, and the result achieved was all but a paragon of equity and justice. As noted by Christoph Schreuer, 'At what time must jurisdiction exist?', in David D Caron et al. (eds), *Practising Virtue Inside International Arbitration* (OUP 2015) 264, 271 there is sufficient support to the notion that '*compliance with a requirement, whether it relates to jurisdiction, admissibility or procedure, may take place after the institution of the proceedings*'. The opposite scenario (the requirement lapses during the proceedings) is normally irrelevant.

735 Although the difference might have been critical with respect to the issue of nationality (a true jurisdictional requirement was perhaps best to be assessed only on the *dies a quo*),

reference to the widespread practice (both at the ICJ and of investment tribunals) to entertain cases when some requirements for jurisdiction, missing at the time of the claim, are subsequently met.[736] The rationale of this exceptional principle, in fact, is premised on fairness and judicial economy (fresh proceedings would be possible after a decision dismissing the case, when the requirement is met, with unnecessary costs and complication).[737] In similar cases, the question is less about the distinction between jurisdiction and admissibility, arguably, and turns on the possibility to carve out a customary exception to the rule that jurisdiction is assessed at the time of the claim. In the *Loewen* case, where such exception could not apply, the tribunal's belated review of jurisdictional matters is more controversial, and apparently lay on a reasoning of admissibility.

Denial of Benefits and Seat or Registration Requirements

The principle of corporate nationality under international law is formalistic (nationality depends only on the place of incorporation). States might insert specific treaty clauses to reserve the safeguards of treaty protection to a narrower category of investments, in order to make nationality-shopping more difficult and benefit only investors who have genuine links with the home State. For instance, in the BIT between Cyprus and Serbia and Montenegro the definition of '*investor*' requires that a company, besides being incorporated in the home State, have '*its seat in the territory of that Contracting Party*'.[738] In the case CEAC *v. Montenegro*[739] it was debated whether the seat requirement should be interpreted in light of domestic law or through an autonomous construction informed by international law and whether, accordingly, it was necessary to show a genuine link with the home State or just the formal incorporation plus a local address of a registered office. Ultimately, the tribunal found that the claimant had failed to prove to have any registered office in Cyprus, thereby failing to discharge its burden irrespective

the claim failed also because the claimant had challenged a non-final judicial measure of the host State.

736 For further examples, see the case law described in Schreuer above (n 734).

737 An obvious exception to this trend is the ICJ's judgment on the preliminary objections in *Georgia v. Russian Federation*, above (n 588).

738 Article 1(3).

739 *Central European Aluminium Company* (CEAC) *v. Montenegro*, ICSID Case No. ARB/14/8, Award of 26 July 2016.

of the applicable standard.[740] In *Alps Finance v. Slovak Republic*[741] at stake was the similar clause in the Slovakia/Switzerland BIT,[742] requiring the investor to have a seat in the home State. The tribunal found that the claimant had provided insufficient evidence to prove that it had a seat '*in the meaning of international business law*'.[743] Whereas the facts of the case might have warranted the same outcome irrespective of the applicable law, it is noteworthy that the tribunal opted for a meaning of the seat requirement autonomous from domestic laws. The claimant similarly failed to satisfy another requirement of the BIT, that of carrying out '*real economic activities*' in the host State.[744] Likewise, in *Orascom v. Algeria*, the Tribunal held that the requirement of a '*registered office*' stipulated by the applicable BIT did not entail a reference to domestic law.[745] The investment treaty can also expressly extend protection only to investments approved by the host State. Whilst technically a requirement *ratione materiae*, similar provisions seek to recoup part of the lost privity between host State and beneficiaries, establishing *intuitus personae* between the two (a sort of denial of benefits in reverse, see below). Non-approved investments are not protected and any attending claim would fall outside the jurisdiction of the tribunal.[746]

740 Even if the claimant had shown a certificate of registered office, the tribunal doubted of its veracity. See ibid., para. 151 ff, referring to a similar reasoning in *Soufraki*, above (n 404).

741 *Alps Finance* above (n 239).

742 See Article I(1)(b).

743 *Alps Finance* above (n 239) para. 216.

744 Ibid., para. 226.

745 *Orascom TMT Investments S.à r.l. v. People's Democratic Republic of Algeria*, ICSID Case No. ARB/12/35, Final Award of 31 May 2017, para. 280–281. Respondent argued that 'registered office' would be a redundant requirement, since the other requirement of local incorporation would necessarily entail establishing a registered office. The tribunal rejected this view (which aimed at reading the formula under Luxembourg law, requiring the stricter element of *siége social reel*, i.e., an effective office) and recalled the *Barcelona Traction* case, where the ICJ also used the combined requirement (incorporation plus registered office). A different conclusion was reached in *Tenaris Talta* above (n 76) para. 169–170, where the tribunal turned to domestic law under Article 32 VCLT, '*in order to confirm the interpretation at which*' it had arrived using Article 31(1) VCLT.

746 See for instance *Yaung Chi Oo Trading Pte Ltd v Government of the Union of Myanmar*, ASEAN Case No ARB/01/1, Award of 31 March 2003 and *Gruslin v. Malaysia*, ICSID Case No. ARB/99/3, Award of 27 November 2000. This issue was discussed also in *Churchill* above (n 13) para. 289, where the tribunal found that the admission requirement refers to the investment's entry into the country.

Another device used to counter nationality-planning is the use of denial of benefits clauses.[747] The parties to a BIT can agree to exclude certain investors from treaty-based protection, normally on grounds of foreign (third State) control or lack of economic connection with the home State.[748] See for instance the clause of the US/Ukraine BIT:

> Each Party reserves the right to deny to any company the advantages of this Treaty if nationals of any third country control such company and, in the case of a company of the other Party, that company has no substantial business activities in the territory of the other Party or is controlled by nationals of a third country with which the denying Party does not maintain normal economic relations.[749]

When the language of the clause refers to the whole treaty, the State's offer to arbitrate is one of the benefits that can be denied.[750] When, as it is the case of Article 17 of the Energy Charter Treaty (ECT), the clause refers only

747 On these clauses, see Anne K Hoffmann, 'Denial of Benefits' in Marc Bungenberg et al. (eds), *International Investment Law* (Nomos 2015) 598. In *Tokios Tokelés v. Ukraine*, ICSID Case No. ARB/02/18, Decision on Jurisdiction of 29 April 2004, the tribunal held that the host State cannot plead a lack of jurisdiction on grounds of a lack of substantive business in the home State, if there is no denial of benefits clause. See para. 36: '... *an international tribunal should exercise, and indeed is bound to exercise, the measure of jurisdiction with which it is endowed.*'

748 For an overview on the practice relating to denial-of-benefits clauses, see Lindsay Gastrell and Paul-Jean Le Cannu, 'Procedural Requirements of 'Denial-of-Benefits' Clauses in Investment Treaties: A Review of Arbitral Decisions' (2015) 30(1) ICSID Review 78–97. The *Ampal* case, above (n 625), provides an overview of the available practice on the matter, referring to the cases *Pac Rim v. El Salvador* above (n 302); *Guaracachi America, Inc. and Rurelec PLC v. The Plurinational State of Bolivia*, UNCITRAL, PCA Case No. 2011–17, Award of 31 January 2014; *Ulysseas, Inc. v. The Republic of Ecuador*, UNCITRAL, Interim Award of 28 September 2010; *Empresa Eléctrica del Ecuador, Inc. v. Republic of Ecuador*, ICSID Case No. ARB/05/9, Award of 2 June 2009; *Plama* above (n 175); *Yukos Universal Ltd. v. Russian Federation*, PCA Case No. AA 227, Interim Award on Jurisdiction and Admissibility of 30 November 2009, para. 456–459; *Hulley v. Russian Federation* above (n 244); *Anatolie Stati et al. v. The Republic of Kazakhstan*, SCC Case No. v. (116/2010), Award of 19 December 2013, para. 717; *Sempra Energy International v. Argentine Republic*, ICSID Case No. ARB/02116, Award of 28 September 2007, para. 386.

749 Article I(2) of the BIT.

750 See *Ulysseas v. Ecuador*, above (n 748) para. 172: '*In the Tribunal's view, since such advantages include BIT arbitration, a valid exercise of the right would have the effect of depriving the Tribunal of jurisdiction under the BIT.*'

to the set of substantive protections, the investor maintains the right to bring arbitration, but its claim might fall outside the scope *ratione materiae* of the treaty. Formally, this distinction would mean that in the former case there is a straightforward lack of jurisdiction *ratione personae*, whereas in the second the investor's claim could fail on the merits.[751] However, even the latter scenario might be framed as one of jurisdiction *ratione materiae* through the *Oil Platforms* test (even if truthful, the claims brought in arbitration are not capable of constituting treaty breaches).

Normally, these clauses do not apply automatically if the conditions are met, but endow the State with a power that it can choose to exercise or not; the host State must express its denial through a specific declaration, which can only operate prospectively.[752] As a result, an investor might bring a claim over State measures occurred before the declaration.

Moreover, the prospective application of denial of benefits declarations affects their availability during proceedings. If a declaration of denial entails a lapse of competence of the tribunal (resulting from the non-application *ratione personae* of the treaty), it must be made before the launch of proceedings. Alternatively, if framed as an obstacle to the admissibility of the claim, it might be made during the proceedings, to raise the corresponding preliminary objection. In *Hulley v. Russia*, the tribunal noted Russia's failure to deny benefits under Article 17 ECT before the arbitration and went as far as noting that it would be useless to do it during the proceedings.[753]

The prospective application of denial of benefits raises some practical issues.[754] If States are unable to deny benefits when a dispute with an investor first arises, they might be forced, to preserve their right to avail themselves of these clauses, to screen all investors in the territory upon entrance. This

---

751 This is the clear instruction issued by the tribunal in *Hulley v. Russian Federation* above (n 244) para. 440.

752 *Plama* above (n 175) para. 159–165; *Hulley v. Russian Federation* above (n 244) para. 455–458.

753 See *Hulley v. Russian Federation* above (n 244) para. 457–458: '*if the passage in Respondent's First Memorial ... is construed as an exercise of the reserved right of denial, it can only be prospective in effect from the date of that Memorial.... that Respondent has not denied and cannot now be heard to deny, and will not be able to deny to Claimant in any merits phase of these proceedings, the advantages and the benefits of Part III of the* ECT *on the basis of Article 17.*'

754 Hoffmann above (n 747) 606–607, referring to the reasoning in Stephen Jagusch and Anthony Sinclair, 'The Limits of protection for Investments and Investors under the Energy Charter Treaty' in Graham Coop and Clarisse Ribeiro (eds), *Investment Arbitration and the Energy Charter Treaty* (Juris Net 2006) 39–40.

would be an unlikely scenario in the age of dematerialised investments, which are the precise target of such clauses. However, this practical problem does not occur when the denial of benefit clause refers to the application of the treaty as a whole (as opposed to its substantive protection only). When access to arbitration is among the benefits of which denial is possible, the State can trigger the clause after the dispute is first raised, but before the launch of arbitration. Normally the cool-off period or the requirement of negotiation will guarantee that some months elapse between the two relevant dates. In *Ampal v. Egypt*, the tribunal rejected Egypt's attempt to deny benefits during the arbitration, noting that the host State had a window of opportunity to do that earlier. Namely, the declaration (and the connected procedural prerequisites) should have been issued during the consultation and negotiations with the investor, after the latter's notification that a treaty dispute had materialised, but before the establishment of the arbitration.[755]

In *Ulysseas v. Ecuador*, instead, the tribunal took no issue with the State's denying '*the BIT's advantages ... at the time when such advantages are sought by the investor through a request for arbitration*.'[756] The retrospective application of the clause did not worry the tribunal either, which noted that investors are aware of the host State's power to trigger the denial if they fit the specific features listed in the dedicated clause. Therefore, they can only count on enjoying the protection of the BIT subject to that *caveat*: they have no legitimate expectations that their benefits will not be denied.[757] The conclusions of the tribunals in *Ampal* and *Ulysseas* are difficult to reconcile, especially with respect to the retroactive application of the denial. The difference, at least with respect to the possibility to raise the denial during the proceedings, might be ascribed to the different language in the applicable clauses; whereas Article 1 of the Protocol to the US/Egypt BIT contains a procedural pre-requisite (consultation with the home State to seek a resolution) Article I(2) of the US/Ecuador BIT does not.

755 *Ampal* above (n 625) para. 160: '*According to Article VII(2) and (3) of the Treaty, Egypt had a window of six (6) months after 18 May 2011* [when the investor notified the State of a treaty dispute] *to seek to resolve the dispute by consultation and negotiation with Ampal. In the opinion of the Tribunal, it was during that six (6) month period that Egypt could also have initiated consultations with the United States pursuant to Paragraph 1 of the Protocol. There is no evidence in the record that such consultations took place during that period*' (the denial of benefits procedure in the US/Egypt BIT provides for consultations and notification with the home State before the denial is formalised).

756 *Ulysseas v. Ecuador* above (n 748) para. 172.

757 Ibid., para. 173.

In *Generation Ukraine*,[758] the tribunal held that control by third country nationals was a prerequisite for this clause to apply, and that it was for the respondent to prove it. The evidence-related point is crucial because it qualifies the requirement as one of admissibility (the host State must prove the existence of the conditions barring the admission of a claim) rather than one of jurisdiction (the prerequisites of which must be proven by the claimant).[759] However, the allocation of evidentiary burdens is not dispositive of whether denial of benefits-based objections go to the jurisdiction of the tribunal or to the admissibility of a claim. For instance, the tribunal in *Ulysseas v. Ecuador*[760] reached the same conclusion but characterised the matter as a jurisdictional one. Whereas claimants would need to prove the requisites of jurisdiction, it falls on respondent to prove the pre-conditions for the denial of advantages, '*as the party advancing* [such] *specific defence to the Tribunal's jurisdiction*.'[761]

In *Isolux*, the tribunal harboured '*no doubt*' that the objection based on Article 17 ECT '*raises a question of admissibility*.'[762] It reasoned that the tribunal must have jurisdiction to pronounce on the denial of benefits issue. If such determination were one of jurisdiction, in the tribunal's view, '*the investor would be deprived of any forum competent to decide on this issue*.'[763] Without prejudice to the conclusion reached by the tribunal, the reasons are not compelling. By virtue of the principle of *Kompetenz-Kompetenz* in general and Article 41 of the ICSID Convention in particular, the tribunal could pronounce on a question of jurisdiction in any case; there is no need to reframe it as one of admissibility solely for the purpose of preserving the tribunal's powers to decide. Ultimately, the tribunal rejected the objection, noting that the respondent had belatedly activated the denial clause, at the time of the Counter-Memorial rather than prior to the dispute.[764]

In the practice, objections based on denial of benefits are interchangeably treated as issues of admissibility, jurisdiction or merits.[765] The doctrinal

---

758 *Generation Ukraine, Inc. v. Ukraine*, ICSID Case No. ARB/00/9, Award of 16 September 2003.

759 Ibid., para. 15(7).

760 *Ulysseas v. Ecuador* above (n 748).

761 Ibid., para. 166. The tribunal refers to the UNCITRAL Rules to support this conclusion, in particular Article 24(1) UNCITRAL Rules (which simply enunciates the *actori incumbit probatio* principle).

762 *Isolux* above (n 47) para. 711.

763 Ibid., para. 712. Our translation. The original reads: '*La solución contraria privaría al inversor de cualquier foro necesario para decidir sobre ésta cuestión*.'

764 Ibid., para. 715.

765 See the discussion in Hoffmann above (n 747).

confusion, however, is not the primary cause of the ambiguity of the case-law. To the contrary, the conceptual flaws seem to depend on (rather than produce) a handful of unresolved matters, such as the possibility that denials apply retroactively, the effectiveness of denial declarations made after the request for arbitration, and the difficulty to determine the allocation of evidentiary burdens in the abstract.

Compulsory Attempts at Local Litigation

Even with respect to a narrow category of procedural objections, like pre-arbitration requirements, the practice reflects normative ambiguity. Born and Šćekić have shown that requirements relating to prior litigation or negotiation, or cool-off periods, are treated alternatively as mandatory or aspirational.[766]

An apt case study is the dispute *Kılıç v. Turkmenistan*, touched upon in the introduction of Part A.[767] In the award, the tribunal rejected the investor's claim for failure to comply with a procedural precondition before starting arbitration. Article VII(2) of the applicable BIT between Turkey and Turkmenistan required—in the tribunal's view—that the investor first bring the claim in the host State's courts. The right to initiate arbitration under the BIT would arise

766 See Born and Šćekić above (n 574) 234–235 and extensive case-law cited therein. For an example, see how the tribunal treated a cooling-off period as a matter of *récevabilité* in *Consortium RFCC v. Royaume du Maroc*, ICSID Case No. ARB/00/6, Decision on Jurisdiction of 16 July 2001, and *Alps Finance* above (n 234) para. 200–211. Conversely, the same requirement is treated as one of jurisdiction in *Enron* above (n 674) para. 88; *Murphy Exploration and Production Company International v. Republic of Ecuador*, ICSID Case No. ARB/08/4, Award on Jurisdiction of 15 December 2010, para. 140 ff. In the case *Mohamed Abdulmohsen Al-Kharafi & Sons Co. v. Libya and others*, Final Arbitral Award of 22 March 2013, the arbitration clause was contained in a contract, and required an attempt at amicable settlement. The tribunal, noting the vagueness of such requirement, relied on the approach prevailing in commercial arbitration and found that '*the fulfillment of the procedural requirements in the arbitration agreement are not considered as a prerequisite of the Arbitral Tribunal's jurisdiction.*' (Section 3 of the tribunal's decision on jurisdiction). In *Western NIS Enterprise Fund v. Ukraine*, ICSID Case No. ARB/04/2, Order of 16 March 2006, the tribunal noted the claimant's failure to notify the respondent of the dispute, for the purpose of reaching an amiable settlement. Instead of rejecting the claim, the tribunal suspended the proceedings and invited the claimant to fulfil the notification duty. A similar procedural defect was treated as grounds for inadmissibility in *Supervision v. Costa Rica* above (n 90) see para. 336–348 (the tribunal considered inadmissible certain claims that the claimant had presented for the first time in arbitration, thus failing to fulfil the prior steps of notification and negotiation established in the BIT).

767 *Kılıç* above (n 4).

only if the local courts, once seised, do not deliver judgment within one year.[768] The tribunal held that the precondition was compulsory and that the claimant could not invoke an exception (e.g., the futility of recourse to local courts). Since the claimant had not brought the claim to Turkmen courts, the claim was unanimously dismissed.

However, a member of the tribunal disagreed with the majority as regards one specific finding, i.e., the legal characterisation of the procedural impediment. He characterised the precondition of Article VII(2) (that the claim could be brought in arbitration '*provided that*' there had been domestic proceedings for twelve months, and no decision therefrom) as one of ripeness or admissibility.[769] The tribunal's majority, instead, considered it a qualifier of consent to arbitrate and, therefore, a jurisdictional condition.[770] Professor Park's *dictum* regarding the difference between admissibility and jurisdiction is worth quoting in full, as it is possible to appreciate how much of the discussion of the previous section of this Part, above, echoed in his remarks:

> Procedural flaws that may be cured during the arbitration are often characterized by reference to notions such as ripeness, *recevabilité* or admissibility. Such terms derive not from technical treaty definition, but from usage as convenient labels to describe steps to be taken either before or after constitution of a tribunal, even if they must be met prior to merits being addressed. These distinctions remain commonplace. Arbitrators often confirm jurisdiction, but proceed to the merits only 'provided that' Terms of Reference are signed, deposits lodged, and/or settlement mechanisms satisfied. Such requirements may be met after exercise of a right to arbitrate. Few requirements introduced by 'provided that' possess an intrinsically jurisdictional quality. Instead, the meaning of a proviso depends on the drafters' intent as evidenced by context, structure and wording, construed in light of all related factors.[771]

---

768 The correct interpretation of this condition and its characterisation as optional (instead of compulsory) were contested in the proceedings. The discussion refers here to the interpretation validated by the tribunal. In another dispute, *Muhammet Çap & Sehil Inşaat Endustri ve Ticaret Ltd. Sti. v. Turkmenistan*, ICSID Case No. ARB/12/6, tribunal held that the same Article VII(2) of the BIT provided for an optional procedure, see Decision on Respondent's Objection to Jurisdiction under Article VII(2) of 13 February 2015.

769 *Kılıç* above (n 4) para. 6.5.1; see the separate opinion of William Park.

770 *Kılıç* above (n 4) para. 6.3.15: '*in order for the necessary consent/agreement in writing to result, the offer must have been accepted on the basis of, and having regard to, the conditions explicitly set out in the BIT*'.

771 Professor Park's separate opinion, para. 27–29. Notes omitted.

The distinction, in this case, came with a practical difference. The claimant's failure to attempt domestic litigation, in Park's view, did not deprive the tribunal of its jurisdiction. The tribunal, duly seised of the claim, could have ordered the suspension of the proceedings for the time necessary to remedy the procedural flaw. According to the majority, instead, the failure to seise Turkmen courts determined the lack of jurisdiction over the dispute, hence the tribunal had no procedural power over the proceedings, such as the power to suspend them.[772] The authority to suspend proceedings would have been relatively uncontroversial if the precondition had been considered one of admissibility.[773]

This distinction between jurisdictional matters (which pertain to the parties' consent) and admissibility matters (which presuppose consent but regulate its exercise) has gained some traction. UNCTAD has produced a publication relating to the use of MFN, in which it distinguished between cases where the clause is invoked to enlarge the tribunal's jurisdiction and cases where it seeks to circumvent admissibility problems.[774] Skipping the requirements of local litigation and waiting periods through MFN clauses would belong to the latter category.[775] The taxonomy was expressly endorsed by the *Teinver v. Argentina* tribunal,[776] which relied on it to allow the investor's attempt to skip the 6-month negotiation requirement and the 18-month domestic litigation pre-conditions in the applicable BIT through the MFN. The UNCTAD taxonomy has some descriptive merit but fails to rely on a principled classification.[777]

A passage from the *Murphy v. Ecuador* (ICSID) award, which addressed the claimant's attempt to characterise the six-month negotiation requirement as merely procedural, is worth reading in full:

772 *Kılıç* above (n 4) para. 6.4.2: '*the conditions for jurisdiction not having been met, the Tribunal has no jurisdiction to suspend the proceedings*'.

773 *SGS v. Philippines* above (n 38); *Western NIS Enterprise Fund v. Ukraine*, ICSID Case No. ARB/04/2, Order of 16 March 2006; *Ethyl Corporation v. The Government of Canada*, UNCITRAL, Award on Jurisdiction of 24 June 1998, para. 58.

774 "Most Favoured-Nation Treatment," UNCTAD Series on International Investment Agreements II, UNCTAD/DIAE/IA/2010/1, 24 January 2011.

775 Ibid., 66–67.

776 *Teinver* above (n 14) para. 168–172.

777 See how the ILC discussed it in the Final Report of the Study Group on the Most-Favoured-Nation clause, Yearbook of the International Law Commission, 2015, vol. II, Part Two, (para. 113): '*there is no explanation in the UNCTAD report as to why it treats cases relating to the 18-month litigation requirement as concerning admissibility rather than as concerning jurisdiction.*'

> The Tribunal also does not accept the consequences Claimant seeks to derive between "procedural" and "jurisdictional" requirements. According to [Claimant], "procedural requirements" are of an inferior category than the "jurisdictional requirements" and, consequently, its non-compliance has no legal consequences. It is evident that in legal practice this does not occur, and that non-compliance with a purely procedural requirement, such as, for example, the time to appeal a judgment, can have serious consequences for the defaulting party.[778]

The tribunal went on to discuss a series of arbitral awards in which similar requirements were alternatively considered compulsory or waivable. Whereas such distinction should not depend on the jurisdiction/admissibility divide, it is often made to depend on it, adding an extra complication to the legal uncertainty described above.

Local Courts (Zoom-in)—the Argentina Cases

Another instance in which the distinction had an impact on the case is the dispute in *Daimler v. Argentina*,[779] selected here as a champion of the several disputes involving the same host State where similar issues were raised.[780]

The matter of contention concerned Article 10(2) and (3) of the German-Argentine BIT. The clauses require the investor to submit the case for 18 months to local courts before bringing arbitration. One of the points raised by the claimant was that this requirement was directive and procedural in nature, rather than mandatory and jurisdictional. This distinction, in the claimant's view, was critical to the application of the BIT's Most Favoured Nation clause. This argument was rejected. The dividing line, according to the *Daimler* tribunal's majority, is firmly rooted in the consent of the parties, as registered in the BIT. Any condition or requirement included in a BIT is by definition a jurisdictional one (a '*sweeping generalisation*,' for the dissenting arbitrator[781]):

> BIT-based dispute resolution provisions [...] are by their very nature jurisdictional. The mere fact of their inclusion in a bilateral treaty indicates that they are reflections of the sovereign agreement of two States—not

778 *Murphy v. Ecuador* (ICSID) above (n 766) para. 142.

779 *Daimler* above (n 779).

780 The ILC report above (n 777) para. 124, noted that in twelve cases (out of eighteen in which the invocation of MFN treatment was successful) investors sought to avoid an 18-month litigation requirement in disputes against Argentina.

781 *Daimler* above (n 779), Dissent by Charles Brower of 15 August 2012, fn 39.

> the mere administrative creation of arbitrators. They set forth the conditions under which an investor-State tribunal may exercise jurisdiction with the contracting state parties' consent, much in the same way in which legislative acts confer jurisdiction upon domestic courts.[782]

The majority of the tribunal distinguished from the treatment of admissibility in domestic jurisdictions. Whereas domestic courts can discard admissibility requirements to preserve the efficiency of their mandate, international tribunals cannot do the same without unilaterally expanding their jurisdiction beyond the limits established by State consent.[783] This remark confirms the impression that procedural requirements qualify necessarily as jurisdictional whenever they are codified in treaty law, and the connected suggestion that it is perhaps useless to observe domestic procedural principles to investigate the operation of their correspondent principles in the international system. The majority cited approvingly the words of the *Wintershall* tribunal, which came to the same conclusion with respect to the same provision: '*the Host State's 'consent' (standing offer) is premised on there being first submitted to the courts of competent jurisdiction in the Host State the entire dispute for resolution in the local courts*'.[784]

In *Daimler*, the issue was crucial to the outcome of the decision (had the 18-month rule qualified as procedural, it could have been waived by the tribunal or bypassed through the MFN); the award was upheld in annulment proceedings, and the specific issue was not examined by the Committee.[785] It is worth observing here that the attempts to frame admissibility conditions as procedural issues aim to justify the tribunal's decision to waive them. A similar approach had emerged in the award of the *Biwater Gauff* tribunal, referring to cooling off requirement:

> [the Respondent's] objection depends upon the characterisation of the six-month period in Article 8(3) of the BIT as a condition precedent to the Arbitral Tribunal's jurisdiction, or the admissibility of BGT's claims. In the Arbitral Tribunal's view, however, properly construed, this six-month period is procedural and directory in nature, rather than jurisdictional and mandatory. Its underlying purpose is to facilitate opportunities

782 *Daimler* above (n 779) para. 193.

783 Ibid., para. 192.

784 *Wintershall* above (n 176) para. 160(2).

785 *Daimler Financial Services AG v. Argentine Republic*, ICSID Case No. ARB/05/1, Decision on Annulment of 7 January 2015.

> for amicable settlement. Its purpose is not to impede or obstruct arbitration proceedings, where such settlement is not possible. Non-compliance with the six month period, therefore, does not preclude this Arbitral Tribunal from proceeding.[786]

Note that the tribunal, which considered the requirement as hortatory, waivable, and certainly non-jurisdictional, avoided pronouncing on whether it affected the admissibility of the claim. Unlike the majority in *Daimler*, the tribunal in *Biwater Gauff* did not go as far as claiming that admissibility requirements are merely procedural and, therefore, non-mandatory. It also noted the futility of any waiting period *in casu* and the implicit waiver of the Respondent, whose action escalated the dispute beyond the possibility of negotiation, making the Claimant's recourse to arbitration '*entirely reasonable*'.[787]

Indeed, the hortatory nature of admissibility requirement is contestable. They regulate, by definition, the admissibility of the claim; as a result it is to be expected that the specific sanction (the case's dismissal) applies in case of non-compliance. It may be true that procedural irregularities can be tolerated,[788] but under general international law inadmissibility is, by definition, sufficient to prevent the analysis of the merits and in any case is not always reducible to a matter of procedure.[789] The tribunal in *Philip Morris v. Uruguay* noted rightly that irrespective of the characterisation (jurisdiction or admissibility) a local litigation requirement was mandatory.[790]

The dissenting arbitrator identified the original sin of the award in the qualification of the 18-month requirement '*as a jurisdictional hurdle rather than*

---

786 *Biwater Gauff (Tanzania) Ltd. v. United Republic of Tanzania*, ICSID Case No. ARB/05/22, Award of 24 July 2008, para. 343.

787 Ibid., para. 347–348.

788 For an application of this approach—not relating to admissibility or jurisdiction, but to the four-minute delay of the claimant's Counter-Memorial—see *Supervision v. Costa Rica* above (n 90) para. 266.

789 Abi Saab noted as much in his dissent to *Abaclat* above (n 11) para. 28.

790 *Philip Morris Brands Sàrl, Philip Morris Products S.A. and Abal Hermanos S.A. v. Oriental Republic of Uruguay*, ICSID Case No. ARB/10/7 (formerly *FTR Holding SA, Philip Morris Products S.A. and Abal Hermanos S.A. v. Oriental Republic of Uruguay*) Decision on Jurisdiction of 2 July 2013, para. 142. See also *Generation Ukraine* above (n 758) para. 14(3): '*Some authorities consider the requirement to consult and negotiate before proceeding to arbitration as "procedural" rather than a condition precedent for the vesting of jurisdiction. This Tribunal would be hesitant to interpret a clear provision of the BIT in such a way so as to render it superfluous, as would be the case if a "procedural" characterisation of the requirement effectively empowered the investor to ignore it at its discretion.*'

an issue of admissibility'[791] and pointed approvingly to the opposite conclusion reached by the *Hochtief* tribunal (interpreting the same provision).[792] In his opinion, Professor Park hinted at the curability of flaws relating to admissibility. It is easy to see that this curability derives from their pertinence to admissibility, and does not constitute it.[793] In other words, these flaws can be remedied because they affect the admissibility of the claim, not vice versa. The qualifying element must be somewhere else: Park mentioned that the touchstone must be the '*drafters' intent as evidenced by context, structure and wording, construed in light of all related factors*'.[794]

In short, whether a requirement pertains to admissibility or jurisdiction would depend primarily on the parties' consent. This conclusion begs the question on how to interpret the silence of the parties—a likely occurrence—and somewhat minimises the practice of international adjudication outside treaty investment arbitration, which might otherwise provide some guidance (see section 1 of this Part). Compared to the proposals by Heiskanen, Paulsson and Shany, described above, Park's implicit proposal makes the dividing line depending not so much on general principles (this makes his suggestion different from Abi Saab's) but only on the contextual interpretation of the specific arrangements of the parties contained in the jurisdictional titles.

An even bolder approach was adopted by the *Abaclat* majority, which qualified the obligations to attempt an amicable settlement and to seek local remedies for at least 18 months as merely procedural, and specified that even if the claimant had breached them, its claim would have been admissible as a matter of fairness[795]:

> a potential non-compliance with the consultation requirement set forth in Article 8(1) BIT would simply express that the premises for an amicable settlement were not given because one or both of the Parties were not willing to give the dispute an amicable end. As such, it could not be considered to constitute per se a hurdle to the admissibility of the claim.[796]

791 Dissent of Professor Park above (n 781) para. 13.

792 *Hochtief* above (n 553) para. 96: '[*the requirement goes*] *to the admissibility of the claim rather than the jurisdiction of the Tribunal*'.

793 In the words of Born and Šćekić above (n 574) 246: '*in most instances, characterization of a procedural requirement as 'jurisdictional' or 'procedural' expresses a conclusion, rather than reasoning for that conclusion.*'

794 Dissent of Professor Park above (n 781) para. 29.

795 *Abaclat* above (n 11) para. 583.

796 Ibid., para. 565. On the 18-month rule, see para. 580.

The *Ambiente Ufficio* and *Alemanni* tribunals, instead, noted that the offer to arbitrate contained in the BIT did not differentiate between jurisdiction and admissibility, nor between mandatory and non-mandatory or procedural requirements.[797] However, the tribunals construed the obligations to negotiate and litigate in domestic courts as obligations of means (rather than obligations of result): '*it cannot be supposed that two sophisticated governments could have intended that foreign investors be required to begin an action before the local courts or administrative authorities just for show*.'[798] The claimants, therefore, were able to plead the futility of the pre-arbitration means of dispute settlement. The tribunal agreed that there would not have been a prospect of resolution and held that the obligations to negotiate and spend 18 months in local courts '*did not act as a jurisdictional bar to … ICSID arbitration*'.[799]

The *ICS* tribunal went as far as using Paulsson's scholarly proposal to probe the nature of the 18-month requirement and determine the consequences of its breach.[800] It expressed concern about the uneasy distinction between jurisdiction and admissibility, and acknowledged that in case of inadmissibility '*the tribunal enjoys some discretion as to how to deal with … non-fulfilment*'[801] of a requirement. Ultimately, it approximated the 18-month rule to a rule of exhaustion of local remedies, and treated it as jurisdictional.

In the case *TSA Spectrum v. Argentina*, instead, the tribunal considered the local litigation requirement as jurisdictional. The investor had breached it, by resorting prematurely to ICSID arbitration. However, the tribunal did not dismiss the claim, and applied a pragmatic reasoning that seemed more apposite to trump admissibility requirements. It noted that '*it would be highly formalistic now to reject the case …, since a rejection … would in no way prevent TSA from immediately instituting new ICSID proceedings on the same matter*'.[802]

Annullability

The *Kılıç* dispute highlights the possible implications that the blur between jurisdiction and admissibility has on the reviewability of awards.

The claimant sought annulment, without success.[803] The claimant argued, among other things, that the majority's view on the jurisdiction/admissibility

797 *Alemanni* above (n 32) para. 304, quoting *Ambiente Ufficio* above (n 569) para. 572.

798 *Alemanni* above (n 32) para. 311.

799 Ibid., para. 317.

800 *ICS* above (n 476) para. 259–262.

801 Ibid., 256.

802 *TSA Spectrum* above (n 42) para. 112.

803 *Kılıç* Decision on Annulment, above (n 6).

issue was flawed. The committee conceded that the reasoning of the majority was controversial and inscribed itself in a contradictory practice. However, the tribunal's finding was not reviewable in annulment proceedings.[804] In other words, the committee held that, even admitting that the Claimant and Professor Park were right in labelling the condition under Art. VII(2) of the BIT as one of admissibility, the tribunal had not manifestly exceeded its powers or departed seriously from a fundamental rule of procedure.[805]

Within the ICSID system, a failure to uphold or exercise jurisdiction can certainly amount to an excess of powers of the tribunal, constituting grounds for annulment under Art. 52(1)(b) of the ICSID Convention.[806] Mistaking admissibility for jurisdiction, instead, might hardly constitute grounds for annulment as such.[807] In either case, the requirement that the tribunal '*manifestly*' exceed its powers makes annulment relatively difficult even in case of wrong characterisations. The *ad hoc* committee deciding on the annulment of the *TECO v. Guatemala* award stated this in the clearest terms:

> ... the Committee wishes to clarify that it cannot accept Guatemala's theory according to which a tribunal's incorrect decision on jurisdiction can never survive annulment because any excess of jurisdiction is necessarily manifest.[808]

It should be clear, through these examples, that the crux of the matter for the purposes of annulment is the gravity of the mistake, not so much whether the mistake related to jurisdiction or admissibility. After all, insofar as a finding on admissibility determines the *exercise* of jurisdiction by the tribunal, a wrong determination will imply a mistaken stance on jurisdiction—one susceptible of annulment. The *Urbaser* tribunal used this approach, and chastised the views of the *Abaclat* tribunal, which distinguished between issues of

---

804 Ibid., para. 166.

805 ICSID Convention, Art. 50(1)(c)(iii).

806 *Lucchetti* Decision on Annulment above (n 273) para. 99; *Alemanni* above (n 32) para. 320.

807 Consider the Decision of the *ad hoc* Committee of 27 May 2007 in the case *Soufraki* above (n 342) para. 42: '*There is, in principle, an excess of power if a tribunal goes beyond its jurisdiction* ratione personae, *or* ratione materiae *or* ratione voluntatis.' Whereas the focus is clearly on jurisdictional matters only, the inclusion of the requirements *ratione voluntatis* might refer to other preconditions to the exercise of jurisdiction that are commonly considered of admissibility.

808 *TECO Guatemala Holdings, LLC v. Republic of Guatemala*, ICSID Case No. ARB/10/23, Decision on Annulment of 5 April 2016, para. 215.

admissibility (which '*usually*'[809] cannot be reviewed) and issues of jurisdiction (which would be more prone to annulment):

> under the ICSID system, a decision stating that a claim lacks admissibility may be brought before an annulment committee based on one of the grounds listed in Article 52(1) of the Convention and in particular when the claimant alleges that the tribunal had 'manifestly exceeded its powers' (lit. b). This feature of ICSID practice renders both the distinction wrong in theory and useless in practice.[810]

The tribunal in *Supervision v. Costa Rica*, however, thought otherwise.[811] Among the differences that the tribunal attached to the distinction between jurisdiction and admissibility, it listed the fact that '*a court may review whether an arbitral tribunal had jurisdiction over the dispute, but not review the admissibility of a claim.*'[812] This is a puzzling statement, not only because it makes annullability dependent on the jurisdictional character of the mistake, but also because it mentions the possibility of a court reviewing arbitral awards, a contingency that could never arise in the ICSID system. At the most, such casual remark could—sometimes—hold true with respect to non-ICSID awards.

Outside the ICSID system, indeed, the distinction between flaws of jurisdiction and inadmissibility can be consequential. Under domestic arbitration regimes, the tribunal's upholding (or refusal) of jurisdiction on the merits can be impugned before a national court. This is what happened in *BG Group v. Argentina*, a case administered through the 1976 UNCITRAL rules. The tribunal upheld jurisdiction, and dismissed the respondent's objection relating to the claimant's failure to resort to local remedies for 18 months, pointing out the absurdity of enforcing this admissibility precondition in the circumstances at stake.[813] Argentina challenged the award in the US, alleging that the tribunal had exceeded its powers.[814] The US Court of Appeal examined the question, subsumed under the US-flavoured label of 'arbitrability' and vacated the

809 *Abaclat* above (n 11) para. 247(ii).

810 *Urbaser S.A. and Consorcio de Aguas Bilbao Bizkaia, Bilbao Biskaia Ur Partzuergoa v. The Argentine Republic*, ICSID Case No. ARB/07/26, Decision on Jurisdiction of 12 December 2012, para. 117.

811 *Supervision y Control S.A. v. Republic of Costa Rica*, ICSID Case No. ARB/12/4, Final Award of 18 January 2017.

812 Ibid., para. 268.

813 *BG Group Plc. v. The Republic of Argentina*, UNCITRAL, Final Award of 24 December 2007, para. 156.

814 Under Section 10(a)(4) of the FAA, 9 U.S.C.

award, holding that the precondition was compulsory.[815] The US Supreme Court reversed the decision, holding that although the determination of the tribunal was not immune from judicial review, domestic judges must review such findings with deference rather than *de novo*. In the instant case, the investment tribunal's determination on admissibility was lawful. In the folds of the Court of Appeal and Supreme Court's decisions it is possible to identify the critical distinction between jurisdiction (the requirement conditioned the consent to arbitrate, and was therefore reviewable by domestic courts) and admissibility (the requirement operated once consent and jurisdiction had already formed, and the tribunal's determination attracted deference in domestic proceedings).

Outside the ICSID circuit, the grounds for setting aside investment awards may vary—as the idiosyncratic and US-law-centred challenge of the *BG* award shows. Errors in the assessment of jurisdiction and errors regarding admissibility might attract a different treatment. The UNCITRAL Model Law, upon which the arbitration law of more than 60 States is shaped,[816] provides for the grounds for setting aside an award.[817] Of interest here are the hypotheses of excess of authority (the dispute—and the award—exceed the terms of the submission of arbitration),[818] the non-arbitrability of the subject-matter of the dispute[819] and the conflict with the State's public policy.[820]

It might be argued that the '*terms of the submission to arbitration*' delimit the competence of the tribunal, rather than the admissibility of the claim. It would follow that alleged mistakes made by the tribunal regarding its jurisdiction might result in a *vacatur* of the award in domestic courts, but mistakes regarding the admissibility of a claim might not. This difference would be all the more likely to operate in jurisdictions where the domestic arbitration law expressly lists '*lack of jurisdiction*' as grounds for annulment, but is silent about errors regarding admissibility matters.[821] It is also possible that domestic courts indeed subscribe to the widespread idea that matters of admissibility

815 Court of Appeals for the District of Columbia Circuit, 665 F. 3d 1363 (2012).

816 See Albert Jan van den Berg, 'Should the Setting Aside of the Arbitral Award be Abolished?' (2014) 29(2) ICSID Review 263–288.

817 These are normally aligned with the grounds for refusing recognition under Article V of the New York Convention.

818 Model Law, Article 34(2)(a)(ii).

819 Article 34(2)(b)(i).

820 Article 34(2)(b)(ii).

821 For instance, see the Swiss Federal Statute on Private International Law, Chapter 12, Article 190 (Action for Annulment). For an overview of domestic arbitration statutes and the available grounds for annulment, see Susan D Franck, 'The legitimacy crisis in

are immune from review, and interpret accordingly the language of their local arbitration laws. For instance, this approach could make the difference when the available grounds for annulment contain a generic reference to the awards resulting from a tribunal's breach of its own mandate, competence or authority.

Mass Claims

In the *Abaclat* dispute, the tribunal was seised with proceedings that aggregated several thousands of similar claims against the host State (initially over 180,000, eventually approximately 60,000). By the tribunal's admission, the investors had brought a mass claim.[822] Argentina challenged the jurisdiction of the tribunal over mass claims, and their admissibility. The instruments setting the tribunal's competence (the ICSID Convention and the Italy-Argentina BIT) do not mention mass claims, and '*the Parties disagree*[d] *on how this silence should be interpreted and what it means with regard to the present mass proceedings*'.[823] The tribunal bifurcated the analysis, linking the review of its own jurisdiction to the parties' consent and the analysis of admissibility to the management of its procedure.

The majority concluded that the issue of mass claim was one of admissibility, arguing *ex hypothesi*: the tribunal would have had jurisdiction over a single one of the claimants' claims, considered alone. Therefore, the tribunal cannot lose its jurisdiction only due to the number of these claims. Moreover, in light of the object and purpose of the ICSID Convention and the BIT, the silence of these instruments could not be interpreted as '*a 'qualified silence' categorically prohibiting collective proceedings*'.[824] The challenge regarding the collective nature of the proceedings, therefore '*must be considered a matter of admissibility and not of jurisdiction*'.[825]

The majority proceeded on the cavalier assumption that admissibility issues boil down to procedural questions. It then relied on Article 44 of the ICSID and Rule 19 ICSID, which empower the tribunal to make procedural determinations when no rule exists on a specific issue.[826] The majority found '*that the silence of the ICSID Convention concerning collective proceedings is to be seen as*

investment treaty arbitration: privatizing public international law through inconsistent decisions' (2005) 73 Fordham Law Review 1521.

822 *Abaclat* above (n 11) para. 296.

823 Ibid., para. 297.

824 Ibid., para. 519.

825 Ibid., para. 249.

826 Ibid., para. 521.

a 'gap'.'[827] Therefore, it invoked its inherent powers to fill the gap and tackle the unprecedented difficulties posed by the claim, without amending any existing rule of procedure.

Once the issue of accepting a mass claim was reframed as one of adapting the standard ICSID rules of procedure,[828] the majority examined the admissibility of such scenario, concluding that—in spite of the necessary procedural restrictions that collective proceedings impose on both parties—the admission of the claim was appropriate:

> the Tribunal finds that not only would it be cost prohibitive for many Claimants to file individual claims but it would also be practically impossible for ICSID to deal separately with 60,000 individual arbitrations. Thus, the rejection of the admissibility of the present claims may equal a denial of justice.[829]

Professor Abi Saab dissented vigorously on this point. In his view, the silence in the applicable instruments was not a gap, but a confirmation that the powers of the tribunal and the standard arbitration rules do not cover mass proceedings. He claimed that a special agreement between the parties would be necessary to dispense with this jurisdictional limitation. Consent might provide for the foundational jurisdiction of the tribunal over mass claims—as a distinct category. In the alternative, the parties could agree on the specific jurisdiction of an existing mechanism over a particular dispute ('*secondary consent*'), thereby granting the tribunal with the power to adjust its procedural framework.[830] In the absence of either expression of consent, the tribunal had no jurisdiction on the claim as presented. Abi Saab took issue with the majority's view that the adjustment of procedure was a question of admissibility. In so far as procedure regulates the arbitration powers of the tribunal and regulates the arbitral function '*it is essentially a question of jurisdiction ... in its first and foremost sense of the legal power to exercise the judicial or arbitral function*'.[831]

827 Ibid., para. 526.

828 Ibid., para. 491: '*with regard to the 'mass' aspect of the present proceedings, the Tribunal considers that the relevant question is not 'has Argentina consented to the mass proceedings?', but rather 'can an ICSID arbitration be conducted in the form of 'mass proceedings' considering that this would require an adaptation and/or modification by the Tribunal of certain procedural rules provided for under the current ICSID framework?*'.

829 Ibid., para. 537.

830 Abi Saab dissent above (n 11) para. 185.

831 Ibid., para. 196.

Abi Saab contested also the majority's conclusion on the admissibility of the procedural adjustments. These adjustments, even assuming jurisdiction, would not fall within the tribunal's inherent powers to conduct the proceedings. The question would not be one of admissibility anyway, but one of abuse of judicial powers.[832]

The latest in the trail of Argentine-bonds cases was the *Alemanni* case. The tribunal did not attribute much weight to the diatribe regarding jurisdiction and admissibility. It noted that the distinction between the two is not very difficult to draw, nor is it very important.[833] Nonetheless, it referred to a '*broad division*,'[834] whereby objections of admissibility are those that invoke the reasons why the tribunal should not exercise a formal competence it possesses. The treatment of the 'mass-claim' objection built upon the arguments of the *Abaclat*'s and *Ambiente Ufficio*'s majorities and dissents, but tried to reframe the issue in simpler terms.

Argentina's argument that mass-claim proceedings would require a special (additional) consent was rejected. Parties' consent cannot expand the foundational jurisdiction of an ICSID tribunal,[835] nor did the multiplicity of claimants drive the claim outside the consent of the host State, as codified in the BIT's arbitration clause. The tribunal, indeed, accepted that the critical question was whether the multiple claims formed '*a* [single] *dispute*' under Article 8 of the Italy/Argentina BIT.[836] This question, which the tribunal joined to the analysis of the merits, went straight to the jurisdiction of the tribunal, not to the admissibility of the claim, as the tribunal held in *Abaclat*.[837]

Abi Saab's characterisation of the majority's reasoning in *Abaclat* is an ideal summary of the issues exposed in this section (and explains the careful reasoning of the *Ambiente Ufficio* majority, which reached the same conclusions but avoided to replicate the reasoning of the *Abaclat* award[838]). The distinction between jurisdiction and admissibility sometimes matters to the outcome of

832 Ibid., para. 262.

833 *Alemanni* above (n 32) para. 257.

834 Ibid., para. 260.

835 Ibid., para. 269.

836 Ibid., para. 292. The application of consent to 'a' dispute is also reflected in the language of the ICSID Institution Rules (Article 2) and ICSID Arbitration Rules (Rule 1).

837 By simply equating the consent to single claims several to the consent to their joint presentation, indeed, '*the Abaclat tribunal begged the question as to jurisdiction that required an answer, and sublimated it into an issue of mere 'admissibility*''; see ibid., para. 289.

838 The attempts of the majority of the *Ambiente Ufficio*'s panel to engage with Abi Saab's dissent are criticised as perfunctory by the dissenting arbitrator. See the dissenting opinion of Torres Bernárdez above (n 36) para. 55 ff.

investment proceedings. Unfortunately, the contours of these legal principles are blurry and contested, and so are the exact legal effects and implications of each (for instance, doubts remain on the sanctions entailed by a breach, and whether the tribunal's discretion or the parties' consent can trump it). The resulting scenario is one of legal uncertainty:

> [the majority wrongly held] that all limitations on the jurisdiction and powers of the Tribunal are obstacles in the way of achieving this object and purpose, that should be 'down-graded', (even with untenable arguments) from 'jurisdictional' to 'admissibility' issues; [it wrongly assumed] that admissibility is less important in its function and legal effects than jurisdiction; [it assumed] wrongly again that questions of admissibility, are at the discretion of the Tribunal, which can dismiss them at will as a result of its own subjective 'balancing of interests' ...[839]

Conclusions

This study showed the tribunals' and scholars' difficulties of telling jurisdiction from admissibility in investment arbitration, and reckoned with the common assumption that the distinction is ultimately useless. Investment treaty arbitration, just like international adjudication at large, would benefit from a clearer taxonomy of these principles of adjudication. The opposite views on jurisdiction and admissibility cannot be reconciled and the clash of the respective implications might even undermine the basic principles of international law:

> As recent investor-host State arbitral decisions and awards have had the occasion to recall, in public international law there *does not exist a default jurisdiction*. The residual default rule is no jurisdiction. To try to fabricate a different rule through arbitral or judicial decisions by means of a free interpretation approach to compromissory clauses in BITs cannot but weaken the ICSID system whose cornerstone is the consent of the Contracting Parties, and general public international law as well, and will

839 Abi Saab dissent above (n 11) para. 261. A similar remark is made in *Ambiente Ufficio* above (n 36) para. 575: '*In no way would the distinction between jurisdictional and admissibility issues suggest a different degree of 'bindingness'*.' However, the tribunal seemed to overlook the other differences that could result from classifying a procedural defect under either category.

> end in a fiasco. *Pacta sunt servanda* and the law of treaties are among the most direct casualties, but there are others as well.[840]

This stall creates an embarrassing recurrence in investment arbitration.[841] The claimant will argue that the preconditions are procedural and dismissible; the respondent will invoke their mandatory and jurisdictional nature. Both parties will have ample support in the form of arbitral precedents and scholarly literature. Tribunals will pretend that all precedents are somewhat distinguishable, and recite the euphemism that '*this area of investment treaty law remains in the process of developing a jurisprudence constant*'.[842] Then, they will do as they deem fit, drawing ammunition from either camp, and in so doing providing ammunition thereto, for future cases.

The study described the practice, and questioned the theory. Whereas it is possible to navigate the former, there are real shortcomings that are caused by the latter, in particular the difficulty in drawing a line between jurisdiction and admissibility in general international law and in investment practice. A fresh start would be desirable, to leave behind DYI solutions and strategic evasion of the unresolved issues. Shany's proposal to oppose the parties' consent and the tribunal's discretion has the merit of doing away from sloppy classifications without undoing all the theoretical efforts expended so far. It is claimed that such distinction should be endorsed in the practice, and inform the analysis of investment tribunals.

Table of Authorities

1 Decisions of Investment Tribunals

Abaclat and Others (Case formerly known as Giovanna Beccara and Others) v. Argentine Republic, ICSID Case No. ARB/07/5, Decision on Jurisdiction and Admissibility of 4 August 2011

ABCI Investments N.V. v. Republic of Tunisia, ICSID Case No. ARB/04/12, Decision on Jurisdiction of 18 February 2011

Accession Mezzanine Capital L.P. and Danubius Kereskedöház Vagyonkezelö Zrt. v. Hungary, ICSID Case No. ARB/12/3, Decision on Respondent's Objection under Arbitration Rule 41(5) of 16 January 2013

840 Dissenting opinion of Torres Bernárdez above (n 36) para. 60.

841 Commenting on the inconsistence practice regarding pre-arbitration requirements, Born and Šćekić above (n 574) 239, note that '[t]*his uncertainty is inconsistent with the objectives of the arbitral process.*'

842 *Philip Morris* above (n 790) para. 134.

Achmea B.V. v. The Slovak Republic, UNCITRAL, PCA Case No. 2013-12 (Number 2), Award on Jurisdiction and Admissibility of 20 May 2014

ADC Affiliate Ltd. and ADC & ADMC Mgmt. Ltd v. Republic of Hungary, ICSID Case No. ARB/03/16, Award of 2 October 2006

AES Corporation and Tau Power B.V. v. Republic of Kazakhstan, ICSID Case No. ARB/10/16, Award of 1 November 2013

Aguas del Tunari, S.A. v. Republic of Bolivia, ICSID Case No. ARB/02/3, Decision on Respondent's Objections to Jurisdiction of 21 October 2005

Mohamed Abdulmohsen Al-Kharafi & Sons Co. v. Libya and others, Final Arbitral Award of 22 March 2013

Giovanni Alemanni and Others v. The Argentine Republic, ICSID Case No. ARB/07/8, Decision on Jurisdiction and Admissibility of 17 November 2014

Rafat Ali Rizvi v Republic of Indonesia, ICSID Case No. ARB/11/13, Award on Jurisdiction of 16 July 2013

Kristian Almås and Geir Almås v. The Republic of Poland, UNCITRAL, Award of 27 June 2016

Alpha Projektholding GmbH v. Ukraine, ICSID Case No. ARB/07/16, Award of 8 November 2010

Alps Finance and Trade AG v. The Slovak Republic, UNCITRAL, Award of 5 March 2011

Álvarez y Marín Corporación S.A. and others v. Republic of Panama, ICSID Case No. ARB/15/14, Reasoning of the Decision on Respondent's Preliminary Objections pursuant to ICSID Arbitration Rule 41(5) of 4 April 2016

Hesham T.M. Al Warraq v. Republic of Indonesia, UNCITRAL, Final Award of 15 December 2014

Ambiente Ufficio S.p.A. and others v. Argentine Republic, ICSID Case No. ARB/08/9 (formerly *Giordano Alpi and others v. Argentine Republic*), Decision on Jurisdiction and Admissibility of 8 February 2013

Ambiente Ufficio S.p.A. and others v. Argentine Republic, ICSID Case No. ARB/08/9 (formerly *Giordano Alpi and others v. Argentine Republic*), Dissenting Opinion of Santiago Torres Bernárdez of 2 May 2013

Amco Indonesia Corporation and others v. Republic of Indonesia, ICSID Case No. ARB/81/1, Decision on Jurisdiction of 25 September 1983, 1 ICSID Reports 389 (1993)

Mohammad Ammar Al-Bahloul v. The Republic of Tajikistan, SCC Case No. V (064/2008), Partial Award of 2 September 2009

Amoco Asia Corporation v Republic of Indonesia, ICSID Case No. ARB/81/1, Decision on Jurisdiction (Resubmitted Case) of 10 May 1988

Ampal-American Israel Corporation and others v. Arab Republic of Egypt, ICSID Case No. ARB/12/11, Award of 1 February 2016

AMTO v. Ukraine, SCC No. 80/2005, Award of 26 March 2008

Alasdair Ross Anderson and others v. Costa Rica, ICSID Case No. ARB(AF)/07/3, Award of 19 May 2010

Ansung Housing Company Limited v China, ICSID Case No. ARB/14/25, Award of 9 March 2017

Apotex Inc. v. The Government of the United States of America, UNCITRAL, Award on Jurisdiction and Admissibility of 14 June 2013

Mr. Franck Charles Arif v. Republic of Moldova, ICSID ARB/11/23, Award of 8 April 2013

Austrian Airlines AG v. The Slovak Republic, UNCITRAL Final Award of 9 October 2009

Autopista Concesionada de Venezuela, C.A. v. Bolivarian Republic of Venezuela, ICSID Case No. ARB/00/5, Decision on Jurisdiction of 27 September 2001

Mr. Hassan Awdi, Enterprise Business Consultants, Inc. and Alfa El Corporation v. Romania, ICSID Case No. ARB/10/13, Decision on the Admissibility of the Respondent's Third Objection to Jurisdiction and Admissibility of Claimant's Claims of 26 July 2013

Mr. Hassan Awdi, Enterprise Business Consultants, Inc. and Alfa El Corporation v. Romania, ICSID Case No. ARB/10/13, Award of 2 March 2015

AWG Group v. The Argentine Republic, UNCITRAL, Decision on Jurisdiction of 3 August 2006

Azurix Corp v. Argentina, ICSID Case No ARB/01/12, Decision on the Application for Annulment of 1 September 2009

Banro American Resources, Inc. and Société Aurifère du Kivu et du Maniema S.A.R.L. v. Democratic Republic of the Congo, ICSID Case No. ARB/98/7, Award of 1 September 2000

Bayindir Insaat Turizm Ticaret Ve Sanayi A.S. v. Islamic Republic of Pakistan, ICSID Case No. ARB/03/29, Decision on Jurisdiction of 14 November 2005

Bayview Irrigation District et al. v. United Mexican States, ICSID Case No. ARB(AF)/05/1, Award of 19 July 2007

Aaron C. Berkowitz, Brett E. Berkowitz and Trevor B. Berkowitz (formerly *Spence International Investments and others*) *v. Republic of Costa Rica*, ICSID Case No. UNCT/13/2, Interim Award of 25 October 2016

Vladimir and Moise Berschader v. The Russian Federation, SCC Case No 080/2004, Award of 21 April 2006

Biloune v. Ghana Investments Centre, Award of 27 October 1989 and 30 June 1990, XIX Yearbook Commercial Arbitration 11, 1994

Biwater Gauff (Tanzania) Ltd. v. United Republic of Tanzania, ICSID Case No. ARB/05/22, Award of 24 July 2008

Blue Bank International & Trust (Barbados) Ltd. v. Bolivarian Republic of Venezuela, ICSID Case No. ARB 12/20, Award of 26 April 2017

Blusun S.A., Jean-Pierre Lecorcier and Michael Stein v. Italian Republic, ICSID Case No. ARB/14/3, Award of 27 December 2016

Luigiterzo Bosca v. Lithuania, PCA Case No. 2011-05, Award of 17 May 2013

Bureau Veritas, Inspection, Valuation, Assessment and Control, BIVAC B.V. v. The Republic of Paraguay, ICSID Case No. ARB/07/9, Decision on the Objections to Jurisdiction of 29 May 2009

Burimi SRL and Eagle Games SH.A v. Republic of Albania, ICSID Case No. ARB/11/18, Award of 29 May 2013

Burlington Resources Inc. v. Republic of Ecuador, (formerly *Burlington Resources Inc. and others v. Republic of Ecuador and Empresa Estatal Petróleos del Ecuador (PetroEcuador)*), ICSID Case No. ARB/08/5 Decision on Jurisdiction of 2 June 2010

Burlington Resources Inc. v. Republic of Ecuador, (formerly *Burlington Resources Inc. and others v. Republic of Ecuador and Empresa Estatal Petróleos del Ecuador (PetroEcuador)*), ICSID Case No. ARB/08/5, Decision on Liability of 14 December 2012

Cambodia Power Company v. Kingdom of Cambodia, ICSID Case No. ARB/09/18, Decision on Jurisdiction of 22 March 2011

Camuzzi International S.A. v. Argentine Republic, ICSID Case No. ARB/03/2, Decision on Jurisdiction of 11 May 2005

Canadian Cattlemen for Fair Trade v. United States of America, UNCITRAL (formerly *Consolidated Canadian Claims v. United States of America*), Award of Jurisdiction of 28 January 2008

Muhammet Çap & Sehil Inşaat Endustri ve Ticaret Ltd. Sti. v. Turkmenistan, ICSID Case No. ARB/12/6, Decision on Respondent's Objection to Jurisdiction under Article VII(2) of 13 February 2015

Cementownia "Nowa Huta" S.A. v. Republic of Turkey, ICSID Case No. ARB(AF)/06/2, Award of 17 September 2009

Central European Aluminium Company (CEAC) v. Montenegro, ICSID Case No. ARB/14/8, Award of 26 July 2016

Champion Trading Company, Ameritrade International, Inc. v. Arab Republic of Egypt, ICSID Case No. ARB/02/9 (formerly *Champion Trading Company, Ameritrade International, Inc., James T. Wahba, John B. Wahba, Timothy T. Wahba v. Arab Republic of Egypt*), see Decision on Jurisdiction of 21 October 2003

Chevron Corporation (USA) and Texaco Petroleum Company (USA) v. The Republic of Ecuador, UNCITRAL, PCA Case No. 34877, Interim Award of 1 December 2008

Chevron Corporation (USA) and Texaco Petroleum Company (USA) v. The Republic of Ecuador, UNCITRAL, PCA Case No. 34877, Partial Award on the Merits of 30 March 2010

Chevron Corporation and Texaco Petroleum Corporation v. The Republic of Ecuador, UNCITRAL, PCA Case No. 2009-23, Third Interim Award on Jurisdiction and Admissibility of 27 February 2012

Churchill Mining PLC and Planet Mining Pty Ltd v. Republic of Indonesia, ICSID Case No. ARB/12/14 and 12/40, Decision on Jurisdiction of 24 February 2014

CMS Gas Transmission Company v. Argentina, ARB/01/8, Decision on Jurisdiction, 17 July 2003

CMS Gas Transmission Company v. The Republic of Argentina, Decision of the ad hoc Committee on the Application for Annulment of the Argentine Republic of 25 September 2007

Compañia de Aguas del Aconquija SA. and Vivendi Universal SA. v. Argentine Republic, ICSID Case No. ARB/97/3, Decision on Annulment of 3 July 2002

Consortium Groupement L.E.S.I.-Dipenta v. People's Democratic Republic of Algeria, ICSID Case No. ARB/03/8, Award of 10 January 2005

Consortium RFCC v. Royaume du Maroc, ICSID Case No. ARB/00/6, Decision on Jurisdiction of 16 July 2001

Consortium RFCC v. Royaume du Maroc, ICSID Case No. ARB/00/6, Award of 22 December 2003

Continental Casualty Company v. The Argentine Republic, ICSID Case No. ARB/03/9, Decision on Jurisdiction of 22 February 2006

Convial Callao S.A. y CCI—Compañía de concesiones de Infraestructura S.A. c. República del Perú, ICSID Case No. ARB/10/2, Laudo Final of 21 May 2013

Copper Mesa Mining Corporation v. Republic of Ecuador, PCA No. 2012-2, Award of 15 March 2016

Corona Materials LLC v. Dominican Republic, ICSID Case No. ARB(AF)/14/3, Award on Preliminary Objections of 31 May 2016

Crystallex International Corporation v. Bolivarian Republic of Venezuela, ICSID Case No. ARB(AF)/11/2, Award of 4 April 2016

Ceskoslovenska Obchodni Banka, A.S. v. The Slovak Republic, ICSID Case No. ARB/97/4, Decision of the Tribunal on Objections to Jurisdictions of 24 May 1999

Consortium RFCC v. Royaume du Maroc, ICSID Case No. ARB/00/6, Decision on Jurisdiction of 16 July 2001

Daimler Financial Services AG v. Argentine Republic, ICSID Case No. ARB/05/1, Award of 22 August 2012

Daimler Financial Services AG v. Argentine Republic, ICSID Case No. ARB/05/1, Decision on Annulment of 7 January 2015

Deutsche Bank AG v. Democratic Socialist Republic of Sri Lanka, ICSID Case No. ARB/09/2, Award of 31 October 2012

Duke Energy International Peru Investments No. 1 Ltd. v. Republic of Peru, ICSID Case No. ARB/03/28, Decision on Jurisdiction of 1 February 2006

Duke Energy Electroquil Partners & Electroquil S.A. v. *Republic of Ecuador*, ICSID Case No. ARB/04/19, Award of 18 August 2008

EDF International S.A., SAUR International S.A. and León Participaciones Argentinas S.A. v. Argentine Republic, ICSID Case No. ARB/03/23, Award of 11 June 2012

EDF (Services) Limited v. Romania, ICSID Case No. ARB/05/13, Award of 8 October 2009

El Paso Energy International Company v. Argentine Republic, ICSID Case No ARB/03/15, Decision on Jurisdiction, 27 April 2006

Emmis International Holding, B.V., Emmis Radio Operating, B.V., MEM Magyar Electronic Media Kereskedelmi és Szolgáltató Kft. v. The Republic of Hungary, ICSID Case No. ARB/12/2, Decision on Respondent's Objection under ICSID Arbitration Rule 41(5) of 11 March 2013

Emmis International Holding, B.V., Emmis Radio Operating, B.V., MEM Magyar Electronic Media Kereskedelmi és Szolgáltató Kft. v. The Republic of Hungary, ICSID Case No. ARB/12/2, Award of 16 April 2014

Empresa Eléctrica del Ecuador, Inc. v. Republic of Ecuador, ICSID Case No. ARB/05/9, Award of 2 June 2009

Enron Corporation and Ponderosa Assets, LP v Argentine Republic, ICSID Case No ARB/01/3, Decision on Jurisdiction of 14 January 2004

Eskosol S.p.A. in liquidazione v. Italian Republic, ICSID Case No. ARB/15/50, Decision on Respondent's Application under Rule 41(5) of 20 March 2017

Ethyl Corporation v. The Government of Canada, UNCITRAL, Award on Jurisdiction of 24 June 1998

Eureko B.V. v Republic of Poland, Ad Hoc Arbitration, Partial Award of 19 August 2005

Europe Cement Investment & Trade S.A. v. Turkey, ICSID Case No. ARB(AF)/07/2, Award of 13 August 2009

Fedax N.V. v. The Republic of Venezuela, ICSID Case No. ARB/96/3, Decision of the Tribunal on Objections to Jurisdiction of 11 July 1997

Fireman's Fund Insurance Company v. The United Mexican States, ICSID Case No. ARB(AF)/02/1, Decision on the Preliminary Question of 17 July 2003

Flemingo DutyFree Shop Private Limited v the Republic of Poland, UNCITRAL, Award of 12 August 2016

Flughafen Zürich A.G. et Gestión e Ingenería IDC S.A. v. Bolivarian Republic of Venezuela, ICSID CASE No. ARB/10/19, Award of 18 November 2014

Fraport AG Frankfurt Airport Services Worldwide v. The Republic of the Philippines (Fraport I), ICSID Case No. ARB/03/25, Award of 16 August 2007

Fraport AG Frankfurt Airport Services Worldwide v. Republic of the Philippines (Fraport II), ICSID Case No. ARB/11/12, Award of 10 December 2014

Gami Inv., Inc. v. The Government of the United Mexican States, UNCITRAL-NAFTA, Final Award of 15 November 2004

Garanti Koza LLP v. Turkmenistan, ICSID Case No. ARB/11/20, Decision on the Objection to Jurisdiction for Lack of Consent of 3 July 2013

Serafín García Armas and Karina García Gruber v. The Bolivarian Republic of Venezuela, UNCITRAL, Caso CPA No. 2013-3, Decision on Jurisdiction of 15 December 2014

Alex Genin, Eastern Credit Limited, Inc. and A. S. Baltoil v. The Republic of Estonia, ICSID Case No. ARB/99/2, Award of 25 June 2001

Getma International and others v. Republic of Guinea, ICSID Case No. ARB/11/29, Decision on Jurisdiction of 29 December 2012

Getma International and others v. Republic of Guinea, ICSID Case No. ARB/11/29, Award of 16 August 2016

Global Trading Resource Corp. and Globex International, Inc. v. Ukraine, ICSID Case No. ARB/09/11, Award of 1 December 2010.

Gold Reserve Inc. v. Bolivarian Republic of Venezuela, ICSID Case No. ARB(AF)/09/1, Award of 22 September 2014

Government of the Province of East Kalimantan v. PT Kaltim Prima Coal and others, ICSID Case No. ARB/07/3, Award on Jurisdiction of 28 December 2009

Grand River Enterprises Six Nations, Ltd., et al. v. United States of America, UNCITRAL, Award of 12 January 2011

Philippe Gruslin v. Malaysia, ICSID Case No. ARB/99/3, Award of 27 November 2000

Rachel S. Grynberg, Stephen M. Grynberg, Miriam Z. Grynberg and RSM Production Company v. Grenada, ICSID Case No. ARB/10/6, Award of 10 December 2010

Guaracachi America, Inc. and Rurelec PLC v. The Plurinational State of Bolivia, UNCITRAL, PCA Case No. 2011-17, Award of 31 January 2014

Guardian Fiduciary Trust, Ltd, f/k/a Capital Conservator Savings & Loan, Ltd v. Macedonia, former Yugoslav Republic of, ICSID Case No. ARB/12/31, Award of 22 September 2015

Gustav F W Hamester GmbH & Co KG v. Republic of Ghana, ICSID Case No. ARB/07/24, Award, 18 June 2010

H&H Enterprises Investments, Inc. v. Arab Republic of Egypt, ICSID Case No. ARB 09/15, Decision on Objections to Jurisdiction of 5 June 2012

Helnan International Hotels A/S v. Arab Republic of Egypt, ICSID Case No. ARB/05/19, Decision on Objection to Jurisdiction of 17 October 2006

Helnan International Hotels A/S v. Arab Republic of Egypt, ICSID Case No. ARB/05/19, Award of 3 July 2008

HICEE B.V. v. The Slovak Republic, UNCITRAL, PCA Case No. 2009-11, Partial Award of 23 May 2011

Hochtief AG v. Argentina, ICSID Case no. ARB/07/31, Decision on Jurisdiction of 24 October 2011

Hulley Enterprises Limited (Cyprus) v. The Russian Federation, UNCITRAL, PCA Case No. AA 226, Interim Award on Jurisdiction and Admissibility of 30 November 2009

Hulley Enterprises Limited (Cyprus) v. The Russian Federation, UNCITRAL, PCA Case No. AA 226, Final Award of 18 July 2014

Iberdrola Energía S.A. v. Republic of Guatemala, ICSID Case No. ARB/09/5, Award of 17 August 2012

Iberdrola Energía S.A. v. Republic of Guatemala, ICSID Case No. ARB/09/5, Decision on Annulment of 13 January 2015

İçkale İnşaat Limited Şirketi v. Turkmenistan, ICSID Case No. ARB/10/24, Award of 8 March 2016

ICS Inspection and Control Services Limited (United Kingdom) v. The Republic of Argentina, UNCITRAL, PCA Case No. 2010-9, Award on Jurisdiction of 10 February 2012

Impregilo S.p.A. v. Islamic Republic of Pakistan, ICSID Case No. ARB/03/3, Decision on Jurisdiction of 22 April 2005

Inmaris Perestroika Sailing Maritime Services GmbH and others v. Ukraine, ICSID Case No. ARB/08/8, Decision on Jurisdiction of 8 March 2010

Inceysa Vallisoletana S.L. v. Republic of El Salvador, ICSID Case No. ARB/03/26, Award of 2 August 2006

International Thunderbird Gaming Corporation v. The United Mexican States, UNCITRAL, Award of 26 January 2006

Isolux Netherlands, BV v. Kingdom of Spain, SCC Case V2013/153, Award of 17 July 2016

Jan de Nul N.V. and Dredging International N.V. v. Arab Republic of Egypt, ICSID Case No. ARB/04/13, Decision on Jurisdiction of 16 June 2006

Joy Mining Machinery Limited v. Arab Republic of Egypt, ICSID Case No. ARB/03/11, Award on Jurisdiction of 6 August 2004

Ioannis Kardassopoulos v. Georgia, ICSID Case No. ARB/05/18, Decision on Jurisdiction of 6 July 2007

Ioannis Kardassopoulos v. Republic of Georgia, ICSID Case No. ARB/05/18, Award of 3 March 2010

Kılıç İnşaat İthalat İhracat Sanayi ve Ticaret Anonim Şirketi v. Turkmenistan, ICSID Case No. ARB/10/1, Award of 2 July 2013

Kılıç İnşaat İthalat İhracat Sanayi ve Ticaret Anonim Şirketi v. Turkmenistan, ICSID Case No. ARB/10/1, Decision on Annulment of 15 July 2015

Klöckner Industrie-Anlagen GmbH and others v. United Republic of Cameroon and Société Camerounaise des Engrais, ICSID Case No. ARB/81/2, Award of 21 October 1983

KT Asia Investment Group B.V. v. Republic of Kazakhstan, ICSID Case No. ARB/09/8, Award of 17 October 2013

Lanco International Inc. v. The Argentine Republic, ICSID Case No. ARB/97/6, Preliminary Decision on Jurisdiction of 8 December 1998

Lao Holdings N.V. v. The Lao People's Democratic Republic, ICSID Case No. ARB(AF)/12/6, Decision on Jurisdiction of 21 February 2014

Lance Larsen v. the Hawaiian Kingdom, PCA case no. 99-001, UNCITRAL 1976 Rules, Award of 5 February 2001, (2001) 119 ILR 566

Renée Rose Levy and Gremcitel S.A. v. Republic of Peru, ICSID Case No. ARB/11/17, Award of 9 January 2015

Liman Caspian Oil BV and NCL Dutch Investment BV v. Republic of Kazakhstan, ICSID Case No. ARB/07/14, Excerpts of Award of 22 June 2010

Loewen Group, Inc. and Raymond L. Loewen v. United States of America, ICSID Case No. ARB(AF)/98/3, Award of 26 June 2003

Empresas Lucchetti, S.A. and Lucchetti Peru, S.A. v. The Republic of Peru, ICSID Case No. ARB/03/4 (also known as *Industria Nacional de Alimentos, A.S. and Indalsa Perú S.A. v. The Republic of Peru*), Decision on Annulment of 5 September 2007

Emilio Agustín Maffezini v. The Kingdom of Spain, ICSID Case No. ARB/97/7, Decision on Jurisdiction of 25 January 2000

Mr. Yosef Maiman and Others v. Egypt, UNCITRAL (confidential)

Malaysian Historical Salvors, SDN, BHD v. The Government of Malaysia, ICSID Case No. ARB/05/10, Award on Jurisdiction of 17 May 2007

Malaysian Historical Salvors, SDN, BHD v. Malaysia, ICSID Case No. ARB/05/10, Dissenting Opinion of Judge Mohamed Shahabuddeen of 19 February 2009

Malaysian Historical Salvors, SDN, BHD v. Malaysia, ICSID Case No. ARB/05/10, Decision on the Application for Annulment of 16 April 2009

Malicorp Limited v. The Arab Republic of Egypt, ICSID Case No. ARB/08/18, Award of 7 February 2011

M.C.I. Power Group L.C. and New Turbine, Inc. v. Republic of Ecuador, ICSID Case ARB/03/6, Award of 31 July 2007

Menzies Middle East and Africa S.A. and Aviation Handling Services International Ltd. v. Republic of Senegal, ICSID Case No. ARB/15/21, Award of 5 August 2016

MetalTech Ltd. v Republic of Uzbekistan, ICSID Case No. ARB/10/3, Award of 4 October 2013

Methanex v. USA, UNCITRAL (NAFTA), First Partial Award, 7 August 2002

Joan Micula, Viorel Micula, S.C. European Food S.A., S.C. Starmii S.R.L. and S.C. Multipack S.R.L. v. Romania, ICSID Case No. ARB/05/20, Decision on Jurisdiction and Admissibility, 24 September 2008

Mihaly International Corporation v. Sri Lanka, ICSID Case No. ARB/00/2, Award of 15 March 2002

Millicom International Operations B.V. and Sentel GSM SA v. The Republic of Senegal, ICSID Case No. ARB/08/20, Decision on Jurisdiction of 16 July 2010

David Minnotte and Robert Lewis v. Republic of Poland, ICSID Case No. ARB(AF)/10/1, Award of 16 May 2014

Patrick Mitchell v. Democratic Republic of Congo, ICSID Case No. ARB/99/7, Decision on the Application for Annulment of the Award of 1 November 2006

MNSS B.V. and Recupero Credito Acciaio N.V. v. Montenegro, ICSID Case No. ARB(AF)/12/8, Award of 4 May 2016

Mobil Corporation, Venezuela Holdings, B.V., Mobil Cerro negro Holding, Ltd., Mobil Venezolana de Petróleos Holdings, Inc., Mobil Cerro Negro, Ltd., and Mobil Venezolana de Petróleos, Inc. v. Bolivarian Republic of Venezuela, ICSID Case No. ARB/07/27, Decision on Jurisdiction of 10 June 2010

Mondev International Ltd. v. United States of America, ICSID Case No. ARB(AF)/99/2, Award of 11 October 2002

MTD Equity Sdn. Bhd. & MTD Chile SA v. Chile, ICSID Case No. ARB/01/7, Award of 25 May 2004

Murphy Exploration & Production Company International v. Republic of Ecuador, ICSID Case No. ARB/08/4, Award on Jurisdiction of 15 December 2010

Murphy Exploration & Production Company International v. Republic of Ecuador, PCA Case No. 2012-16 (formerly AA 434), Partial Final Award of 6 May 2016

Mytilineos Holdings SA v. The State Union of Serbia & Montenegro and Republic of Serbia, UNCITRAL, Partial Award on Jurisdiction of 8 September 2006

National Gas S.A.E v. Arab Republic of Egypt, ICSID Case No. ARB/11/7, Award of 3 April 2014

National Grid plc v. The Argentine Republic, UNCITRAL, Decision on Jurisdiction of 20 June 2006

Nations Energy Corporation, Electric Machinery Enterprises Inc., and Jamie Jurado v. The Republic of Panama, ICSID Case No. ARB/06/19, Award of 24 November 2010

Niko Resources Ltd. v. Bangladesh Petroleum Exploration & Production Company Limited and Bangladesh Oil Gas and Mineral Corporation, ICSID Case No. ARB/10/11, Decision on Jurisdiction of 19 August 2013

Noble Ventures, Inc v. Romania, ICSID Case No ARB/O 1/11, Award of 12 October 2005

Nordzucker v. Poland, UNCITRAL, Partial Award on Jurisdiction of 10 December 2008

Nova Scotia Power Incorporated (Canada) v. República Bolivariana de Venezuela, UNCITRAL, Decision on Jurisdiction of 22 April 2010

Nova Scotia Power Incorporated v. Bolivarian Republic of Venezuela, ICSID Case No. ARB(AF)/11/1, Award of 30 April 2014

Occidental Exploration and Production Company v. The Republic of Ecuador, LCIA Case No. UN3467, Award of 1 July 2004

Jan Oostergetel and Theodora Laurentius v. The Slovak Republic, UNCITRAL Decision on Jurisdiction of 30 April 2010

OPIC Karimum Corporation v. The Bolivarian Republic of Venezuela, ICSID Case No. ARB/10/14, Award of 28 May 2013

Orascom TMT Investments S.à r.l. v. People's Democratic Republic of Algeria, ICSID Case No. ARB/12/35, Final Award of 31 May 2017

Oxus Gold plc v. Republic of Uzbekistan, the State Committee of Uzbekistan for Geology & Mineral Resources, and Navoi Mining & Metallurgical Kombinat, UNCITRAL, Award of 17 December 2015

Pac Rim Cayman LLC v. Republic of El Salvador, ICSID Case No. ARB/09/12, Decision on the Respondent's Jurisdictional Objections of 1 June 2012

Pan American Energy LLC and BP Argentina Exploration Company v. The Argentine Republic, ICSID Case No. ARB/03/13, Decision on Preliminary Objections of 27 July 2006

Pan American Energy LLC v. Plurinational State of Bolivia, ICSID Case No. ARB/10/8, Decision on the Respondent's Preliminary Objections of 26 April 2013

Pantechniki S.A. Contractors & Engineers (Greece) v. The Republic of Albania, ICSID Case No. ARB/07/21, Award of 30 July 2009

Sergei Paushok, CJSC Golden East Company and CJSC Vostokneftegaz Company v. The Government of Mongolia, UNCITRAL, Award on Jurisdiction and Liability of 28 April 2011

Victor Pey Casado and President Allende Foundation v. Republic of Chile, ICSID Case No. ARB/98/2, Award of 8 May 2008

Philip Morris Asia Limited v. The Commonwealth of Australia, UNCITRAL, PCA Case No. 2012-12, Award on Jurisdiction and Admissibility of 17 December 2015

Philip Morris Brands Sàrl, Philip Morris Products S.A. and Abal Hermanos S.A. v. Oriental Republic of Uruguay, ICSID Case No. ARB/10/7 (formerly *FTR Holding SA, Philip Morris Products S.A. and Abal Hermanos S.A. v. Oriental Republic of Uruguay*) Decision on Jurisdiction of 2 July 2013

Phoenix Action Ltd v. Czech Republic, ICSID Case No. ARB/06/5, Award of 15 April 2009

Ping An Life Insurance Company, Limited and Ping An Insurance (Group) Company, Limited v. The Government of Belgium, ICSID Case No. ARB/12/29, Award of 30 April 2015

PJSC Ukrnafta v. The Russian Federation, UNCITRAL, PCA Case No. 2015-34, Award on Jurisdiction of 4 July 2017

PJSC Ukrnafta v. The Russian Federation, UNCITRAL, PCA Case No. 2015-34, Award on Jurisdiction of 4 July 2017

Plama Consortium Limited v. Republic of Bulgaria, ICSID Case No. ARB/03/24, Decision on Jurisdiction of 8 February 2005

Plama Consortium Limited v. Republic of Bulgaria, ICSID Case No ARB/03/24, Award of 27 August 2008

Poštová Banka, a.s. and Istrokapital SE v. The Hellenic Republic, ICSID Case No. ARB/13/8, Award of 9 April 2015

Quiborax S.A., Non Metallic Minerals S.A. and Allan Fosk Kaplún v. Plurinational State of Bolivia, ICSID Case No. ARB/06/2, Decision on Jurisdiction of 27 September 2012

Renta 4 S.V.S.A, Ahorro Corporación Emergentes F.I., Ahorro Corporación Eurofondo F.I., Rovime Inversiones SICAV S.A., Quasar de Valors SICAV S.A., Orgor de Valores SICAV S.A., GBI 9000 SICAV S.A. v. The Russian Federation, SCC No. 24/2007, Award on Preliminary Objections of 20 March 2009

Romak S.A. (Switzerland) v. The Republic of Uzbekistan, PCA Case No. AA280 (UNCITRAL Rules), Award of 26 November 2009

Rompetrol Group N.V. v. Romania, ICSID Case No. ARB/06/3, Decision on the Respondent's Preliminary Objections on Jurisdiction and Admissibility of 18 April 2008

RosInvestCo UK Ltd. v. The Russian Federation, SCC Case No. V079/2005, Award on Jurisdiction of 1 October 2007

Spyridon Roussalis v. Romania, ICSID Case No. ARB/06/1, Award of 7 December 2011

RSM Production Corporation v. Grenada, ICSID Case No. ARB/05/14, Award of 13 March 2009

Rusoro Mining Ltd. v. Bolivarian Republic of Venezuela, ICSID Case No. ARB(AF)/12/5, Award of 22 August 2016

Mr. Saba Fakes v. Republic of Turkey, ICSID Case No. ARB/07/20, Award of 14 July 2010

Saipem S.p.A. v. The People's Republic of Bangladesh, ICSID Case No. ARB/05/07, Decision on Jurisdiction and Recommendation on Provisional Measures of 21 March 2007

Salini Costruttori S.p.A. and Italstrade S.p.A. v. The Hashemite Kingdom of Jordan, ICSID Case No. ARB/02/13, Decision on Jurisdiction of 9 November 2004

Salini Costruttori s.p.a. and Italstrade S.p.A. v. The Kingdom of Morocco, ICSID Case No. ARB/00/4, Decision on Jurisdiction of 23 July 2001

Saluka Investments B.V. v. Czech Republic, UNCITRAL, Partial Award of 17 March 2006

Sanum Investments Limited v. Lao People's Democratic Republic, UNCITRAL, PCA Case No. 2013-13, Jurisdictional Award of 13 December 2013

S.A.R.L. Benvenuti & Bonfant v. People's Republic of the Congo, ICSID/ARB/77/2, Award of 8 August 1980

Werner Schneider, acting in his capacity as insolvency administrator of Walter Bau Ag (In Liquidation) v. The Kingdom of Thailand, UNCITRAL (formerly *Walter Bau AG (in liquidation) v. The Kingdom of Thailand*), Award of 1 July 2009

S.D. Myers, Inc. v. Government of Canada, UNCITRAL, Partial Award of 13 November 2000

S.D. Myers, Inc. v. Government of Canada, UNCITRAL, Second Partial Award of 21 October 2002

Sempra Energy International v. The Argentine Republic, ICSID Case No. ARB/02/16, Decision on Objections to Jurisdiction of 11 May 2005

Sempra Energy International v. Argentine Republic, ICSID Case No. ARB/02116, Award of 28 September 2007

SGS Société Générale de Surveillance SA v. Islamic Republic of Pakistan, ICSID Case No ARB/01/13, Decision on Jurisdiction of 6 August 2003

SGS Société Générale de Surveillance SA v. The Republic of Paraguay, ICSID Case No ARB/07/29, Award of 12 February 2012

SGS Société Générale de Surveillance SA v. Republic of the Philippines, ICSID Case No ARB/02/6, Decision on Jurisdiction, 29 January 2004

Waguih Elie George Siag and Clorinda Vecchi v. The Arab Republic of Egypt, ICSID Case No. ARB/05/15, Decision on Jurisdiction, and Partial Dissenting Opinion of Professor Francisco Orrego Vicuña of 11 April 2007

Waguih Elie George Siag and Clorinda Vecchi v. The Arab Republic of Egypt, ICSID Case No. ARB/05/15, Award of 1 June 2009

Soabi v. Republic of Senegal, ICSID Case No. ARB/82/1, Decision on Objections to Jurisdiction of 19 July 1984

Société Civile Immobilière de Gaëta v. Republic of Guinea, ICSID Case No. ARB/12/36, Award of 21 December 2015

Société Générale in respect of DR Energy Holdings Limited and Empresa Distribuidora de Electricidad del Este, S.A. v. The Dominican Republic, UNCITRAL, LCIA Case No. UN 7927, Award on Preliminary Objections to Jurisdiction of 19 September 2008

Hussein Nuaman Soufraki v. The United Arab Emirates, ICSID Case No. ARB/02/7, Award of 7 July 2004

Hussein Nuaman Soufraki v. The United Arab Emirates, ICSID Case No. ARB/02/7, Decision of the ad hoc Committee on the Application for Annulment of Mr Soufraki of 5 June 2007

Southern Pacific Properties (Middle East) Limited v. Arab Republic of Egypt, ICSID Case No. ARB/84/3, Decision on Jurisdiction of 27 November 1985

ST-AD GmbH v. Republic of Bulgaria, UNCITRAL, PCA Case No. 2011-06, Award on Jurisdiction of 18 July 2013

Anatolie Stati et al. v. Republic of Kazakhstan, Arbitration SCC V (116/2010), Award of 19 December 2013

Suez, Sociedad General de Aguas de Barcelona S.A., and InterAguas Servicios Integrales del Agua S.A. v. The Argentine Republic, ICSID Case No. ARB/03/17, Decision on Jurisdiction of 16 May 2006

Supervision y Control S.A. v. Republic of Costa Rica, ICSID Case No. ARB/12/4, Final Award of 18 January 2017

Técnicas Medioambientales Tecmed, S.A. v. United Mexican States, ICSID Case No. ARB (AF)/00/2, Award of 29 May 2003

TECO Guatemala Holdings, LLC v. Republic of Guatemala, ICSID Case No. ARB/10/23, Award of 19 December 2013

TECO Guatemala Holdings, LLC v. Republic of Guatemala, ICSID Case No. ARB/10/23, Decision on Annulment of 5 April 2016

Teinver S.A., Transportes de Cercanías S.A. and Autobuses Urbanos del Sur S.A. v. Argentine Republic, ICSID Case No. ARB/09/1, Decision on Jurisdiction of 21 December 2012

Teinver S.A., Transportes de Cercanías S.A. and Autobuses Urbanos del Sur S.A. v. Argentine Republic, ICSID Case No. ARB/09/1, Award of the Tribunal of 21 July 2017

Telefónica S.A. v. Argentine Republic, ICSID Case No. ARB/03/20, Decision on Jurisdiction of 25 May 2006

Telenor Mobile Communications A.S. v. The Republic of Hungary, ICSID Case No. ARB/04/15, Award of 13 September 2006

Tenaris S.A. and Talta—Trading e Marketing Sociedade Unipessoal Lda. v. Bolivarian Republic of Venezuela, ICSID Case No. ARB/12/23, Award of 29 January 2016

Tidewater Inc., Tidewater Investment SRL, Tidewater Caribe, C.A., et al. v. The Bolivarian Republic of Venezuela, ICSID Case No. ARB/10/5, Decision on Jurisdiction of 8 February 2013

Tokios Tokelés v. Ukraine, ICSID Case No. ARB/02/18, Decision on Jurisdiction of 29 April 2004

Tradex Hellas S.A. v. Republic of Albania, ICSID Case No. ARB/94/2, Decision on Jurisdiction of 24 December 1996

Transglobal Green Energy, LLC and Transglobal Green Energy de Panama, S.A. v. The Republic of Panama, ICSID Case No. ARB/13/28, Award of 2 June 2016

Trans-Global Petroleum, Inc. v. Hashemite Kingdom of Jordan, ICSID Case No. ARB/07/25, Decision on the Respondent's Objection Pursuant to Rule 41(5) of 12 May 2008

TSA Spectrum de Argentina SA v. Argentina Republic, ICSID Case No. ARB/ 05/5, Award of 19 December 2008

Tulip Real Estate and Development Netherlands B.V. v. Republic of Turkey, ICSID Case No. ARB/11/28, Decision on Bifurcated Jurisdictional Issue of 5 March 2013

Tulip Real Estate and Development Netherlands B.V. v. Republic of Turkey, ICSID Case No. ARB/11/28, Award of 10 March 2014

Señor Tza Yap Shum v. The Republic of Peru, ICSID Case No. ARB/07/6, Decision of Jurisdiction of 19 June 2009

Ulysseas, Inc. v. The Republic of Ecuador, UNCITRAL, Interim Award of 28 September 2010

Marion Unglaube v. Republic of Costa Rica, ICSID Case No. ARB/08/1, Award of 16 May 2012

United Parcel Service of America Inc. v. Government of Canada, Award on the Merits of 24 May 2007

Urbaser S.A. and Consorcio de Aguas Bilbao Bizkaia, Bilbao Biskaia Ur Partzuergoa v. The Argentine Republic, ICSID Case No. ARB/07/26, Decision on Jurisdiction of 12 December 2012

Cem Cengiz Uzan v. Republic of Turkey, Award on Respondent's Bifurcated Preliminary Objection of 20 April 2016

Vacuum Salt Products Ltd. v. Republic of Ghana, ICSID Case No. ARB/92/1, Award of 16 February 1994

Vannessa Ventures Ltd. v. Bolivarian Republic of Venezuela, ICSID Case No. ARB(AF)04/6, Decision on Jurisdiction of 22 August 2008

Venezuela Holdings, B.V., et al v. Venezuela (case formerly known as *Mobil Corporation, Venezuela Holdings, B.V., Mobil Cerro Negro Holding, Ltd., Mobil Venezolana de Petróleos Holdings, Inc., Mobil Cerro Negro, Ltd., and Mobil Venezolana de Petróleos, Inc. v. Venezuela*), ICSID CASE NO. ARB/07/27, Award of 9 October 2014

Venezuela US, S.R.L. (Barbados) v. Bolivarian Republic of Venezuela, PCA Case No. 2013-34, Interim Award on Jurisdiction on the Respondent Objection to Jurisdiction *Ratione Voluntatis* of 26 July 2016

Venoklim Holding B.V. v. Bolivarian Republic of Venezuela, ICSID Case No. ARB/12/22, Award of 3 April 2015

Vigotop Limited v. Hungary, ICSID Case No. ARB/11/22, Award of 1 October 2014

Yaung Chi Oo Trading Pte. Ltd. v. Government of the Union of Myanmar, ASEAN Case No ARB/01/1, Award of 31 March 2003

Yukos Universal Ltd. v. Russian Federation, PCA Case No. AA 227, Interim Award on Jurisdiction and Admissibility of 30 November 2009

Waste Management, Inc. v. United Mexican States, ICSID Case No. ARB(AF)/98/2, Dissenting Opinion of Keith Highet, of 8 May 2000

Wena Hotels LTD. v. Arab Republic of Egypt, ICSID Case No. ARB/98/4, Award of 8 December 2000

Western NIS Enterprise Fund v. Ukraine, ICSID Case No. ARB/04/2, Order of 16 March 2006

White Industries Australia Limited v. The Republic of India, UNCITRAL, Final Award of 30 November 2011

William Ralph Clayton, William Richard Clayton, Douglas Clayton, Daniel Clayton and Bilcon of Delaware Inc. v. Government of Canada, UNCITRAL, PCA Case No. 2009-04, Award on Jurisdiction and Liability of 17 March 2015

Wintershall Aktiengesellschaft v. Argentine Republic, ICSID Case No. ARB/04/14, Award of 8 December 2008

WNC Factoring Limited v. The Czech Republic, PCA Case No. 2014-34, Award of 22 February 2017

World Duty Free Company v Republic of Kenya, ICSID Case No. ARB/00/7, Award of 4 October 2006

World Wide Minerals v. Republic of Kazakhstan, UNCITRAL (Case 1), Award of 22 December 2010

World Wide Minerals v. Republic of Kazakhstan, UNCITRAL (Case 2), Decision on Jurisdiction of 15 October 2015

2 Decisions of Other Courts and Tribunals

Ad hoc arbitration, *Delimitation of the Continental Shelf between the United Kingdom of Great Britain and Northern Ireland, and the French Republic* (UK, France) 30 June 1977-14 March 1978 UNRIAA, Volume XVIII pp. 3–413

Arbitral Tribunal for the Agreement on German External Debts, *United States of America v. the Federal Republic of Germany* (16 May 1980) 59 ILR 495 (Young Loan Arbitration)

European Commission of Human Rights, case *Macit and 53 others v. Turkey*, App. No. 19934/92, Decision on admissibility of 31 March 1993

European Court of Human Rights, *Klass and Others v. Germany*, 6 September 1978, Series A no. 28

European Court of Human Rights, *Chrysostomos Papachrysostomou and Loizidou v. Turkey*, App. Nos. 15299/89, 15300/89 and 15318/89 (joined), Admissibility Decision of 4 March 1991, D.R. 68, 216

European Court of Human Rights, *Agrotexim and Others v. Greece*, 24 October 1995, Series A no. 330-A

European Court of Human Rights, *Loizidou v. Turkey*, App. No. 25781/94, Series A no. 310, Preliminary Objections

European Court of Human Rights, *Banković and Others v. Belgium and Others* (dec.) [GC], no. 52207/99

European Court of Human Rights, *Tahsin Acar v. Turkey* (preliminary objections) [GC], no. 26307/95, ECHR 2003-VI

European Court of Human Rights, *Tahsin Acar v. Turkey* [GC], no. 26307/95, ECHR 2004-III

High Court of Justice (UK), Queen's Bench Division, Commercial Court, *Standard Chartered Bank v Ceylon Petroleum Corporation* [2011] EWHC 1785 (Comm) (11 July 2011)

Human Rights Committee *Kennedy v. Trinidad and Tobago* Communication No. 845/1998, 26 March 2002, CCPR/C/74/D/845/1998

Human Rights Comiitee, *Husseini v. Denmark*, Communication No. 2243/2013, 26 November 2014, CCPR/C/112/D/2243/2013

Inter-American Court on Human Rights, *Ivcher Bronstein*, Competence, Judgment of September 24, 1999, (Ser. C) No. 54 (1999)

Inter-American Court on Human Rights, *Constitutional Court*, Competence, Judgment of September 24, 1999, (Ser. C) No. 55 (1999)

International Court of Justice, *Corfu Channel case* (United Kingdom v. Albania), Judgment on Preliminary Objection, I.C.J. Reports 1948, 15

International Court of Justice, *Anglo-Iranian Oil Co. Case* (United Kingdom v. Iran), Order of 5 July 1951, I.C.J. Reports 1951, 89

International Court of Justice, *Case of the monetary gold removed from Rome in 1943* (Italy v. France, United Kingdom of Great Britain and Northern Ireland and United States of America) Preliminary Question, Judgment of 15 June 1954, I.C.J. Reports 1954, 19.

International Court of Justice, *Nottebohm* (Liechtenstein v. Guatemala), Preliminary Objections, I.C.J. Reports 1955, 26.

International Court of Justice, *Advisory Opinion on Judgements of the Administrative Tribunal of the I.L.O. upon complaints made against the U.N.E.S.C.O.*, 1956 I.C.J. Reports, 77

International Court of Justice, *Interhandel* (Switzerland v. USA), Judgment, Preliminary Objections, I.C.J. Reports 1959, 6

International Court of Justice, *South West Africa Cases* (Ethiopia v. South Africa; Liberia v. South Africa), Preliminary Objections, Judgment of 21 December 1962, I.C.J. Reports 1962, 319

International Court of Justice, *Case concerning the Northern Cameroons* (Cameroon v. United Kingdom), Preliminary Objections, Judgment of 2 December 1963 I.C.J. Reports 1963, 15

International Court of Justice, *South West Africa*, Second Phase, Judgment of 18 July 1966, I.C.J. Reports 1966, 6

International Court of Justice, *Barcelona Traction, Light and Power Company, Limited*, (Belgium v. Spain), Second Phase, Judgment, I.C.J. Reports 1970, 3

International Court of Justice, *Nuclear Tests* (Australia v. France), Interim Protection, Order of 22 June 1973, I.C.J. Reports 1973, 99

International Court of Justice, *Nuclear Tests* (Australia v. France), I.C.J. Reports 1974, 253

International Court of Justice, *Aegean Sea* (Greece v. Turkey), 1978 I.C.J. Reports, 3

International Court of Justice, *Military and Paramilitary Activities in and against Nicaragua* (Nicaragua v. United States of America), Jurisdiction and Admissibility, Judgment, I.C.J. Reports 1984, 392

International Court of Justice, *Border and Transborder Armed Actions* (Nicaragua v. Honduras), Jurisdiction and Admissibility, Judgment, I.C.J. Reports 1988, 69

International Court of Justice, *Case concerning Elettronica Sicula* (United States of America v. Italy), Judgment, I.C.J. Reports 1989, 15

International Court of Justice, *Certain Phosphate Lands in Nauru* (Nauru v. Australia), Preliminary Objections, Judgment, I.C.J. Reports 1992, 240

International Court of Justice, *Application of the Convention on the Prevention and Punishment of the Crime of Genocide* (Bosnia and Herzegovina v. Serbia and Montenegro), Order of 13 September 1993 (Further Requests for the Indication of Provisional Measures), Separate opinion of Judge ad hoc Lauterpacht, 416

International Court of Justice, *East Timor* (Portugal v. Australia), Judgment, I.C.J. Reports 1995, 90

International Court of Justice, *Oil Platforms* (Islamic Republic of Iran v. United States of America), Preliminary Objection, Judgment, I.C.J. Reports 1996, 803

International Court of Justice, *Questions of Interpretation and Application of the 1971 Montreal Convention arising from the Aerial Incident at Lockerbie* (Libyan Arab Jamahiriya v. United Kingdom), Preliminary Objections, Judgment, I.C.J. Reports 1998, 16

International Court of Justice, *Land and Maritime Boundary between Cameroon and Nigeria*, Preliminary Objections, Judgment, I.C.J. Reports 1998, 275

International Court of Justice, *Legality of Use of Force (Yugoslavia v. United States of America)*, Provisional Measures, Order of 2 June 1999, I.C.J. Reports 1999, 916

International Court of Justice, *LaGrand (Germany v. United States of America)*, Judgment, I.C.J. Reports 2001, 466

International Court of Justice, *Case Concerning the Arrest Warrant of 11 April 2000* (Democratic Republic of Congo v. Belgium), Judgment, 14 February 2002, I.C.J. Reports 2002, 3

International Court of Justice, *Legal Consequences of the Construction of a Wall in the Occupied Palestinian Territory*, Advisory Opinion, I.C.J. Reports 2004, 136

International Court of Justice, *Armed Activities on the Territory of the Congo (New Application: 2002)* (Democratic Republic of the Congo v. Rwanda), I.C.J. Reports 2006, 39

International Court of Justice, *Territorial and Maritime Dispute* (Nicaragua v. Colombia), Preliminary Objections, Judgment, I.C.J. Reports 2007, 832

International Court of Justice, *Certain Questions of Mutual Assistance in Criminal Matters* (Djibouti v. France), Judgment, I.C.J. Reports 2008, 177

International Court of Justice, *Application of the Convention on the Prevention and Punishment of the Crime of Genocide* (Croatia v. Serbia), Preliminary Objections, Judgment, I.C.J. Reports 2008, 412

International Court of Justice, *Application of the International Convention on the Elimination of All Forms of Racial Discrimination* (Georgia v. Russian Federation), Preliminary Objections, Judgment, I.C.J. Reports 2011, 70

International Court of Justice, *Application of the Convention on the Prevention and Punishment of the Crime of Genocide* (Croatia v. Serbia), Judgment of 3 February 2015, I.C.J. Reports 2015, 3

International Court of Justice, *Question of the Delimitation of the Continental Shelf between Nicaragua and Colombia beyond 200 Nautical Miles from the Nicaraguan Coast (Nicaragua v. Colombia)*, Judgment on the Preliminary Objections of 17 March 2016, I.C.J. Reports 2016, 100

International Court of Justice, *Obligations concerning Negotiations relating to Cessation of the Nuclear Arms Race and to Nuclear Disarmament* (Marshall Islands v. India), Jurisdiction and Admissibility, Judgment, I.C.J. Reports 2016, p. 255

Permanent Court of International Justice, *Status of Eastern Carelia*, Advisory Opinion of 23 July 1923, P.C.I.J. Series B, No. 527, 22

Permanent Court of International Justice, *Mavrommatis Palestine Concessions*, Greece v. United Kingdom, Objection to the Jurisdiction of the Court, Judgment, P.C.I.J. 1924 Series A, No 2, 10

Permanent Court of International Justice, *German Interests in Upper Silesia* (Germany v. Poland), Judgment of 25 August 1925, P.C.I.J. Series A, No. 6

Permanent Court of International Justice, *Case of the S.S. Lotus* (*France v. Turkey*), P.C.I.J. (ser. A) No. 10 (1927)

Permanent Court of International Justice, *Factory at Chorzów*, Jurisdiction, Judgment No. 8, 1927, P.C.I.J., Series A, No. 9, 32

Permanent Court of International Justice, *Interpretation of Judgments Nos. 7 and 8* (*Factory at Chorzów*) 1927 PCIJ Series, No. 13, 23

Permanent Court of International Justice, *Rights of Minorities in Upper Silesia* (*Minority Schools*), *Germany v. Poland*, Judgment of 26 April 1928, P.C.I.J. Series A, No 15, 23

Permanent Court of International Justice, *Panevezys-Saldutiskis Railway* (Estonia v. Lithuania), Preliminary objections, Order of 30 June 1938, P.C.I.J. Series A/B, No. 75, 16

International Tribunal for the Law of the Sea, *The M/V 'SAIGA'* (No 2), Saint Vincent and the Grenadines v. Guinea, Merits, Judgment, ITLOS Case No. 2, ICGJ 336 (ITLOS 1999), 1st July 1999

ICTY, *Prosecutor v. Dusko Tadić a/k/a* 'Dule', decision on the defence motion for interlocutory appeal on jurisdiction, ICTY Appeals Chamber, 2 October 1995

Iran—US Claims Tribunal, *Flexi Van Leasing v. Iran et al.*, 82-0463 (D.D.C.)

Iran—US Claims Tribunal, *Iran and United States*, Case No. A/18, Decision No. DEC 32-A18-FT (6 April 1984), 5 Iran-US Cl. Trib. Rep. 251

London Court of International Arbitration, *Citibank N.A. v. Ceylon Petroleum Corporation*, First Partial Award, LCIA ab# 81215, 31 July 2011

Paris Court of Appeal, Decision on the Set Aside Application of 25 April 2017, *Venezuela v. Garcia Armas* and *Garcia Gruver*, Reg. No. 15/01040

Singapore Court of Appeal, *Sanum Investments Ltd v Government of the Lao People's Democratic Republic* [2016] SGCA 57

UNCLOS arbitration, *Arbitral Tribunal Southern Bluefin Tuna Case* (Australia and New Zealand v. Japan) Award on Jurisdiction and Admissibility of 4 August 2000

UNCLOS arbitration, *MOX Plant* (Ireland v. UK), Order No. 3, 42 ILM 1187, 1190 (2003) (PCA, 24 June 24)

Court of Appeals for the District of Columbia Circuit, *BG Group PLC v. Republic of Argentina*, 665 F. 3d 1363 (2012)

World Bank Administrative Tribunal, *George Kavoukas et al. v. International Bank for Reconstruction and Development*, Decision No. 3 of 5 June 1981

World Bank Administrative Tribunal, *Elizabeth Tweddle v. International Bank for Reconstruction and Development*, Decision No. 508 of 29 May 2015 (Preliminary Objection)

WTO Appellate Body, *EC—Measures Concerning Meat and Meat Products*, WT/DS26/AB/R, WT/DS48/AB/R, report of 16 January 1998

3 Other Authorities

Roberto Ago, 'Eccezioni 'non esclusivamente preliminari'' in *Il Processo internzionale, Studi in onore di Gaetano Morelli, Comunicazioni e Studi, vol. XIV* (Giuffré 1975) 1

Chittharanjan F Amerasinghe, *International Arbitral Jurisdiction* (Brill 2011) 71

Cyrus Benson, Penny Madden and Ceyda Knoebel, 'Covered investment' in Barton Legum (ed), *The Investment Treaty Arbitration Review* (Law Business Research 2016) 15

Gary Born and Marija Šćekić, 'Pre-Arbitration Procedural Requirements 'A Dismal Swamp'' in David D Caron et al. (eds), *Practising Virtue, Inside International Arbitration* (OUP 2015) 227

Chester Brown, 'The Inherent Powers of International Courts and Tribunals' (2005) 76 British Yearbook of International Law 195

Chester Brown, *A Common Law of International Adjudication* (OUP 2007)

Luigi Crema, 'Disappearance and new sightings of restrictive interpretation(s)' (2010) 21(3) European Journal of International Law 681

Zachary Douglas, *The International Law of Investment Claims* (CUP 2009)

Patrick Dumberry and Gabrielle Dumas-Aubin, 'The Doctrine of "Clean Hands" and the Inadmissibility of Claims by Investors Breaching International Human Rights Law' (2013) 10(1) Transnational Dispute Management 1

Gerald G Fitzmaurice, *The Law and Procedure of the International Court of Justice* (Grotius 1986) Vol. 2, 439

Filippo Fontanelli and Attila Tanzi, 'Jurisdiction and Admissibility in Investment Arbitration. A View from the Bridge at the Practice' (2017) 16(1) The Law and Practice of International Courts and Tribunals 3

Filippo Fontanelli and Paolo Busco, 'The function of procedural justice in international adjudication' (2016) 15(1) The Law and Practice of International Courts and Tribunals 1

Filippo Fontanelli, 'Reflections on the indispensable party principle in the wake of the judgment on preliminary objections in the *Norstar* case' [2017] 1 Rivista di Diritto Internazionale 163

Serena Forlati, *The International Court of Justice—An Arbitral Tribunal or a Judicial Body?* (Springer 2014)

Susan D Franck, 'The legitimacy crisis in investment treaty arbitration: privatizing public international law through inconsistent decisions' (2005) 73 Fordham Law Review 1521

Giorgio Gaja, 'General Principles of Law' (2013) Oxford Encyclopedia of Public International Law

Lindsay Gastrell and Paul-Jean Le Cannu, 'Procedural Requirements of 'Denial-of-Benefits' Clauses in Investment Treaties: A Review of Arbitral Decisions' (2015) 30(1) ICSID Review 78

Lucy Greenwood, 'Does Bifurcation Really Promote Efficiency?' (2011) 28 Journal of International Arbitration 105

Veijo Heiskanen, 'Jurisdiction v. Competence: Revisiting a frequently neglected distinction (1994) 5 Finnish Yearbook of International Law 1

Veijo Heiskanen, 'Dealing with Pandora: The Concept of 'Merits' in International Commercial Arbitration' (2006) 22 Arbitration International 597

Rosalyn Higgins, 'Respecting Sovereign States and Running a Tight Courtroom' (2001) 50 International and Comparative Law Quarterly 121

Anne K Hoffmann, 'Denial of Benefits' in Marc Bungenberget al (eds), *International Investment Law* (Nomos 2015) 598

Juan Pablo Hugues Arthur, 'The legal value of prior steps to arbitration in international law of foreign investment: Two (different?) approaches, one outcome' (2015) 15 Anuario Mexicano de Derecho Internacional 449

International Law Commission, Final Report of the Study Group on the Most-Favoured-Nation clause, Yearbook of the International Law Commission, 2015, vol. II

Stephen Jagusch and Anthony Sinclair, 'The Limits of protection for Investments and Investors under the Energy Charter Treaty' in Graham Coop and Clarisse Ribeiro (eds), *Investment Arbitration and the Energy Charter Treaty* (Juris Net 2006) 39

Neha Jain, 'Judicial Lawmaking and General Principles of Law in International Criminal Law' (2016) 57(1) Harvard Journal of International Law 119

Ian Laird, 'A Distinction without a Difference? An Examination of the Concepts of Admissibility and Jurisdiction in Salini v. Jordan and Methanex v. USA' in Todd Weiler (ed), *International Investment law and Arbitration: Leading Cases from ICSID, NAFTA and Customary International Law* (Cameron May 2005) 201

Christopher J Larouer, 'In the Name of Sovereignty? The Battle over *In Dubio Mitius* Inside and Outside the Courts' (2009) Cornell Law School Inter-University Graduate Student Conference Papers 22

Aloysius P Llamzon, *Corruption in International Investment Arbitration* (OUP 2014)

Campbell McLachlan, Laurence Shore and Matthew Weiniger, *International investment arbitration: substantive principles* (OUP 2007)

Herman Melville, *Moby Dick; or, The Whale* (1851, ed. Simonds 1922)

Maurice Mendelson, 'Runaway Train: The 'Continuous Nationality' Rule from the Panavezys-Saldutiskis Railway case to Loewen' in Todd Weiler (ed), *International Investment Law and Arbitration* (Cameron May 2005) 97

Cameron A Miles, 'Corruption, Jurisdiction and Admissibility in International Investment Claims' (2012) 3(2) Journal of International Dispute Settlement 329

Alexander Orakhelashvili, 'The Concept of International Judicial Jurisdiction: A Reappraisal' (2003) 3 The Law and Practice of International Courts and Tribunals 501

William W Park, 'Determining an Arbitrator's Jurisdiction: Timing and Finality in American Law' (2007) 8 Nevada Law Journal 135

Jan Paulsson, 'Jurisdiction and Admissibility' in Gerald Aksen et al (eds), *Global Reflections on International Law, Commerce and Dispute Resolution: Liber Amicorum in Honour of Robert Briner* (International Chamber of Commerce 2005) 601

Alain Pellet, 'The Case Law of the ICJ in Investment Arbitration' (2013) 28 ICSID Review 223

Cesare PR Romano, 'The Shift from the Consensual to the Compulsory Paradigm in International Adjudication: Elements for a Theory of Consent' (2006) 39 New York University Journal of International Law & Policy 791

Shabtai Rosenne and Yael Ronen, *The Law and Practice of the International Court, 1920–2005* (Brill 2006)

Shabtai Rosenne, 'International Courts and Tribunals, Jurisdiction and Admissibility of Inter-State Applications' (2006) Oxford Encyclopaedia of Public International Law

Luiz E Salles, *Forum Shopping in International Adjudication: The Role of Preliminary Objections* (CUP 2014)

Arman Sarvarian and Rudy Baker, 'Arbitration between Croatia and Slovenia: Leaks, Wiretaps, Scandal' (2015) EJIL: Talk! of 28 July 2015, at http://www.ejiltalk.org/arbitration-between-croatia-and-slovenia-leaks-wiretaps-scandal/

Oscar Schachter, *International Law in Theory and Practice* (Martinus Nijhoff 1991)

Christoph Schreuer, *The ICSID Convention: A Commentary* (CUP 2001)

Christoph Schreuer, 'At what time must jurisdiction exist?', in David D Caron et al. (eds), *Practising Virtue Inside International Arbitration* (OUP 2015) 264

Yuval Shany, 'Jurisdiction and Admissibility', in Cesare Romano, Karen Alter, and Yuval Shany, *Oxford Handbook of International Adjudication* (OUP 2014) 782

Yuval Shany, *Questions of Jurisdiction and Admissibility before International Courts* (CUP 2015)

Giuseppe Sperduti, 'La recevabilité des exceptions préliminaires de fond dans le procès international' (1970) 53 Rivista di Diritto Internazionale 461

Andrea Marco Steingruber, 'Some remarks on Veijo Heiskanen's Note 'Ménage à trois? Jurisdiction, Admissibility and Competence in Investment Treaty Arbitration' (2014) 29 ICSID Review 675

Attila Tanzi, 'The Relevance of the Foreign Investor's Good Faith' in Attila Tanzi, Andrea Gattini, Filippo Fontanelli (eds), *General Principles of Law and International Investment Arbitration* (Brill 2018) 193

Hugh Thirlway, 'The Law and Procedure of the International Court of Justice' (1998) British Yearbook of International Law 4

UNCTAD, "Most Favoured-Nation Treatment," UNCTAD Series on International Investment Agreements II, UNCTAD/DIAE/IA/2010/1, 24 January 2011

Albert Jan van den Berg, 'Should the Setting Aside of the Arbitral Award be Abolished?' (2014) 29(2) ICSID Review 263

Jorge E Viñuales, 'International Investment Proceedings: Converging Principles?' (Morelli Lectures 2016), in Enzo Cannizzaro (ed), *International Procedural Law: Common Principles of General Principles?* (Sapienza Università Editrice 2017)

Jorge E Viñuales, 'Investor Diligence in Investment Arbitration: Sources and Arguments' (2017) 32(2) ICSID Review-Foreign Investment Law Journal 346

Michael Waibel (in 'Investment Arbitration: Jurisdiction and Admissibility', in August Renisch et al. (eds), *Handbook on International Investment Law* (Hart 2015) 1212

Gregory S Weber, 'Who Killed the Friendly Settlement? The Decline of Negotiated Resolutions at the European Court of Human Rights' (2007) 7(2) Pepperdine Dispute Resolution Law Journal 1

Gerold Zeiler, 'Jurisdiction, Competence and Admissibility of Claims in ICSID Arbitration Proceedings' in Christina Binder and others (eds), *International Investment Law for the 21st Century: Essays in Honour of Christoph Schreuer* (OUP 2009) 76

www.ingramcontent.com/pod-product-compliance
Lightning Source LLC
LaVergne TN
LVHW102227300926
849160LV00005B/57